PATTON'S DRIVE

PATTON'S DRIVE

THE MAKING OF AMERICA'S GREATEST GENERAL

ALAN AXELROD

THE LYONS PRESS
Guilford, Connecticut
An imprint of The Globe Pequot Press

The Lyons Press is an imprint of The Globe Pequot Press.

Text designer: Sheryl P. Kober
Layout artist: Kim Burdick

Library of Congress Cataloging-in-Publication Data is available on file.

ISBN 978-1-59921-539-6

Printed in the United States of America

10 9 8 7 6 5 4 3 2 1

For Anita and Ian
21 guns—each

CONTENTS

NOLI ME TANGERE

In World War II, George C. Marshall held the title of Chief of Staff, and Dwight D. Eisenhower, Supreme Allied Commander in Europe, but it is General George S. Patton Jr. who is remembered as America's Warrior.

It is not an official title, of course, but a universal accolade that puts him in company with the likes of Hannibal, Caesar, Genghis Khan, Attila the Hun, William Wallace, Napoleon, Horatio Nelson, Stonewall Jackson, and Geronimo—history's great fighting "captains," men who masterminded victory and always led from the front, in person, where the spears, or arrows, or bullets flew, and where men got killed. For better or worse, war was their vocation and their destiny. They could not help themselves. They had to fight, and they had to lead others in the fighting.

Patton's Drive is in part a meditation on the nature and the role of the pure warrior, the frankly atavistic man of war in a modern army, the army of a rational democracy, no less. It is a theme that Shakespeare adumbrated in such military tragic heroes as Othello, Julius Caesar, and Titus Andronicus, but it is a theme that few of Patton's many biographers have broached, let alone explored. Yet I believe it is the key to understanding Patton as a man and as a soldier. Thus, *Patton's Drive* is intended to contribute to the understanding of Patton psychologically and culturally, but also in the narrower context of military history.

Less famous than the near-legendary Erwin Rommel, Field Marshal Gerd von Rundstedt was nevertheless one of the most formidable of Germany's generals of World War II, mastermind of the daring Ardennes Offensive—the "Battle of the Bulge"—which inflicted on the American army the heaviest losses it suffered in Europe before General George S. Patton Jr. succeeded in pounding the offensive into absolute defeat. Captured at the end of the war and asked to name the American commander who had most impressed him, Rundstedt did not pause before he snapped back: "Patton was your best."

In Patton, the American army had precisely the kind of general the Germans most desperately wanted for themselves, a brilliant, innovative, and daring master of modern tactics who possessed the powerfully charismatic soul of an ancient warrior. Carlo D'Este put it into the title of his 1996 biography of the general: Patton had a "genius for war."

Genius. The term is worth contemplating, because it stands at the crux that is the meeting place of the Patton personality and the Patton vocation. "I belong to a different class," West Point cadet Patton wrote in a letter to his father in July 1904. A different *class*? Like all creative geniuses, Patton seemed to belong to a different world, a different time, a different place, almost a different species. He took to combat as if he had been born to it. It was peace that was, for him, the alien element. In the absence of war, he did not know what to do in the world, and the world did not know what to do with him. In war alone did he live fully, gaining victory by deliberately courting defeat. His achievements in World War II are familiar through the many histories of the conflict, through several biographies and biographical works (including my own 1999 *Patton on Leadership* and 2006 *Patton: A Biography*), and not least of all through the monumental 1970 film, *Patton*, starring George C. Scott and directed by Franklin Schaffner.

Even reduced to a few summary lines, Patton's martial prodigies are staggering in their scope: Early in the war, he created a desert warfare training center outside of Indio, California, and turned out America's first generation of desert warriors. When the U.S. II Corps, in the American army's first major contest against the Germans, suffered humiliating defeat at Kasserine Pass, Tunisia, it was Patton on whom Eisenhower called, and, in the space of ten days, he transformed the thoroughly demoralized American force into the kernel of a victorious army capable of defeating no less than Rommel's vaunted Afrika Korps. When Anglo-American forces stepped off from North Africa to invade Sicily, Patton unilaterally revised the subordinate role his Seventh Army had been assigned and, with lightning speed, took Palermo, then beat British general (later field marshal) Sir Bernard Law Montgomery to the conquest of Messina.

Following the D-Day landings at Normandy, Patton was given command of a force created for him, the Third Army, which he used to amplify Operation Cobra, Omar Bradley's initially modest plan for breaking out of the Norman hedgerow country. In Patton's hands, Cobra was expanded into the most spectacular and productive advance of World War II. *The Third Army's After Action Report*, the official account, begins: "In nine months and eight days of campaigning, Third U.S. Army compiled a record of offensive operations that could only be measured in superlatives, for not only did the Army's achievements astonish the world but its deeds in terms of figures challenged the imagination." During this brief period,

Patton's men liberated or gained 81,522 square miles in France, 1,010 in Luxembourg, 156 in Belgium, 29,940 in Germany, 3,485 in Czechoslovakia, and 2,103 in Austria. The Third Army liberated or captured some 12,000 cities, towns, and villages, 27 of which contained more than 50,000 people. It captured 1,280,688 prisoners of war between August 1, 1944, and May 13, 1945. It killed 47,500 enemy soldiers and wounded 115,700 more. During this same period, Third Army logistics troops brought in by rail, truck, and air 1,234,529 tons of supplies, including 533,825 tons of ammunition. Its engineers built 2,498 bridges—about 8.5 miles of bridges—and repaired or reconstructed 2,240 miles of road and 2,092 miles of railroad. Its Signal Corps troops laid 3,747 miles of open wire and 36,338 miles of underground cable. Its telephone operators handled an average of 13,986 calls daily. Its ambulances evacuated 269,187 patients. Its officers and men administered civil affairs in Belgium, Czechoslovakia, France, and Luxembourg, as well as providing military governments for parts of Germany and Austria, ultimately regulating the lives and welfare of some thirty million men, women, and children. As Patton himself repeatedly remarked in various ways, next to war, all other human endeavors pale into insignificance.

And there was yet more.

In the very midst of the great Allied eastward drive, Rundstedt launched the Ardennes offensive during the Christmas season of 1944, hitting the American line at its weakest point and threatening to split the Allied forces in two with an all-out advance targeting the crucial Allied-held port of Antwerp. Patton performed a miracle of tactics, logistics, and human endurance when he turned the bulk of his army, troops exhausted by three months of continual battle and advance, ninety degrees north to launch a bold counterattack into the southern flank of the German advance. The Battle of the Bulge, which began as a stunning catastrophe for the Allies, was converted into a U.S. victory that broke the back of the German army.

It was as if he had been born to all of this. Certainly, Patton himself was convinced that greatness in battle was his destiny, his birthright—or, more accurately, the right of many births; for he believed himself to be only the latest reincarnation of a line of warriors stretching back through Napoleonic times to ancient Rome and probably beyond.

Strange as it may seem, Patton's vision of himself has become the popularly accepted view of him. It is of a piece, really, with the way most of us look upon all cases of genius. Where did van Gogh learn to be van Gogh? Who taught Beethoven to be Beethoven? Such questions seem unanswerable, if not just silly. With regard to the analysis of genius, writers have traditionally observed the equivalent of the Latin proverb, *Noli me tangere*— Touch me not.

And such, by and large, has been the prevailing attitude toward Patton. He has been written about and marveled at over and over again, but the unspoken assumption has always been that we will never—*can* never—know the sources of his "genius for war." *Patton's Drive: The Making of America's Greatest General* challenges this assumption by exploring precisely these sources.

Beginning with the general's spectacular trans-European drive, we step backward to survey Patton's military origins—a heritage that extends to the American Revolution and the Civil War—and his Virginia Military Institute and West Point experience, then we concentrate on what was his double baptism of fire, in the Punitive Expedition pursuing Pancho Villa during 1916–1917 and in his personal leadership of the first American "Tank Service" in World War I, 1917–1918.

In contrast to George C. Marshall, Dwight D. Eisenhower, and Omar Bradley, none of whom had ever personally commanded troops in combat, Patton entered World War II knowing firsthand what it meant to lead men in what he liked to call "desperate battle." From his very first encounter, a full-on shootout with Villa's men in Mexico, Patton forged together the military cutting edge with the atavism of a primal warrior. His successful attack on a top Villa general and his men at the San Miguelito Ranch on May 14, 1916, made use of three automobiles and so is counted as the first mechanized assault in U.S. military history, yet it culminated in an intense gun battle eminently suited to the bygone era of the Wild West. Similarly, in the Great War, Patton achieved rapid mastery of the embryonic technology, tactics, and doctrine of tank warfare, yet when it came to leading the men and machines into combat, he advanced on foot, armed with nothing more than his swagger stick and Colt revolver, sometimes leaping from tank to tank, perpetually defying snipers and machine-gun fire to provide the eyes, ears, and brain needed to direct America's maiden armored battle effectively.

Patton paid a high price for his genius, and not just in blood and lives. Who is not familiar with the romantic cliché of the "tortured," self-destructive creative genius, the van Gogh, the Jackson Pollock, the Arthur Rimbaud, the Charlie Parker, who can truly exist only in his art and who is otherwise tragically dysfunctional in life as ordinarily lived? For Patton, war was his art, and his commitment to it utterly unfitted him for a life in peace.

Society has rarely been kind to pure genius in any field, and when that genius expresses itself in a warrior, society responds with outright fear and loathing—at least in times of peace, when a warrior's countrymen recognize little need for him. Everywhere and at all times it has been hard to be a soldier between wars, but in the army of a modern, rational democracy, it is hardest of all. Patton believed it his destiny to be a warrior, but to be an American warrior proved a dark destiny indeed.

In his *Agricola* of the year 98, the Roman historian Tacitus put into the mouth of a British tribal chieftain named Calgacus a malediction delivered to an assembly of legionnaires and intended to be heard in Rome itself. "To ravage, to slaughter, to usurp under false titles, they call empire," Calgacus said, "and where they make a desert, they call it peace." For Patton, this could serve as the very definition of peace. Where others regarded it as a longed-for oasis, to him it was a desert, dreaded and parching to his very soul.

So much we can surmise from the emotionally tempestuous, ill-tempered, self-destructive, and profoundly unfulfilling life Patton lived between the two world wars. We cannot know the life he would have led after World War II—though we know he dreaded the prospect of it—because he died on December 21, 1945, from injuries sustained in an otherwise trivial automobile accident twelve days earlier. A car wreck en route to a pheasant hunt was not the way George S. Patton Jr. wanted to die. On May 8, 1945, the very day the war ended in Europe, Patton had turned to an aide. "The best end for an old campaigner," he said to him, "is a bullet at the last minute of the last battle." Succumbing to pulmonary edema and congestive heart failure brought on by traumatic quadriplegia was, as he put it, "a helluva way to die." Bad as it was, unlucky as it was, for the likes of Patton, it was quite possibly a fate preferable and more fortunate than life without a war.

CHAPTER 1

"I AM DESTINED TO ACHIEVE SOME GREAT THING"

"It is Hell to be on the side lines and see all the glory eluding me, but I guess there will be enough for all . . . I guess I will read the Bible."

> —PATTON, LETTER TO BEATRICE PATTON,
> JUNE 6, 1944

Not Alexander, not Caesar, not Napoleon—none of history's "great captains" had ever led a waterborne invasion of the magnitude and consequence of the assault on Normandy, June 6, 1944. It was, in fact, the biggest invasion in the biggest war in history, and George Smith Patton Jr. was given no active part in it—other than inclusion among an array of brilliant stage props: wooden dummy aircraft, inflatable rubber dummy tanks, and phony radio traffic from one fictitious division to another, all designed to deceive the Germans into believing that the invasion of France would come not at Normandy, where the English Channel was broad and hazardous, but up the coast, at Pas de Calais, where the Channel was much narrower and the beach so much closer to the principal objectives of any invasion: direct routes across France, into the Low Countries, and on to the German border.

Everyone knew that Patton was the man to command such an invasion. Most of all, the Germans knew it. Thanks to a well-developed espionage apparatus, they knew as well as Patton's own superiors knew that he had performed head and shoulders above the other commanders in the major

Texas-Louisiana maneuvers of 1941 that had preceded American entry into the war. They knew what he had done in North Africa in 1943, how in the space of ten days he transformed the thoroughly demoralized II Corps, humiliated at the Kasserine Pass and mocked by the British as "our Italians," into the spirited and disciplined fighting unit that triumphed at El Guettar and, under Patton's successor Omar Bradley, was instrumental in pushing the Afrika Korps off the continent. They knew Patton as the conqueror of Sicily, who led the Seventh U.S. Army in the landings of Operation Husky—a dress rehearsal for Normandy—and, though assigned merely to support the British Eighth Army of Bernard Law Montgomery, had seized the initiative, leading his army in the capture of Palermo then beating Montgomery to the capture of Messina, springboard to the Italian mainland.

Patton was not only the obvious choice to lead the assault of *Festung Europa*—Fortress Europe—he was manifestly the inevitable choice. But that is precisely what made him such a good decoy.

Even as the June 6 invasion poured onto the Norman beaches, German headquarters continued to insist that the "real" invasion was yet to come and, when it came, would do so at Pas de Calais under Patton's command. So Wilhelm Keitel, head of the Armed Forces High Command (*Oberkommando der Wehrmacht*, the OKW), and Alfred Jodl, chief of the OKW Operations Staff, ignored the pleas of Field Marshal Erwin Rommel and held in the north, far from Normandy, the whole of Hans von Salmuth's Fifteenth Army to defend against an invasion that would never be.

It was a daring play, using Patton as nothing more than a decoy, like bringing Babe Ruth to bat in the bottom of the ninth, only to have him bunt. But it was hard to tell whether it was the product of strategic brilliance or something of a punishment—perhaps a no-confidence vote—imposed on Patton by the supreme Allied commander, Dwight D. Eisenhower.

The legend of Patton's erratic misbehavior cast a shadow that surely stretched as far as Normandy. He had come into the war already notorious for exuberant profanity, hard drinking, and an ego as enormous as his countervailing superego was vanishingly small. Self-censorship, let alone basic discretion, in word and deed was unknown to him.

President Franklin D. Roosevelt sent Patton his personal "thanks and enthusiastic approbation" at the end of the Sicily campaign, but even more welcome was a note from his archrival, Bernard Law Montgomery: "The Eighth sends its warmest congratulations to you and your splendid Army for the way you captured Messina and so ended the campaign in Sicily." What, then, would be his next assignment? Patton did not know, and Ike wasn't saying. When Patton learned that his Seventh Army would play no part in the campaign on the Italian mainland, he guessed that meant he would have a big part in the planned cross-Channel invasion. Ike, however, kept silent for weeks before finally delivering the bombshell order that Patton was to remain in Sicily with bare-bones garrison units only and was to send the rest of the Seventh Army's men and equipment to Mark Clark's Fifth Army for the invasion of the Italian mainland.

Patton had a reputation for fearlessness, but he never claimed to be unafraid. In fact, he often remarked that he took chances with his own life in the front lines mainly to reassure himself that he was not a coward. Patton continually placed himself in danger, always subjecting himself to tests aimed at finding out if he possessed the kind of courage his father had told him about, the courage to "face death from weapons with a smile."

But fear in battle was one thing; Patton had learned to deal with it as he dealt with any other problem of war. The anxiety created by consignment to the sidelines was another proposition altogether. For this feeling, Patton had no sovereign remedy. He passed the time in Sicily as best he could with administrative duties and by visiting the wounded. "Old Blood and Guts," they called him, a sobriquet Patton himself relished as part of his warrior image, but the hyper-tough appellation hid the high esteem in which Patton held the officers and men of his army—"The soldier is the army," he often said—and it hardly hinted at the remarkable fact that Patton made the rounds of the field hospitals far more often than any other senior commander in the war.

He sincerely believed that his presence among the convalescing wounded lifted morale. "Inspected all sick and wounded," he noted in his diary on August 2, 1943. "Pinned on some 40 Purple Hearts on men hurt in air raid. One man was dying and had an oxygen mask on, so I knelt down and pinned the Purple Heart on him, and he seemed to understand although he could not speak." The visits took a toll on him. "One man had the top of his head blown off," Patton noted in his diary on August 6, "and they were just waiting for him to die. He was a horrid bloody mess and was not good to look at, or I might develop personal feelings about sending men to battle. That would be fatal for a General."

If "personal feelings" were a dread disease for a general, maybe Patton was already infected. On August 3, he learned that General Eisenhower intended to award him the Distinguished

Service Cross for "extraordinary heroism." He took this news oddly, writing about the forthcoming decoration to his wife, Beatrice, that he "rather" felt he "did not deserve it, but won't say so."

What did this reveal about the state of Patton's mind the morning of August 3? All we know is that, later in the day, he visited the 15th Evacuation Hospital near Nicosia, where, among the grievously wounded was one Charles H. Kuhl, private first class, Company L, 26th Infantry Regiment (1st Division). What struck the general about Kuhl was the complete absence of any wounds.

In a document titled "Mistreatment of Patients in Receiving Tents of the 15th and 93rd Evacuation Hospitals," Lieutenant Colonel Perrin H. Long, a senior medical officer, reported the encounter between general and private:

> *[Patton] came to Pvt. Kuhl and asked him what was the matter. The soldier replied, "I guess I can't take it." The General immediately flared up, cursed the soldier, called him all types of a coward, then slapped him across the face with his gloves and finally grabbed the soldier by the scruff of his neck and kicked him out of the tent.*

A pair of medics intervened, grabbing Kuhl by both arms, and hustling him out of sight into a ward tent. There, on subsequent examination, he was found to have a fever and reported having suffered from severe diarrhea for a month. "A blood smear," Long observed, was "positive for malarial parasites."

It never occurred to Patton that Kuhl might be sick. The night after slapping the soldier, he expressed no regret, recording the event in his diary as an encounter with "the only arrant coward I have ever seen in this Army" and observing that "such men . . . should be tried for cowardice and shot." If Patton sensed any connection between having just received what he felt was an undeserved decoration for heroism and his outburst against Kuhl, he did not record it in his diary or anywhere else. But there Patton had been, pinning medals on the dying, knowing that he was about to receive such a medal himself.

He had been born on November 11, 1885, at Lake Vineyard, his family's home outside of Los Angeles. They had come to California from Virginia, which had sent a long line of Pattons into the army, stretching back to the American Revolution. George was named after both his father (who had changed his middle name from William to Smith to honor both his father and his stepfather, George Hugh Smith) and his grandfather, George Smith Patton. Grandfather had graduated from the Virginia Military Institute in 1852, having been a student of Thomas "Stonewall" Jackson, commanded the 22nd Virginia Infantry in the Civil War, was wounded, captured, and then exchanged, only to meet his end on September 19, 1864, at the Third Battle of Winchester. Grandfather's brother, Waller Tazewell Patton, also fought in the Confederate army, sustained a wound at the Second Battle of Bull Run, then fell with so many others at Gettysburg, in Pickett's Charge.

Patton was wounded on the Western Front near the village of Cheppy in September 1918, so he entered World War II knowing well what it meant to be wounded. But because his wound had not been mortal, he did not know what it was to die in battle, and, at the 15th Evac, near Nicosia, as he pinned medals on the dying, what he may well have felt was the gnawing consciousness that here before him were the *real* heroes, the men about to join *his* own ancestors. And the medal Ike was going to give him? It must have seemed a mockery as he came upon Private Kuhl, a sick, scared soldier in the wrong place at the wrong time. For Patton, Kuhl's presence was an ambush, and he found himself face to face with the only enemy that really mattered: the coward he always feared he himself was.

Striking a soldier was a court-martial offense, but, beyond shocking those who had actually witnessed the episode, it produced no further consequence. Eight days later, however, the general assaulted another soldier, this one at the 93rd Evacuation Hospital.

According to Lieutenant Colonel Long's official report, Private Paul G. Bennett, C Battery, 17th Field Artillery, II Corps, a veteran of four years, "never had any difficulties until August 6th, when his buddy was wounded."

> *He could not sleep that night and felt nervous. The shells going over him bothered him. The next day he was worried about his buddy and became more nervous. He was sent down to the rear echelon by a battery aid man and there the medical officer gave him some medicine which made him sleep, but still he was nervous and disturbed. On the next day the medical officer ordered him to be evacuated, although the boy begged not to be evacuated because he did not want to leave his unit.*

Feverish, dehydrated, exhausted, and disoriented, Bennett, despite his protests, was in no condition to return to the front. As in the case of Kuhl, Patton knew nothing of the man's condition other than that he appeared uninjured.

Patton positioned himself a matter of inches from Bennett's face, as superior officers do, and demanded to know the private's problem.

"It's my nerves," Bennett replied, sobbing.

"What did you say?"

"It's my nerves, I can't stand the shelling any more."

The general regarded the crying man with profound disgust. "Your nerves, hell; you are just a Goddamned coward, you yellow son of a bitch."

With that, he slapped him across the face. The sobbing would not stop.

"Shut up that Goddamned crying. I won't have these brave men here who have been shot at seeing a yellow bastard sitting here crying."

He slapped him again, this time with sufficient force to send his helmet liner flying into the next tent. Turning to the doctor who had admitted him, Patton barked out an order: "Don't admit this yellow bastard; there's nothing the matter with him. I won't have the hospitals cluttered up with these sons of bitches who haven't got the guts to fight." Returning his gaze to Bennett, Patton drilled his words into him: "You're going back to the front lines and you may get shot and killed, but you're going to fight. If you don't, I'll stand you up against a wall and have a firing squad kill you on purpose."

Then, as if seizing on a passing thought, he reached for his revolver, an ivory-handled Colt that was as much his trademark as his scowl, the well-rehearsed mask he called his "war face."

"In fact, I ought to shoot you myself, you Goddamned whimpering coward."

The hand went for the ivory handle, but Patton wheeled around and stormed out of the tent without taking the weapon out of its holster. "Send that yellow son of a bitch back to the front line," he shouted over his shoulder.

This second episode affected Patton far more strongly than the first. He continued his round of the tent wards, but he couldn't stop talking about Bennett, his eyes repeatedly tearing up as he did.

"I can't help it," he said, "but it makes my blood boil to think of a yellow bastard being babied."

It was as if he saw cowardice as an infection—doubtless an infection to which he had no special immunity.

"I won't have those cowardly bastards hanging around our hospitals," he declared to Colonel Donald E. Currier, the hospital's commanding officer (CO). "We'll probably have to shoot them some time anyway, or we'll raise a breed of morons."

And the effect of the second incident would reach far beyond his own emotions. This episode, coming as it did less than a week after the first, prompted Lieutenant Colonel Long to write a report and send it through Medical Corps channels, where someone saw to it that the document reached the desk of Omar Bradley, now commanding II Corps. As we will see, Bradley, who would soon rise over Patton to become his commanding officer, had profoundly ambivalent feelings toward him, but, whether out of loyalty, an awareness of Patton's importance to the war, or fear of igniting a public relations powder keg, he read the report and then locked it in his safe, along with other eyes-only papers. What Bradley did not know was that his wasn't the only copy. Medical officers had also sent the report directly to Eisenhower, who received it on August 16.

The very next day, Ike wrote a "personal and secret letter" to Patton, attached to which was Long's report, which the supreme Allied commander described as "shocking in its allegations against your personal conduct. I hope you can assure me that none of them is true . . ." because "if there is a very considerable element of truth in the allegations . . . I must so seriously question your good judgment and your self discipline as to raise serious doubts in my mind as to your future usefulness."

Patton described it as "a very nasty letter," but the fact was that Eisenhower had done him the great service of filing neither the letter nor the report with Allied Headquarters; moreover, he included in the letter an assurance that it was "*not* my present intention to institute any formal investigation." Later, when Demaree Bess of the *Saturday Evening Post*, along with other correspondents, learned of both episodes, Eisenhower moved quickly to dissuade them from publishing stories. He explained that the war effort could not afford to lose Patton. The reporters complied—at least for a time.

Ike closed his letter by noting that nothing he had ever written in his military career had caused him so much "mental anguish," and he warned Patton that such conduct "will *not* be tolerated in this theater no matter who the offender may be."

The 1970 film, *Patton*, presents the letter as having included orders that Patton deliver a round of apologies for his behavior. In fact, Eisenhower issued no such order or even made such a request. It was Patton himself who deemed that personal, even humbling apologies were called for—though he seems to have reached this decision primarily as a means of placating his commander. "I hate to make Ike mad when it is my earnest study to please him," he wrote in his diary on

August 20. Patton called on the medical personnel of the hospitals involved and apologized to them, then he summoned both Kuhl and Bennett for private meetings, at which he insisted on their shaking hands with him—in effect ordering them to accept his apology. At the end of August, he addressed the eighteen thousand men of the 1st Division, Seventh Army, and made what division CO Clarence R. Huebner called "a very good speech, in which he explained that he was sorry." There was, Huebner noted, "no applause. They knew Patton was wrong, but they also knew it was something to get over and forget as soon as possible."

Yet it was Patton, first and foremost, who would not let it drop. On August 30, he addressed the 3rd Division, but, this time, when the men sensed that he was about to embark on his apology, a chant, completely spontaneous, rose up from nearly twenty thousand throats, "No, General, no, no; no, General, no, no," and continued in an increasingly earnest crescendo until Patton, overcome with emotion, stepped away from the rostrum. By September, when he addressed troops assembled for a USO show, he had learned to temper his apology with humor. "I thought I would stand here," he began, "and let you see what a son of a bitch looks like and whether I am as big a son of a bitch as you think I am."

To Eisenhower himself, Patton wrote a letter of thanks for the "fairness and generous consideration" shown by his writing a personal letter rather than an official, and career-ending, censure. He then continued in an abject vein—"I am at a loss to find words with which to express my chagrin and grief at having given you, a man to whom I owe everything and for whom I would gladly lay down my life, cause for displeasure with me"—only to conclude with a series of excuses: In striking the two soldiers, he had had "no intention of being either harsh or cruel"; his "sole purpose was to try and restore in them a just appreciation of their obligations as men and soldiers." He went on to relate a story, of

> *a dear friend and former schoolmate who lost his nerve in an exactly analogous manner, and . . . after years of mental anguish, committed suicide. . . . Both my friend and the medical men with whom I discussed his case assured me that had he been roundly checked at the time of his first misbehavior, he would have been restored to a normal state.*

"Naturally," Patton continued, "the memory actuated me when I inaptly tried to apply the remedies suggested." Thus, as Patton would have Eisenhower believe, the two assaults had actually been merciful attempts to save two endangered lives.

As if the anecdote were not improbable enough, Patton tripped himself up by having his "friend" explain how his own suicide might have been prevented. Was all of this intended to explain away his behavior to Eisenhower—or to himself? In either case, the incident could not be explained away or otherwise made to go away.

Ike might have refrained from issuing an official reprimand, but the indisputable fact was that he had named Mark Clark, not George Patton, to command the Fifth Army on the Italian mainland. Even more pointedly, Ike chose Omar Bradley, not Patton, to organize an army for the cross-Channel invasion. While these major combat operations were in the hands of these other commanders, Patton was pinioned to the island he had conquered, ordered to preside over the dismemberment of the very army with which he had conquered it.

For months, the newspapers had been filled with Patton. Lately, they hardly mentioned him. Perhaps getting Patton out of the limelight in the wake of the slapping incidents was a stroke of deliberate strategy on the part of Eisenhower. It has been the traditional assumption, however, that benching Patton was punishment for his bad behavior. Most recent historians have labeled this interpretation a myth, arguing that Eisenhower's motive was the same as it would be during the Normandy invasion: to deceive the enemy. If American newspapers had stopped talking about Patton, the German OKW buzzed with his name. What was *Patton* doing? What army and what operation would *Patton* lead next? When would *Patton* attack? Indeed, although Eisenhower kept Patton out of the action, he hardly kept him under wraps. Instead, he ordered him on highly visible junkets to Algiers, Tunis, Corsica, Cairo, Jerusalem, and Malta, knowing that these disparate locations had one thing in common. They all loomed in the enemy's consciousness as plausible jumping-off places for a major Allied operation. Patton's appearance in one after another of them kept the Germans guessing, compelling them not only to spread their resources thin, but to engage in the most energy- and resource-consuming activity any army undertakes: moving from place to place.

If his peripatetic status made the Germans uncomfortable, it threw Patton into an agony of anxious anticipation. No one, not Ike and not Bradley, assured him that he *would* get into the war, sooner or later. So Patton waited and wandered from one Mediterranean bastion to another.

Then, late in November 1943, broadcasting from Washington on a Sunday evening, the popular columnist and liberal gadfly Drew Pearson, without warning, broke the long-suppressed news of the slapping incidents. With the memory of North African and Sicilian triumphs already fading from the public consciousness, Patton now appeared to be the incarnation of the very fascist mentality America's sons were fighting. Even worse, Pearson castigated not only Patton, but Eisenhower as well, for having covered up the shameful episode by failing to file an official reprimand. In the wake of the Sunday broadcast, the House and Senate rang with calls for Patton's dismissal, some politicians even comparing him to Adolf Hitler. Pressured, secretary of war Henry Stimson asked Eisenhower for a full report.

It would have been expedient for Ike to fire Patton. Instead, he defended him on the basis of his record. Yes, he admitted to Stimson, he had issued a personal rather than an official reprimand. His intention had not been to cover up the episodes, but to preserve for the war effort an extraordinarily effective commander. He argued that Patton, the slapper of soldiers, was far more importantly a savior of soldiers, his victories achieved as much by rapid movement as by battle; therefore, his casualties were low, especially when balanced against his tactical achievements.

In the end, Eisenhower and Patton weathered the storm. After roiling through most of November and part of December, the tumult began to subside—or, more importantly, to shift. Letters continued to arrive in the office of the president and the secretary of war, but, increasingly, they expressed support for Patton and forgiveness for what many judged to have been the unfortunate product of the stress of war and command.

Ike stood by Patton, but the slapping incidents surely gave him pause and, because of this, the episodes did shape Patton's destiny. It was not that Ike had lost all confidence in Patton, but that his outbursts had confirmed in his mind what he had long felt about him. The very qualities that drove him, that made Patton a master of hit-and-run tactics—of moving fire, which swept away the enemy while preserving the lives of his own soldiers—were also associated with volatility, even instability, of personality. Patton was not so much a loose cannon as he was a cannon charged with a propellant so dangerously explosive that it always threatened to blow up in the faces of those who fired it.

The slapping incidents confirmed Ike's already existing sense that Patton was the wrong man to lead Operation Overlord—the invasion of Normandy. Planning, logistics, the management of landings on an unprecedented scale, comradely coordination with British commanders—all of this required the patient head and steady hand of someone as competently ordinary as Patton was flamboyantly incendiary. Omar Bradley filled the bill. But, and this was key, once the landings had been made, the beachheads secured, and the lodgments established—in short, as soon as the odds of instantaneous catastrophe had been reduced—the explosive Patton, matchless mover of men and machines, was just the officer to drive a breakout from beachhead and lodgment and into and through the continent held by Hitler.

The cost of holding Patton back, of transforming him into a decoy, was high. For eleven months after the capture of Messina, he was out of the shooting war. As far as Patton himself could tell, by slapping those GIs, he had sustained a self-inflicted wound. But the question of whether his prolonged hiatus ultimately advanced or retarded the Allied war effort is open to speculation.

The agony of suspense significantly eased in January 1944, when Patton was at last ordered from Sicily to London. On the twenty-sixth he was told that he would command the Third United States Army, a force created for him. As to what, exactly, he was expected to do with his army, Patton was left in the dark, and, though he knew that the invasion of Europe was being planned, he was given little more than the role of auditor in the planning—and not always that much. He and his army were domiciled in the tranquil Cheshire town of Knutsford, five hours outside of London. Patton was billeted at Peover Hall, which he described as "a huge house last repaired in 1627 or there abouts."

The weeks spent in dismal, drafty, dilapidated Peover Hall turned into months. Patton had an army, but nothing for it to do—beyond train and drill. Eisenhower instructed him to keep an ultra-low profile. Although he had a real command, the truth was that Ike was still using him as a decoy. Operation Fortitude was the name given to the vast campaign of deception designed to dupe the Germans into believing that the invasion of Europe would come via the Pas de Calais, not Normandy. Phony assembly points for a Pas de Calais invasion were laid out and jammed with plywood aircraft, inflatable rubber tanks, empty tents, and hollow buildings, all elaborate decoys designed and crafted by scenic artists from Hollywood and the British film industry. Patton, whose actual Peover Hall headquarters was remote from this charade, took care to avoid revealing his true location. But, toward the end of April 1944, he reluctantly accepted an invitation from a delegation of local ladies to make an appearance at the dedication of a Knutsford "Welcome Club" for American GIs. Doubtless, he was motivated by a desire to maintain friendly relations with his army's hosts, and also by the knowledge that Ike was very keen on any courtesies that would reduce friction between U.S. military personnel and British civilians. "There are only three things wrong with Americans," the British man and woman on the street were fond of saying. "They are overpaid, oversexed, and over here." Above all else at the moment, Patton wanted to please Eisenhower. Besides, he had taken the precaution of accepting the invitation on strict condition that he would not preside over the ceremony, and that it would not be covered by the press.

On the appointed day, Patton took an additional precautionary measure. He deliberately arrived fifteen minutes late, a tactic he hoped would allow him to dodge most of the proceedings. To his dismay, the Knutsford ladies swarmed him as he emerged from his staff car and ushered him to a podium, where he was welcomed, introduced—and asked to speak. Unwilling to give offense, Patton did not demur, but ad-libbed what he believed were a handful of innocuous remarks.

Because his brief speech was unscripted, only Patton's own recollection of it survives. He seized on the theme of "welcoming" and remarked that "until today" his "only experience in welcoming has been to welcome Germans and Italians to the 'Infernal Regions.'" It was a good line for a laugh, and the anticipated response must have heartened the general, because he warmed to his task and declared next that "such clubs as this are a very real value, because I believe with Mr. Bernard Shaw, I think it was he, that the British and Americans are two people separated by a common language."

Had he stopped there, the world would have little noted nor long remembered what was said in sleepy Knutsford. But, riding the momentum of his audience's approval, he continued, and, by his own recollection, he went on to say, "and since it is the evident destiny of the British and Americans, and, of course, the Russians, to rule the world, the better we know each other, the better job we will do."

The newspapers—despite a ban on the presence of the press, journalists were on the job nevertheless—reported the speech very differently. On April 26, U.S. Army PR officers showered Patton, Eisenhower, *and* prime minister Winston Churchill with press clippings proclaiming that Patton had announced that the British and the Americans would rule the postwar world, pointedly excluding the Russians.

Churchill, who liked nothing about the Soviets, dismissed the reported omission as of no consequence, but American newspapers, thrilled to put the general they loved to hate in the headlines again, trumpeted Patton's "insult" to "our gallant Soviet allies." And even those papers that did not particularly object to such an insult sputtered in self-righteous indignation over the concept of "ruling the world." This, they observed, was a phrase and a sentiment better suited to Mussolini, Hitler, and Tojo than to a top commander of an army fighting to restore liberty and democracy.

Patton was at a loss. Slapping a pair of dogfaces was one thing. He understood why that made people mad. But a few remarks to a few old ladies? Besides, he insisted, the fault was not in what he had said—which had included the Russians—but in the reporting, which had not. Still, Patton had every reason to believe that this would blow over, if anything even sooner than the furor over the slapping incidents had.

He was wrong. "This last incident was so trivial in its nature," he later remarked, "but so terrible in its effect." Eisenhower, who had found it in himself to defend Patton even after he had assaulted two men in hospitals—acts truly heinous—now cabled Army chief of staff General George C. Marshall that he was "seriously contemplating" relieving Patton and sending him home. Marshall responded in a way that wisely aimed at removing emotion from Eisenhower's impending decision. Marshall replied that if he was convinced that Courtney Hodges could lead the Third Army as effectively as Patton, then he should fire Patton. If, on the other hand, he believed Patton to be the better commander for the Third Army, then it was best to bear "between us . . . the burden of the present unfortunate reaction" against Patton's latest gaffe.

Eisenhower summoned the general to his headquarters on May 1, 1944. Patton later recalled that Ike started by declaring, "George, you have gotten yourself into a very serious fix."

Even now, fighting to be allowed to fulfill what he believed to be his destiny, Patton drove forward, hard, into the teeth of the battle. He broke in before Eisenhower could begin another sentence: "I want to say that your job is more important than mine, so if in trying to save me you are hurting yourself, throw me out."

His "enemy" did not retreat, however. Instead, Eisenhower replied that it was not a matter of his being hurt by Patton, "but of hurting you and depriving me of a fighting Army commander." Nor did he let up. Ike said that General Marshall believed that his "repeated mistakes have shaken the confidence of the country and the War Department." Eisenhower then implied that he did intend to relieve Patton, telling him that if he were sent home, he would recommend against a reduction in rank to colonel so as to reserve the option of assigning him command of another army—someday, should the need ever arise.

Patton recorded in his diary that he responded to this by announcing his wish to be busted to colonel, if that would keep him from being sent home and allow him to get into combat as commander of one of the assault regiments. When Ike failed to take this bait, Patton became more insistent, verging on insubordination: "I told him that if I was reduced to a Colonel, I demanded the right to command one of the assault regiments." This, he insisted, "was not a favor but a right."

Thus Patton recalled the exchange as one in which he came out swinging and refused to break off the attack. "You are not beaten until you surrender," Patton once wrote in his field notebook. "Hence, don't." But Eisenhower, in his own recollection of the interview, remembered only how, "in a gesture of almost little-boy contriteness, [Patton] put his head on my shoulder," and doing so caused "his helmet to fall off—a gleaming helmet I sometimes thought he wore in bed."

> *As it rolled across the room I had the rather odd feeling that I was in the middle of a ridiculous situation . . . his helmet bounced across the floor into a corner. I prayed that no one would come in and see the scene. . . . Without apology and without embarrassment, he walked over, picked up his helmet, adjusted it, and said: "Sir, could I now go back to my headquarters?"*

"When I came out [of Eisenhower's office], I don't think anyone could tell that I had just been killed. . . . My final thought on the matter is that I am destined to achieve some great thing—what, I don't know, but this last incident was so trivial in its nature, but so terrible in its effect, that it is not the result of an accident but the work of God. His Will be done."

Forty-eight hours crawled by before Patton received Eisenhower's cable: "I am once more taking the responsibility of retaining you in command in spite of damaging repercussions resulting from a personal indiscretion. I do this solely because of my faith in you as a battle leader and from no other motives."

And in case he didn't get the message, Eisenhower sent Colonel Justus "Jock" Lawrence, a senior PR officer, to Peover Hall to verbally convey Ike's order that neither Patton nor his staff were to make any public statements until he, the supreme Allied commander, issued orders to the contrary.

"Come on, Jock," Patton goaded, "what did Ike *really* say?"

"He said that you were not to open your goddamned mouth again publicly until he said you could!"

The reprieve failed to produce immediate relief. "I felt all tense," Patton recorded in his diary on May 4, "so took pills with a bromide, with no effect so far." Nevertheless, he threw himself into training the Third Army, fearful that their edge would grow dull with waiting and inaction. It was during this interval that he delivered the most famous speech of his career. Actually, it was a series of speeches, variations on a single theme, delivered personally to each unit of the Third Army. It was never written out. A lifelong sufferer from what today would be diagnosed as dyslexia, Patton had great difficulty reading from a script. He therefore spoke from a mixture of memory and the inspiration of the moment.

Men, this stuff some sources sling around about America wanting to stay out of the war and not wanting to fight is a lot of baloney! Americans love to fight, traditionally. All real Americans love the sting and clash of battle. America loves a winner. America will not tolerate a loser. Americans despise a coward, Americans play to win. That's why America has never lost and never will lose a war.

You are not all going to die. Only two percent of you, right here today, would be killed in a major battle. Death must not be feared. Death, in time, comes to all of us. And every man is scared in his first action. If he says he's not, he's a goddamn liar. . . . The real hero is the man who fights even though he's scared. . . .

All through your Army careers, you've been bitching about what you call "chicken-shit drill." That, like everything else in the Army, has a definite purpose. That purpose is Instant Obedience to Orders and to create and maintain Constant Alertness! This must be bred into every soldier. A man must be alert all the time if he expects to stay alive. If not, some German son-of-a-bitch will sneak up behind him with a sock full o' shit! There are four hundred neatly marked graves somewhere in Sicily, all because ONE man went to sleep on his job . . . but they are German graves, because WE caught the bastards asleep! An Army is a team, lives, sleeps, fights, and eats as a team. This individual hero stuff is a lot of horse shit. The bilious bastards who write that kind of stuff for the Saturday Evening Post *don't know any more about real fighting under fire than they know about fucking!*

Every single man in the Army plays a vital role . . . even the guy who boils the water to keep us from getting the G.I. shits!

Remember, men, you don't know I'm here. . . . I'm not supposed to be commanding this Army. . . . Let the first bastards to find out be the Goddamn Germans. I want them to look up and howl, "ACH, IT'S THE GODDAM THIRD ARMY AND THAT SON-OF-A-BITCH PATTON AGAIN!"

We want to get this thing over and get the hell out of here, and get at those purple-pissin' Japs!!! The shortest road home is through Berlin and Tokyo! We'll win this war, but we'll win it only by showing the enemy we have more guts than they have or ever will have!

There's one great thing you men can say when it's all over and you're home once more. You can thank God that twenty years from now, when you're sitting around the fireside with your grandson on your knee and he asks you what you did in the war, you won't have to shift him to the other knee, cough, and say, "I shoveled shit in Louisiana."

It was, of course, a marvelous speech, but it was intended to be heard by men on the very eve of battle, whereas the dismal fact was that the Third Army and George S. Patton were going nowhere. They had been assigned no role in the cross-Channel invasion.

On June 4, as D-Day drew near, with Bradley already having set up his First U.S. Army command post on board the cruiser USS *Augusta*, Patton sought solace in church.

"I am awfully restless," he recorded in his diary that evening, "and wish I were leading the assault." To Beatrice that same evening, he wrote of the impending invasion not as what it was, a desperate epic enterprise on which the future of civilization depended, but as a personal disappointment. "Don't get excited when the whistle blows. I am not in the opening kick off."

On June 6—D-Day—Patton filled his diary with nothing but himself. "I have horrible feelings," he wrote, "that the fighting will be over before I get in . . ." and, over the next month, from June 6 to July 6, a span in which hundreds of thousands fought and bled and died in an effort to scratch into the Norman sand a foothold on the imprisoned continent, the pages of the Patton diary echoed dully over and again with the same burden, "Time drags terribly."

23

CHAPTER 2

"A VERY TIMID OPERATION"

"There is nothing to do at the moment but be a secret weapon."

—PATTON, LETTER TO BEATRICE PATTON,

JULY 10, 1944

On June 6, 1944, American, British, and Canadian forces stormed the beaches at Normandy in the most spectacular and consequential landing in modern history. Precisely one month later, on July 6, 1944, Patton, together with aides Colonel Charles R. Codman and Major Alexander C. Stiller, and Patton's bull terrier Willy, drove quietly to an airfield near Salisbury and found seats among the cargo loaded in a C-47 "Gooney Bird." With two other C-47s and an escort of four P-47 "Jugs," Patton's plane took off on an hour-long flight to an airstrip just behind Omaha Beach, Normandy. Two days earlier, the men and the equipment of the Third Army had begun slipping out of their British embarkation areas and onto landing ships (LSTs—"landing ships, tank") for the stomach-churning voyage across the English Channel to join the European invasion already in progress. Rarely have a commander and his army moved into battle with so little fanfare.

Patton appreciated the need for secrecy. Operation Fortitude was still in effect—and was obviously still working astoundingly well. One month after the Normandy landings, the Germans were *still* holding their entire Fifteenth Army behind the Pas de Calais. Hitler and his high command remained convinced that Patton would soon land there with the main invasion force. The longer they labored under this delusion the better—especially since the initial invasion forces were having a very tough time making progress.

Between June 6 and June 12, the Allies managed to weld together their five beachheads—Utah, Omaha, Gold, Juno, and Sword—into a lodgment eighty miles wide with an average depth of ten miles. With eight additional combat divisions having landed since June 6, Omar Bradley had reason to be confident that no German effort would succeed in driving the invaders back into the sea. But he also perceived that German resistance was stiffening everywhere, and it was clear to him that the clock was running out on the opportunity for a swift, clean breakout inland.

The key, he knew, was to quickly capture Caen and Cherbourg on the Cotentin Peninsula. Breaking through Caen would open up to the invaders ideal terrain for a high-speed armor advance to Paris, about 120 miles inland. Capturing Cherbourg would assure the armies of a capacious, readily defended port to supply and reinforce the invasion for the long term. Britain's Bernard Law Montgomery had almost casually promised that he would capture Caen within a very few days after D-Day, thereby securing a hub around which the armies were to wheel toward their various objectives. The plan was for the First Canadian Army to pivot on Caen before turning east-northeast for a march to the Seine, targeting Rouen. Simultaneously, the Second British Army would advance south-southwest, striking through German strong points at Falaise and Argentan in an advance to the Seine. While Montgomery carved out this great swath of territory, the First U.S. Army would drive the main movement of the breakout inland. It was to sweep south past Avranches, from where it would send units up the Brittany Peninsula, through Rennes, to take Brest on the tip of the peninsula. At the same time, another First Army force was to march toward Nantes on the Loire, which would cut off Brittany, thereby foiling any German counterattack on the rear of the inland advance. Finally, a pair of First Army contingents were to break away from Brittany and advance toward the Seine. One would target Paris, while the other would move south of Paris, to close what Bradley called the "Paris-Orléans gap." Once Avranches had been taken, Patton's Third Army would swing into action, beginning the major thrust through the rest of France and points east.

That was the plan—all of which depended on Montgomery doing what he said he would do: take Caen quickly. Unfortunately for both Bradley and Montgomery, Erwin Rommel understood that Caen would have to be the first battleground following the landings themselves. He therefore transferred three divisions from Brittany to augment the two already defending Caen. This was sufficient to keep Montgomery's Second British Army out of Caen for weeks following the landings.

Thus deprived of the hub of his plan, Bradley decided to focus on taking the village of Carentan, in the American battle sector. Once this objective was obtained, he planned to send three First Army corps to establish and defend a perimeter extending from Carentan to Caumont on the southeastern neck of the Cotentin Peninsula. Despite Montgomery's failings, this operation provided the appearance of rapid progress, prompting Winston Churchill, British general Alan Brooke, Eisenhower, George C. Marshall, Admiral Ernest J. King, and USAAF general Henry H. "Hap" Arnold to predict, when they visited the front on June 12, the defeat of Germany by Christmas. Though he said nothing to dampen the spirits of his distinguished visitors, Bradley was less sure. Without Caen in his possession, he had no clear idea of how to restore momentum to the invasion. Worse, no sooner had his visitors left, than Bradley received intelligence indicating that Rommel had just shifted the 17th SS Panzer Grenadier Division and the 6th Parachute Regiment from Brittany to the First U.S. Army front. Clearly, Rommel meant to take back Carentan. If he succeeded, he could then drive between First Army's V and VII Corps, and, by splitting and flanking them, push them all the way back to the beaches. Unwilling to allow this, Bradley turned from offense to defense, sending a tank battalion and an armored infantry battalion to Carentan to reinforce the lightly armed 101st Airborne there. Thus bolstered, the 101st repulsed Rommel's attack, but took heavy losses in the effort. This was only part of the cost of shifting to defense. Borrowing the tank and infantry battalions had weakened the First Army's position near Caumont. This time it was Montgomery who came to the rescue, sending elements of the British 7th Armoured Division to cover the left flank of the U.S. 1st Division at Caumont. The timely action held Rommel at bay until additional British and American divisions could come into position and put a period to the German commander's already vanishing hope of bottling up the invasion.

While the drama at Carentan played out, the U.S. VII Corps, positioned north of Carentan, attacked to the west, across the base of the Cotentin Peninsula. Its progress, however, was slowed by the *bocage*—hedgerows—in what was the American army's first experience with hedgerow country. In many places, the marshy Norman farmlands were networked by ancient man-high stone walls overgrown with tangled vines and thick bushes, which demarcated property lines, separating one farm from another. Intensely picturesque, these hedgerows also made virtually impenetrable anti-tank obstacles. Tanks as well as other vehicles and even infantry became entangled in the bocage and were often torn up by German defensive fire. Even when a tank was able to climb over a hedgerow, doing so exposed its unarmored underside to fire—sometimes for several minutes as the vehicle struggled to clear the obstacle.

As a West Point instructor, Bradley became well known for his use of sand tables in preference to flat maps in tactical exercises, because he believed it imperative for a commander to fully understand the topography of the battlefield in three dimensions. It is, therefore, difficult to fathom why Bradley failed to take the bocage, the region's dominant topographical feature, into account when he planned the breakout from the Normandy lodgments. The Americans were able to struggle through the hedgerows en route to Cherbourg, the defenses of which the 9th, 79th, and 4th Infantry Divisions battered from June 22 to June 27, when the key port town yielded. Yet these troops soon discovered that, as troublesome as the hedgerows were in the advance up the Cotentin Peninsula toward Cherbourg, they presented a far more formidable obstacle on the way back down the peninsula.

And this was a very bad thing. Bradley's tactical method of choice was to identify a soft spot in the enemy's positions and concentrate his attack on it. Believing he had found such a spot on the west Cotentin coast from La Haye du Puits down to the moorlands of Coutances, Bradley decided to make his first major breakthrough there. So dense were the hedgerows, however, that an attacker could not face more challenging ground whereas a defender could not ask for ground more congenial. On July 3, Bradley began his attack southward, down the western Cotentin coast. Impeded by the hedgerows, he got no farther than Lessay, a meager distance south of La Haye du Puits, his starting point.

The Norman hedgerows threatened to do what Rommel could not: bottle up the invasion. It was in this agonizing circumstance that Bradley writhed on July 6 as Patton's C-47 touched down.

"Well, come on," Patton turned to Codman and Stiller as he moved toward the door. "Let's see if there is still a war going on."

Patton, who loved uniforms, had dressed down in a nod toward maintaining a low profile. He wore an ordinary Class A uniform, officer's Oxfords instead of shiny cavalry boots, and a single automatic pistol in a shoulder holster in lieu of his flashy ivory-handled Colt. To his dismay—but also his delight—his descent down the Gooney Bird's boarding stairs was greeted by a barrage of clicking camera shutters. He recorded in his diary that a "great many people seemed to know me and wanted to take photographs." Most of them were GIs "with $5.00 Leicas, but there were some professionals present" as well. These reporters he "warned off by assuring them I was still a secret." It was, however, too late. News of Patton's arrival had leaked, and soldiers as well as sailors gathered in abundance at the airport for a glimpse of the most famous general in the American army.

Patton could not ignore any substantial group of assembled troops. "I'm proud to be here to fight beside you," he told the crowd gathered near his aircraft. "Now let's cut the guts out of those Krauts and get the hell to Berlin. And when we get to

Berlin, I am going to personally shoot that paper-hanging god-damned son of a bitch just like I would a snake." The shutter clicks gave way to cheers.

Depressed by what he considered the ignominy of his anonymous flight into battle over the Channel, Patton was greatly buoyed by the reception he received. But he was even more stirred by what he saw as he was driven along the landing beaches. It was not the wreckage of ships in the shallows or the remnants of the carnage in the sand that moved him, but the "character of the [German] defensive works." This was Hitler's vaunted "Atlantic Wall," the titanic labor of slaves. Patton saw formidable pillboxes made of concrete reinforced with stout rebar—each pillbox "taken by American infantry," which went to prove "that good American troops can capture anything." Even more important, the ruined pillboxes demonstrated that "no beach can be defended if seriously attacked." This was a key element of Patton's vision of the world-as-battlespace. No defense could withstand a truly determined attack. For time out of mind, military men had been awed by castles, fortresses, and bunkers, but Patton viewed them with contempt. Such structures were the enemies, not the allies, of victory. As he saw it, the pillboxes carried within them the seeds of defeat. As he looked at them from his jeep, he pondered the "psychological effect of concrete defenses on the defenders. If a man gets inside a concrete pillbox, ten feet thick, his first reaction is that: 'The enemy must be very strong or I wouldn't have to hide.'" For Patton, this was no mere intellectual analysis. He never had to imagine what it felt like to attack for the simple reason that he *had* attacked, so he *knew* what it felt like. Defending in place, however, was another matter. He had never done it. Looking at the twisted orange-brown rebar protruding from the shattered concrete, he could only imagine what a soldier felt "when the

line he is defending is pierced." It was, he believed, "a creeping feeling in his spine, knowing that he is surrounded and not
knowing from where an attack is coming." In fact, he "must
feel very much like a turtle who has been picked up on the
road by small boys; and like the turtle, he is very apt to experience a fire on his back, but from a flamethrower rather than
from matches."

To hole up, to cower in battle was not merely contemptible,
it was fatal. First, it reduced one to cowardice, a state of fear;
then it deprived one not merely of manhood, but of humanity.
The defender was not a human warrior, but a box turtle, whose
shell might provide adequate defense against lesser animals,
but was powerless against the human ingenuity of small boys
armed with matches.

The whole world had seen an example of the folly of reli-
ance on defensive fortifications in the spectacular irrelevance
of the vaunted Maginot Line, which the Germans simply
circumvented in 1940. Patton had personally seen another
example close up when Ike Eisenhower had called on him
to replace Major General Lloyd Fredendall in Tunisia after
the humiliating defeat of his II Corps at Kasserine Pass (February 19–25, 1943). Just at the time that a policy of relentless
advance against Erwin Rommel's Afrika Korps was called for,
Fredendall had instead commandeered an entire company of
the 19th Engineer Regiment to build him an elaborately hardened bunker seventy miles behind the front lines at a place
the troops called Speedy Valley, southeast of Tébessa. While II
Corps idled, awaiting its leader's orders, the bunker was laboriously drilled and blasted out of solid rock over three weeks
to create a pair of U-shaped tunnel structures that ran 160 feet
into a hillside. The general also assembled one full anti-aircraft
battalion for the exclusive purpose of protecting him and his

headquarters. During the Kasserine Pass debacle, Fredendall did not command in the front lines, but stewed in his bunker. Ike dispatched 2nd Armored Division commander Major General Ernest Harmon to see what was going on with II Corps. The blunt officer, whose neatly trimmed mustache gave him the look of a younger Pershing, reported back to Eisenhower that Fredendall was a "son-of-a-bitch" unfit for command. (To Patton, whom he greatly admired, Harmon spoke even more brutally. Fredendall, he said, was a "moral and physical coward.") When Eisenhower turned to British general Harold Alexander for a second opinion, the reply was more refined but just as uncompromising: "I'm sure you must have better men than that."

Like Harmon, Bradley was particularly appalled by the bunker, which, he reported to Eisenhower, was "an embarrassment to every American soldier." Patton agreed. The bunker was defeat in dirt and concrete.

Bradley hosted Patton in his First Army headquarters on July 6, then the two met with Montgomery on the 7th. Patton had little patience for the British commander, who, he recorded in his diary, "went to great length explaining why the British had done nothing. Caen was their D-Day objective, and they have not taken it." This, together with the hedgerows, prompted Bradley himself to recall in his autobiography, *A General's Life*, that "we faced a real danger of a World War I–type stalemate."

During the lunch and the conference that followed, it became clear to Patton that the fight with the Germans wasn't the only war going on in Normandy. Bradley and Montgomery were at swords' point, and it was crystal clear to Patton that both Montgomery and Bradley eyed him with skepticism. Patton "had not been my first choice for Army commander," Bradley wrote in another postwar memoir, *A Soldier's Story.* "I feared that too much of my time would probably be spent in curbing his impetuous habits." But as if realizing that impetuosity was precisely what was needed to break the congealing stalemate, Bradley continued: "At the same time I knew that with Patton there would be no need for my whipping Third Army to keep it on the move. We had only to keep him pointed in the direction we wanted to go."

The last sentence is particularly revelatory. Over the next several months, Bradley would often be at odds with Patton and, at one point, would even nudge Eisenhower into sending him home. Ultimately, however, Bradley learned to regard Patton as a powerful weapon, which, like any such weapon, was potentially as dangerous to the user as it was to the target. The trick was to keep the weapon pointed in the right direction. Patton was a force, an elemental energy that could neither be created nor destroyed, but only transformed—shaped, used, aimed. The catch was that doing this was no easy task.

As Patton himself saw the situation, he, Patton, was still "in the doghouse," guilty in the eyes of his seniors and colleagues until proven otherwise. The required proof, he told VII Corps commander J. Lawton Collins, was for him "to do something spectacular."

If Patton was dismayed by the ill-tempered wrangling into which he had suddenly been dropped, he never let on. To Collins he remarked, "You know, . . . you and I are the only people around here who seem to be enjoying this goddamned war," and all that really seemed to worry him was that the failed July 20 assassination attempt against Hitler at his "Wolf's Lair" command complex (news of which quickly arrived at Bradley's headquarters) heralded an imminent end to the war—before he could get into it.

Yet even this caused him no real anxiety. Despite the miasma of ill will hanging over Bradley's headquarters, despite the arguments, despite the delays, Patton was, in effect, already in the battle. In 1818, John Adams wrote, "The Revolution was effected before the war commenced. The Revolution was in the minds and hearts of the people. . . ." And so the invasion of Europe had been in the mind and heart of George Patton months earlier, well before he left England.

At Peover Hall, Patton devoured maps, as if he meant to burn a picture of the prospective battlespace into his memory. As he recounted in his posthumously published memoir, *War as I Knew It*, he showed assistant secretary of war John J. McCloy a Michelin map of France when he visited Peover Hall and pointed to Rennes, telling him that "the first big battle of the Third Army" would be fought there. (As it turned out, Patton noted, this was "actually . . . the second big battle.") "Many other points, at most of which we subsequently fought, were selected . . . . It is of interest to note that this study was made on a road map of France, scale 1:1,000,000, and if 'The greatest study of mankind is man,' surely the greatest study of war is the road net."

Whereas most commanders demanded the most detailed, largest-scale maps they could obtain, Patton declared his "opinion that, in the High Command, small-scale maps are best because from that level one has to decide on general policies and determine the places, usually road centers or river lines, the capture of which will hurt the enemy most." Large-scale maps were suited to the "lower echelons," whose job was to determine how to capture the objectives high command had designated based on the big picture supplied by study of a small-scale map.

If Patton habitually pulled back in space so as to get in his mind before battle the biggest possible picture, so he also pulled back in time. While he was still at Peover Hall, he read Edward A. Freeman's 1879 *History of the Norman Conquest*, "paying particular attention to the roads William the Conqueror used in his operations in Normandy and Brittany." Patton's absorption in military history is nearly legendary, going hand in hand with his celebrated belief that he was the reincarnation of warriors stretching back to the Crucifixion and earlier. But his study of the Norman Conquest was more than a product of an amateur's interest in history. "The roads used in those days," he explained, "had to be on ground which was always practicable. Therefore, using these roads, even in modern times, permits easy by-passing when the enemy resorts, as he always does, to demolition." For Patton, looking backwards was a means of ensuring that he could always move ahead.

As for the maps he had studied and marked at his leisure in Peover Hall, those who examined them after the war in Europe had ended were stunned by how accurately they anticipated the movements of the Third U.S. Army, from the Channel coast to Germany.

As Bradley continued to struggle through the bocage on his right (Cotentin) flank, his center (consisting mainly of XIX Corps) managed to capture the strategically important village of Saint-Lô on July 18, though at substantial cost. On July 8, the Second British Army finally took at least the portion of Caen that lay west of the Orne River; on the 20th, Montgomery at long last occupied the rest of the town. This was a relief to Bradley, but it was an objective that was supposed to have been attained almost immediately after D-Day. As of July 20, therefore, the invaders held a bit more than 20 percent of the territory they had planned to control by this date.

There was at this time a heartening development in the war against the hedgerows. Engineers had devised a device dubbed the "salad fork," a pair of stout timber prongs fitted onto the front of a tank, which was then driven into a hedgerow, piercing two small tunnels through it. Into these, soldiers slid fifteen pounds of high explosive, which had been packed into the empty fiberboard cylinders used to transport 105-mm artillery ammunition. When the charges were detonated, they blasted out a gap in the hedgerow sufficiently wide to allow passage of tanks. This procedure was better than being stuck and exposed to fire, but it was still time-consuming and hazardous. Looking at the situation, Sergeant Curtis G. Culin Jr. of the 102nd Cavalry Reconnaissance Squadron had a brainstorm.

The beaches and shallows of Normandy were thickly sown with a variety of steel obstacles intended to rip out the hulls of landing craft and to impede the advance of amphibious vehicles. The traditional collective name for these was *chevaux de fries* (literally, "horses of Friesland," a name adopted from their first use in the seventeenth-century Dutch Revolt); but whereas the original chevaux de fries had been made of sharpened timbers, Rommel's were fabricated out of hard steel. Culin salvaged one of these obstacles and fashioned it into a set of steel prongs, which he welded onto the front of a tank. The result was variously called a Culin cutter, hedgerow prongs, hedgerow cutters, and a Rhinoceros. (The tanks eventually fitted with the prongs were dubbed Rhinos.) Culin's company commander brought the prototype cutter to the attention of higher command, and Bradley, desperate for any solution to the hedgerow problem, came down to see a demonstration on July 14. He judged the Culin cutter superior to the salad fork because it required no explosives. You just aimed the tank and plowed right through the hedgerows. It was therefore faster and less hazardous to use. Without further testing, he ordered First Army Ordnance to build as many cutters as quickly as possible, using scavenged beach obstacles. By July 25, more than five hundred tanks had been converted to Rhinos. Although they did not magically overcome the hedgerow problem, the Rhinos were an important advance in coping with the terrain.

Patton was hard on Eisenhower as well as Bradley. "Neither Ike or Brad has the stuff," he wrote in his diary on July 12. "Ike is bound hand and foot by the British and does not know it. Poor fool. We actually have no Supreme Commander—no one who can take hold and say that this shall be done and that shall not be done." As for Bradley, he and his deputy First Army commander Courtney Hodges were "such nothings," Patton complained to his diary on July 14.

Their one virtue is that they get along by doing nothing. I could break through in three days if I commanded. They try to push all along the front and have no power anywhere. All that is necessary now is to take chances by leading with armored divisions and covering their advance with air bursts. Such

an attack would have to be made on a narrow sector, whereas
at present we are trying to attack all along the line.

A few days after Patton made this diary entry, Bradley
revealed to him his new approach to the Normandy breakout,
one in which his thinking dovetailed with Patton's. Having
failed to break out along a broad front (as Patton had observed
in the privacy of his diary), Bradley now decided to concentrate
on a much narrower six-thousand-yard front five miles west of
Saint-Lô. The breakout would begin with intensive bombing
against German defensive positions, followed by an infantry
thrust to rip a hole into the weakened enemy line. Through
this gap, armor and mechanized units would roll to the west
coast of the Cotentin Peninsula, targeting for assault the territory between Coutances and Brehal. The idea was to isolate the
German LXXXIV Corps, which held the road between Saint-Lô
and Perriers-Lessay. Once control of this thoroughfare had been
seized, the breakthrough could continue rapidly along it and,
as more men and machines were poured onto the highway, the
breakthrough would expand into a general breakout into the
French interior. Bradley called the plan Operation Cobra.

Patton wrote in his diary on July 23 that it was "really a very
timid operation, but Bradley and Hodges consider themselves
regular devils for having thought of it." Then Patton, perhaps
recognizing that Cobra actually harmonized quite well with
his own insistence on boldly breaking through a narrow front
rather than trying to hammer away along a broad line, turned
more charitable. "At least it is the best operation which had
been planned so far, and I hope it works."

CHAPTER 3

GIVING COBRA ITS VENOM

"The best is the enemy of the good. By this I mean that a good plan violently executed now is better than a perfect plan next week. War is a very simple thing, and the determining characteristics are self-confidence, speed, and audacity. None of these things can ever be perfect, but they can be good."

—PATTON, "REFLECTIONS AND SUGGESTIONS,"
IN *WAR AS I KNEW IT*, 1947

In World War I, the great assaults—the attempts of one side to overrun the trenches of the other—were invariably preceded by "artillery preparation," the heavy bombardment of the enemy's positions to soften them up for the infantry's attack. It was, of course, hell to be on the receiving side of such a preparation, but the tactic could also be self-defeating for the attacker because it sacrificed the element of surprise by signaling to the enemy his intention to attack. For this reason, late in the war, attackers began to substitute a "rolling barrage" for the traditional artillery preparation. Instead of hammering the enemy lines for hours—sometimes days—before attacking, the attacking side would begin the artillery barrage almost simultaneously with the infantry attack. The trick was to time and coordinate the operation so that the artillery shells bracketed the infantry advance, rolling forward with the assault wave and aimed such that shells fell both ahead of the attackers and behind them, but not on them. The object of the rolling barrage was to soften up the defensive line ahead of the attackers *and* prevent the enemy from counterattacking from the rear.

The tactic of the rolling barrage preserved the element of surprise, but if the timing and coordination were off—if something went wrong (and, in war, something almost always went wrong)—the forward barrage would fall on friendly troops in the front while the rearward barrage would prevent their withdrawing from the friendly fire.

At the opening of World War II, advances in weapons technology enabled the Germans to employ an alternative to both the preparatory barrage *and* the rolling barrage. Journalists—not the German military—labeled it "blitzkrieg": *lightning war*.

It was a doctrine and tactic of attack intended both to overawe and overwhelm defenders with rapid, violent, and, above all, intensely mobile action coordinated among armor, mechanized infantry, massed firepower, and air power, with special forces units thrown into the mix to disrupt the defenders' communication and supply, thereby increasing confusion during the onslaught. Simultaneous with a relentless advance, blitzkrieg disabled the enemy's capacity to coordinate defenses effectively. By *paralyzing* defensive capability, an attacker did not have to be delayed by a costly campaign aimed at *destroying* defenses. In this way, the attack could be accelerated to achieve maximum penetration.

Some recent military historians have argued that the opening action of World War II, the German invasion of Poland beginning on September 1, 1939, was not so much innovative blitzkrieg as an exceptionally vigorous application of more traditional warfare practices. This is not how it was seen in 1939. According to Omar Bradley, who that year was a member of Army chief of staff George C. Marshall's inner administrative circle, the War Office was rocked to its core by the spectacle of blitzkrieg in Poland. "We were amazed, shocked, dumbfounded, shaking our heads in disbelief," Bradley recalled. "Here was modern open warfare—war of maneuver—brought to the ultimate. To match such a performance, let alone exceed it, the U.S. Army had years of catching up and little time in which to do it."

Bradley may have been shocked by blitzkrieg, but by no means shocked into incomprehension, as so many of his colleagues were. The combination of his training and, paradoxically, his *lack* of combat experience in the trenches of France made the difference. He had graduated from West Point in 1915 and served in various posts in Washington State and Arizona through 1918. Like his West Point classmate Dwight David Eisenhower, Bradley was keenly disappointed by not being sent to France to lead troops in combat in World War I. Marshall (who was in France, but as one of American Expeditionary Force [AEF] commander John J. Pershing's staff, not as a combat commander), Ike, and Bradley, three top-level commanders in World War II, had one thing in common: None had led men in combat.

In 1919, Bradley was assigned as a military instructor in the ROTC program at South Dakota State College, then returned to West Point as an instructor (1920–1924), was graduated from the Infantry School at Fort Benning in 1925, and, from 1925 to 1928, served in Hawaii, where he met George S. Patton Jr.

Bradley did not much like him. Major Patton, G-2 (chief intelligence officer) of the army's Hawaiian Division, lived with his wife across the street from the Bradleys' Schofield Barracks quarters. The two couples ran in very different circles and so saw little of each other. The wealthy Pattons were at the center of Hawaii's polo-playing elite, whereas the humble Bradleys were on the outside and not much interested even in just looking in. Bradley's chief outdoor recreation was a friendly round of golf, a sport Patton detested. As a cavalry-man, Patton believed that a man's time was best spent on the back of a horse, preferably risking his neck in hell-for-leather steeplechase competitions or, even better, in polo played the way war is fought. An infantryman, Bradley had no fondness for horses.

What worked to keep the two men furthest apart, despite their being neighbors and brother officers, was the fact that Patton had seen combat in the Great War and Bradley had not. This was the great divide in the post-1918 army. Those who had fought looked with contempt on those who had not.

Nevertheless, the paths of the two majors (Patton, a colonel in the wartime AEF reverted after the war to his regular army rank of captain, but was soon promoted to major) crossed when Patton, always restless for any competition with mar-tial overtones, decided to recruit a trapshooting team. Having heard that Bradley was a good shot—Bradley's father had put a BB rifle into his hands when he was just six and a .22 not very much later—Patton invited him to try out for the team. Brad-ley missed his first two shots, then hit numbers three through twenty-three in rapid succession. Patton neither grinned nor extended his hand, but merely muttered, "You'll do."

Put off, Bradley gave no reply. In fact, his initial impulse was to take a pass. As it always did and always would, Pat-ton's reputation preceded actual acquaintance with him. An abundance of anecdotes woven around the major's flamboy-ant arrogance, his showboating, impulsive temper, fondness for drink, and what seemed an irresistible compulsion to utter outrageous, often profane pronouncements gave Brad-ley pause. "I was not certain I wanted to be on the team," he recalled years later. "Patton's style did not at all appeal to me." In the end, though, he "signed on for the sport of it."

Still, nothing like a friendship developed between them in Hawaii. Yet if Patton the Great War warrior regarded Bradley, who had stayed home in 1917–1918, with contempt, he did not show it. For his part, Bradley did not look upon those who had fought, such as Patton, with the customary attitude of admiration, envy, or resentment. Instead, he managed to persuade himself that his exclusion from the war in France had actually given him an advantage. The officers who had experienced trench warfare seemed ever afterward committed to the tactics of trench warfare, the static doctrine of attack against an entrenched defender. In contrast, Bradley, innocent of trench experience, was free to look ahead to what he believed the next war would bring: open warfare, a war of maneuver—in short, blitzkrieg.

This tactical and doctrinal orientation evolved in the course of the two assignments Bradley drew after leaving Hawaii. During 1928–1929 he attended the Command and General Staff School at Fort Leavenworth. The "trite, predictable and often unrealistic" problems and exercises to which he was exposed there convinced him that the American army was mired in the experience of the Great War and needed desperately to get prepared for the very different kind of combat situation the next war would present. After graduation, Bradley was appointed to the faculty of the Infantry School at Fort Benning, Georgia. From 1929 to 1933, he came under the influence of the school's assistant commandant, George Catlett Marshall, whom Bradley believed was "one of the greatest military minds the world has ever produced."

Marshall was eager to disseminate the innovative ideas General Pershing had developed during the war, especially his concept of combat built on firepower and maneuverability. This was squarely opposed to the static nature of trench warfare as practiced by the French and the British, and Pershing himself had found the concept nearly impossible to implement in actual combat because American military officers had received no training in "open warfare" or the "war of maneuver." It was this training Marshall was determined to provide. Like Bradley, he believed the future of combat was in offensive movement, not static defense.

The future Marshall and Bradley envisioned was not the result of a change in military fashion, but the product of technological progress. The weapons technology of the "Great War" had favored defenders over attackers. The trench was a highly effective defensive fortification, and the machine gun, the most advanced infantry weapon of the war, was principally a defensive weapon. Fired from a tripod, it allowed a crew of two or three men, operating from the cover of a trench, to kill hundreds of highly mobile attackers. By the end of the war, however, the balance of technology had begun to shift dramatically, so that weapons of attack—the weapons of movement—were starting to overtake those of defense. The airplane, the tank, and other motorized vehicles had already begun to emerge and were quickly being developed and improved. Pershing was highly critical of the Allies' stubborn adherence to static trench tactics, which he blamed for transforming the war into a bloody stalemate.

Inspired by his boss's beliefs, Marshall had no doubt that the next war would *begin* with attack and movement on a vast scale. Whichever side mastered these tactics was destined to win. Lifelong, Bradley never forgot the thrill of a typical Marshall Fort Benning lecture. "Picture the opening campaign of a war," Marshall would invite students and instructors alike.

It is a cloud of uncertainties, haste, rapid movements, congestion on the roads, strange terrain, lack of ammunition and supplies at the right place at the right moment, failures of communications, terrific tests of endurance, and misunderstandings in direct proportion to the inexperience of the officers and the aggressive action of the enemy. Add to this a minimum of preliminary information of the enemy and of his dispositions, poor maps, and a speed of movement in alteration of the situation, resulting from fast flying planes, fast moving tanks, armored cars, and motor transportation in general. There you have warfare of movement. . . . That, gentlemen, is what you are supposed to be preparing for.

Marshall was determined to inoculate Bradley and the other eighty instructors under his command with the gospel of open warfare, the doctrine that was anathema to those arrogant officers who had "seen action" in France. Back in Hawaii, had Bradley been able to get past Patton's obnoxious exterior, he would have discovered in this particular combat veteran not an arrogant conservative, but a forward-looking spirit kindred with both Marshall and himself. Like Marshall, Patton had been close to Pershing, and, like Marshall as well, he deeply admired him—in fact, modeled himself on him.

In many ways, Patton was an atavistic warrior, who immersed himself in military history stretching back to the beginning of recorded warfare. He sincerely believed himself to have fought in past lives, as a Roman legionnaire and as a soldier in Napoleon's army. He was thoroughly steeped in the lore of his own military ancestors, who had fought in the Revolution and the Civil War. From West Point, he had chosen a commission in the most romantically traditional service branch, the cavalry. He had made himself an expert in the most traditional of weapons, the sword, and in 1912, competed in the Olympics at Stockholm, Sweden, making a particularly strong impression with his fencing. Before returning to the United States after the games, he made a stop at Saumur, home of the French army's cavalry school, where he took two weeks of private fencing lessons from the school's chief fencing instructor, known to history only as Adjutant Cléry, a man generally conceded in his time to be the greatest swordsman in Europe. Patton absorbed Cléry's method of instruction, which he brought back to the U.S. Army. On his return to Fort Myer, Virginia, he wrote a detailed report of his experience with Cléry and set about revising mounted saber technique as it was being taught in the American cavalry (see Chapter 8). Patton himself was appointed "master of the sword," a title and instructional position the army created expressly for him. But most important of all was the fact that, while Patton's enthusiasm for the sword and for swordsmanship was grounded in martial tradition, he genuinely believed that there was still an important role for the weapon in *modern* combat. For great as his love of the traditional weapon was, *modern* combat interested him much more, and this throwback warrior, the knightly "master of the sword," did not hesitate to embrace in its early infancy what he considered the most promising ground-war weapon: the tank.

In fact, the potential of the tank was actually similar to that of the sword as he had redesigned it. Both were meant to be used in the attack. And that is what interested him about both.

Once Bradley had exchanged his original broad-front strategy for a breakthrough on a narrow front, Operation Cobra closely resembled blitzkrieg. As executed by German forces early in the war, "blitzkrieg" was aimed at thrusting through a relatively narrow front using armor, motorized artillery, and aircraft. The air component was critical to the attack. In Poland, the Luftwaffe made extensive use of the Ju 87 "Stuka," the fearsome ground-attack aircraft whose broad gull wings and large fixed landing gear, with their bulbous spats, gave it the appearance of a hawk descending on its prey, even as its "Jericho trumpet," a wind-actuated siren, wailed chillingly during its predatory dive. The objective of concentrating the combined attack modalities—infantry, armor, and air—on a single point of attack, called the *"Schwerpunkt"* (strong point), was to tear a gap in which defenders were fatally weakened. Before the enemy could repair the gap, the attacker followed the initial puncturing attack with wide, rapid sweeps by massed tanks rapidly succeeded by an influx of swiftly moving mechanized infantry, including specially trained "shock troops." The combination of tank sweeps and shock troop action widened the initial Schwerpunkt and tore out other gaps, fatally disrupting the enemy's line of defense, creating areas in which defenders were trapped, immobilized, and ultimately cut off from one another. For these now-isolated troop pockets, the only option was surrender; and because surrender tended to breed surrender, soon the entire line would collapse.

As the practitioners of blitzkrieg saw it, the beauty of the tactic was that, while it relied on extreme violence, its speed, which neutralized rather than destroyed a defender, was actually a highly economical form of warfare, creating the impression of total defeat and thereby bringing surrender sooner rather than later. This spared casualties on both sides, and the tactic was seen as an alternative to the less efficient but more destructive war of stalemate that had been allowed to develop along the Western Front in World War I.

For his part, Patton was delighted that Bradley had finally abandoned what he regarded as the both overly ambitious and overly cautious broad-front approach and was determined instead to concentrate on a Schwerpunkt. Patton was always more inclined to think tactically than strategically, planning battles in terms of concentration rather than dilution. The combat doctrine of Napoleon and Ulysses Grant, that the aim of battle was not to capture territory (the obsession of so many generals) but to destroy the enemy army, was congenial to him. So, even if he initially derided Cobra as "timid" albeit better than anything else yet proposed, he was now generally pleased by it. Indeed, in a July 28 letter to Eisenhower, Patton praised Cobra, generously remarking that "Bradley certainly has done a wonderful job," adding good-naturedly (if rather more than half seriously), "My only kick is that he will win the war before I get in."

Undeniably, Operation Cobra had borrowed from blitzkrieg, but Bradley had not been a slavish imitator. In particular, he had greatly expanded the air component of the operation in a radical and daring way. Instead of using tactical ground-attack aircraft, the equivalent of the Germans' single-engine Stukas, to disrupt enemy lines, he defined as *the* "key feature" of Cobra "the saturation bombing of the German concentration opposite us." This required strategic aircraft, the medium and heavy bombers that were being used to bomb German cities. What Bradley called "saturation bombing"—also known as carpet bombing—was generally defined as the exact opposite of "precision bombing." In fact, the strategic bombing of Germany had been divided between the RAF and the USAAF precisely along the lines of carpet bombing versus precision bombing. Attacking by night, the RAF carpet bombed German cities; attacking by day, the USAAF practiced precision bombing, specifically targeting factories and other high-value objectives. What the Cobra plan required was a demanding combination of saturation *and* precision bombing. As Bradley explained, it was a "risky" proposition, calling for "pinpoint saturation bombing of a rectangle three and a half miles wide and one and a half miles deep, south of the St. Lô-Périers road to which . . . troops would advance prior to jump-off." The margin for error was zero. A "mistake on the part of the aviators could bring a rain of bombs on our own troops." And, as Bradley saw it, a mistake was certainly possible: "For all their boasting, the aviators were not skilled in pinpoint bombing." It was, in short, the World War II equivalent of the World War I tactic of the rolling barrage, requiring both great intensity and great accuracy of destruction.

Hedging his bet, Bradley proposed introducing a safety factor by specifying that the bombers would approach the target rectangle on a course parallel to the east-west St. Lô-Périers road rather than via a more direct route, which would fly over the advancing U.S. troops. In this way, "if the aviators dropped bombs long or short of the target area (as they were wont to do)," the misdrops would fall on the German side of the road, not the American.

Rain, heavy and incessant, repeatedly imposed delays on the launch of Cobra. Patton agonized. "Raining like any thing," he scribbled in a letter to his wife. With greater equanimity, Bradley used the delay to fly back over the Channel to Stanmore to meet with RAF vice air marshal Trafford Leigh-Mallory, who had overall command of the air component of Cobra, air marshal Arthur Tedder, and U.S. commander of Strategic Air Forces in Europe Carl A. Spaatz, in addition to all senior air commanders. Bradley pressed on them his requirement that the bombers fly a course parallel with rather than perpendicular to troop formations. When he was met with objections, he dug in, refusing to agree to any plan that took the bombers *over* the troops. Leigh-Mallory was out of the room when the other airmen finally gave in and agreed to the parallel approach. They also agreed to use no bombs larger than 100 pounds, to avoid cratering the landscape through which men and machines had to advance.

On account of the weather, Cobra was rescheduled for July 21, but a thick cloud cover once again grounded the bombers. The 22nd and 23rd offered no break, and now Bradley's outward calm finally began to crack. He became increasingly concerned that the enemy would discover his troop build-up and that the element of surprise would be lost. Fortunately, weather officers predicted a clear day for July 24, and so Bradley authorized the bombers to take off from their English bases. J. Lawton "Lightning Joe" Collins, commanding VII Corps, the spearhead of Cobra, pulled his men back from the St. Lô-Périers road to provide an extra margin of safety when the bombs started dropping. On the 24th he and his men both heard and felt the rhythmic drone of the first wave of a planned attack by more than two thousand aircraft. The men on the ground heard and felt the planes, but they did not see them. Despite the predictions of clear weather, the cloud cover remained so thick that the aircrews in the first waves were unable to identify the limits of their target area. An abort order was transmitted, and the bombers began turning back across the Channel.

What happened next is not entirely clear. Either Leigh-Mallory's orders recalling the bombers failed to reach all of the groups or some just did not receive the order. In any case, a group of the "heavies" dropped their ordnance through the cloud cover—and directly on the U.S. 30th Division, killing twenty-five American GIs and wounding 131 others.

Patton would have agreed with Confederate general Nathan Bedford Forrest that "war means fightin' and fightin' means killin'," but the loss of men to friendly fire affected him deeply. For Bradley, the tragedy was amplified by the fact that not only had some bombers either failed to receive or heed the recall order, but that the whole first wave had approached the target area not on a course parallel to the ground troops, as agreed, but perpendicular to them, flying directly over the heads of the soldiers. When Bradley confronted Leigh-Mallory about this, the air chief marshal explained to him that the promised parallel approach had in the end proved impossible because it would have taken more than two and a half hours to funnel the heavies along the narrow course prescribed. On one level, Bradley understood. Nevertheless, he was enraged that the airmen had not anticipated this in planning. Moreover, he experienced an emotion of paranoia that might have been expected in the volatile Patton, but not in Bradley, the cool plodder. He suspected that he had been deliberately deceived, that Leigh-Mallory *never* intended to fly the parallel course and had, in fact, slipped out of the room just in time to avoid having to make any promise himself.

Bradley was in no mood to do what he now knew had to be done: authorize a second extremely hazardous carpet bombing very close to his own lines, and do so knowing that the bombers would be flying directly over the ground troops to reach

51

their target. He seethed as Leigh-Mallory asked: "Shall I tell them to go ahead in the morning?"

The price of the short drops had been even greater than the men killed and wounded by the bombs themselves. In withdrawing from the perimeter of the drop zone, Collins had been forced to relinquish some hard-won ground north of the St. Lô-Périers road. After the aborted bombing raid, he wasted no time in regaining the territory and reestablishing his front. Patton empathized with Collins. Like him, he hated "paying for the same real estate twice." In this instance, he also learned that Colonel Harry A. "Paddy" Flint, CO of the 39th Infantry Regiment, 9th Division, had been killed in retaking the lost ground. Flint was both a legendary infantryman and a dear friend. Back in Sicily, in 1943, when Patton was at his lowest, forced for the first time to play decoy in the wake of the slapping incidents, his mess sergeants surprised him with a giant cake on his fifty-eighth birthday. It was, they said, in recognition not only of the birthday, but also of the magnificent achievements of his Seventh Army. This being the case, Patton turned to Flint, handed him the knife, and insisted that he do the honors of slicing the cake. Shortly after this celebration, a Seventh Army chaplain, knowing that Patton read his Bible and liked to write verse, asked the general to compose a "Soldier's Prayer" for a wreath-laying and memorial service to honor those who had fallen in the capture of Sicily. Patton complied:

God of our Fathers, who by land and by sea has ever led us on to victory, please continue Your inspiring guidance in this the greatest of our conflicts.

Strengthen my soul so that the weakening instinct of self-preservation, which besets all of us in battle, shall not blind me to my duty, to my own manhood, to the glory of my calling, and to my responsibility to my fellow soldiers. . . .

Let me not mourn for the men who have died fighting, but rather let me be glad that such heroes have lived. . . .

And now it was Paddy who was dead. He "was hit in the left side of the helmet by an automatic pistol bullet," Patton wrote to Beatrice on July 25, delving into the gory details as if he were trying to make sense of the death of his friend, a hard death for Patton to accept because it was, in a roundabout way, ultimately the result of an accident. The shot, he reasoned, "must have been short range. It gouged some bone out of his head and a piece entered his brain. . . . He never regained consciousness and did not suffer." As if to rationalize the loss—even to suggest that it had somehow been for the best—Patton observed that his friend "was about at the end of his strength and would have been sent home for a rest soon. I guess it was the best end he could have had. . . . A lot more will go before this show is over. Those who go as well and as bravely will be fortunate."

"Shall I tell them to go ahead in the morning?" Leigh-Mallory asked Bradley about the bombers.

"We've got no choice." Just as he often called American GIs "doughboys," Bradley preferred the World War I French term for the Germans: "The Boche will build up out front if we don't get this thing off soon. But we're still taking an awful chance. Another short drop could ruin us."

Bradley paused, then made the only decision he could: "Let it go that way. We'll be ready in the morning."

That morning of July 25 the air "throbbed with heavy bombers while I fidgeted," Bradley recalled, "within easy reach of the telephone." The mission consisted of 1,500 heavy and 380 medium bombers as well as 550 fighter-bombers. These 2,430 aircraft flew perpendicular to the target, directly over the American troops, then dropped four thousand tons of high-explosive and fragmentation bombs as well as napalm, the jellied gasoline that adhered to its target when it blazed, whether that target was the wood of a field headquarters or the flesh of a soldier, the wood of a French farmer's house or the clothes on the farmer's back.

"The thunder had scarcely rolled away when the casualty reports began trickling in."

Handing Bradley a teletype, Truman C. "Tubby" Thorson, one of his longtime staff officers, grimly announced: "They've done it again."

"Oh Christ," Bradley moaned, "not another short drop?"

Thorson nodded. Among the 111 American soldiers killed (490 were wounded) was Lieutenant General Lesley McNair, commanding officer of Army Ground Forces—the man responsible for the organization, training, and preparation of all soldiers for overseas service. He had come to the European front to see firsthand what his stateside training programs had produced. He occupied a foxhole far forward, and he didn't have a chance.

The deep shadow of this second catastrophe seemed to close over Operation Cobra, as if to smother it. Patton noted in his diary, "Some Germans must have survived. The bombing was not a success." His pessimism was backed up by the initial disappointing damage estimates. German defenses, the analysts believed, had been little diminished. Bradley took to his bed on the night of July 25 feeling that Cobra would prove an abortive failure.

For strategic planning, Patton believed in using small-scale maps. Tactics, however, required "the study of large-scale maps or, better still, [the view] from the ground" itself. From headquarters, Operation Cobra looked doomed, but from the ground itself, the situation appeared very different. As the air attacks continued through July 26, the infantry advanced according to plan, pushing the badly battered German defenders into full retreat. On the morning of July 27, VII Corps commander "Lightning Joe" Collins saw the German line beginning to break under the pressure of his infantry. He knew the time had come to throw in his armor—just as Bradley had planned. The tanks roared through the broken lines of retreating Wehrmacht and SS troops. Omar Bradley had his breakthrough.

A *breakthrough* was all that Bradley had hoped and planned for. Earlier in the month, Montgomery had launched Operation Goodwood, an attempt to break through German lines adjacent to Saint-Lô by carpet bombing southeast of town, then rolling through the resulting gap with three armored divisions. The operation did not exactly fail, but neither did it produce the definitive breakthrough hoped for. In some ways, Operation Cobra was little more than an amplification of Goodwood, planned so as to more effectively exploit the gap blasted into the German lines. Bradley decided to dedicate two entire infantry divisions to holding the gap open, so that three divisions—two of armor and one of mechanized infantry—could storm through. The mechanized infantry would take Coutances, and the armor would target Avranches, which was to serve as the jumping-off point for Patton and his Third Army. But Lawton's crash through the defenders' line was so unexpectedly rapid and wide that Bradley decided to expand Cobra from a breakthrough—nothing more than an escape from the bocage—into a breakout, the first steps of the main advance across Europe.

At noon on July 27, he quickly rewrote his operational orders. Originally, VII Corps was to advance to Coutances, cutting across VIII Corps' route of advance. Now Bradley ordered both corps to advance down the Cotentin peninsula together, pushing south, all the way to Avranches, which was the portal to all Brittany.

Up to this point, Patton had been on the bench, waiting for Coach Bradley to put him in the game. For his part, Bradley had not been eager to put Patton—his powerful but dangerous weapon—into the war. The longer Operation Cobra could get along without him, the better. But now that Cobra had suddenly proven bigger than Bradley had intended it to be, now that it had achieved a faster and bigger breakthrough than he had imagined possible, Bradley recognized that Patton was precisely the force of nature he needed to push Cobra over the threshold.

Historians of World War II typically paint Bradley as a drab but necessary plodder and Patton as a brilliant but volatile genius. They point out that Patton "dismissed" Operation Cobra as "timid." They suggest that it was Patton who, *in spite* of Bradley and his timid plan, broke out, broke away, and began in earnest the reconquest, redemption, and rescue of Europe. As with most myths, there is a significant grain of truth in this interpretation. But it is also true that Bradley deserves credit for doing more than "letting" Patton make him look good. Patton, after all, joined Operation Cobra at *Bradley's* invitation and, indeed, at *Bradley's* insistence. Bradley knew what his plan needed.

According to the schedule by which the invasion was operating, the Third Army was not to be activated until August 1.
But seeing Cobra suddenly open up before him, Bradley, hitherto content to keep Patton at arm's length, telephoned Hugh
J. Gaffey on July 28 to get hold of his boss Patton. Bradley did
not want to wait until August 1. He wanted Patton to take
over command—unofficially, but actually—of VIII Corps right
away—today, in fact. Troy Middleton, VIII Corps' designated
commander, was a fine officer, competent and stable. Bradley
knew him as a slow and steady motor, the kind of engine well
suited to heavy hauling. But Patton, Patton was volatile, hot,
brilliant. He was a machine built for full-out racing.

Gaffey tapped one of his junior officers to locate Patton. At
3:30 in the afternoon—1530—the young man found the general
at the gas dump and told him that he was needed in headquarters "at once." He arrived at 1645. Gaffey passed on Bradley's
message: He was taking over VIII Corps.

Without delay, Patton visited VIII Corps to arrange the
takeover, "but conducted everything very casually so as to not
get people excited at the change." Of course it was Patton himself who was excited: "Felt much happier over the war," he
noted in his diary. "May get in it yet."

As with his entry into France from England, Patton's step into
combat was quiet. The deceptions of Operation Fortitude were
still in effect, and Eisenhower did not want to trumpet the
general's presence. His cable to Patton on July 30 was marked
secret and began by thanking him for sending a report of Paddy
Flint's death—on the verge of finally entering the invasion
of Europe, which he wanted more than anything else in life,

Patton's thoughts were nevertheless with the friend who had been killed by friendly fire. "As I understand it," Ike's cable continued, "you will take over your Sector day after tomorrow; the best good luck to you! I don't have to urge you to keep them fighting. That is one thing I know you will do."

It was a well-intentioned message; however, the phrasing— "That is one thing I know you will do"—implied that there were many other things about Patton's prospective performance that worried Ike, who had covered up for his misbehavior once and had nearly sacked him on another occasion. Moreover, the message made clear that Ike was still under the impression that Patton was not going into action until the Third Army was activated on August 1. In fact, on July 29, Patton had already noted in his diary that "Bradley came up . . . and told me his plans. They are getting more ambitious but are just what I wanted to do . . . so I am very happy. . . ." From "timid," Operation Cobra had progressed to "more ambitious"—a credit to Bradley, all the more so because it was now "just what" *Patton* wanted to do. The two men, so very different in temperament, were coming together in war, and that made Patton "very happy."

Bradley had put him in the game at just the right time, when the shackles of the hedgerows had been broken, and the breakthrough had begun toward Avranches, at the angle formed by the Gulf of St. Malo, the gateway to all Brittany, and Coutances, to the north, adorning the neck of the Cotentin Peninsula. Securing these two towns would clear the enemy from the invaders' rear by taking Brittany, thereby enabling the grand eastward advance.

Patton's genius as a commander was founded in part on his ability to conceptualize the big picture—those small-scale maps he devoured to get the war in his mind and heart long before he ever walked the field of battle—and then to translate the concept into the smallest action details on the ground. He drove out to Coutances on July 29 to monitor the progress of the 6th Armored Division. On the way, he ran across an infantry battalion, well behind the front lines, digging what he characterized in his diary as "tomb-like slit trenches." Patton stopped his jeep, got out, and "told them to stop it, as it was stupid to be afraid of a beaten enemy."

All armies, Patton believed, but especially the American army, put too much emphasis on entrenchment and too little on movement. "The trick expression, 'Dig or die,' is much over-used and much misunderstood," he wrote. It was a "trick" because, in situations of perceived danger, the natural impulse was to hide, to dig in, but, Patton believed, this was precisely the opposite of the action most likely to save your life. "Personally, I am opposed to digging," even when a soldier "thinks he may be strafed from the air or is within artillery range of the enemy." For one thing, "the chance of getting killed while sleeping normally on the ground is quite remote, and the fatigue from digging innumerable slit trenches is avoided." Moreover, "the psychological effect on the soldier is bad." As with the ruined German pillboxes that had impressed him so on the Norman beaches, digging trenches made the soldier "think the enemy is dangerous, which he usually is not." Digging in, as Patton saw it, was literally self-defeating because "Wars are not won by defensive tactics" and "Digging is primarily defensive."

Patton did not even like to take cover. "'Hit the dirt,'" he complained, "is another expression which has done much to increase our casualties." He believed that the enemy was all too familiar with "our custom of hitting the dirt. What they do is wait until we have arrived at a predetermined spot on which they have ranged rockets, mortars, or artillery and then they put on a sudden and violent machine-gun fire—frequently straight up in the air. The soldier, obsessed with the idea of hitting the dirt, lies now and waits supinely for the arrival of the shells from the mortars, rockets, etc. He usually does not have to wait long."

Keep moving, and you won't be "ranged," won't be targeted. Keep moving, even into the teeth of the enemy, and you have a much better chance of staying alive. "The only time it is proper for a soldier to drop is when he is caught at short range—under three hundred yards—by concentrated small-arms fire," Patton wrote. "But even then he must not hit the dirt and stay supine. He must shoot fast at the enemy, or in the direction of the enemy." Patton cited Commodore David Farragut of the Union navy in the Civil War: "'The best armor (and the best defense) is a rapid and well-directed fire.'" When a unit is "caught in a barrage . . . the surest way to get out of it is to go forward fast, because it is almost the invariable practice of the enemy to increase rather than decrease his range." And when a soldier moves forward, he should always be shooting. "Marching fire," Patton called it. "The proper way to advance, particularly for troops armed with that magnificent weapon, the M-1 rifle, is to utilize marching fire and keep moving." It was, Patton thought, a bad idea to pause even to take aim. Shoot in the general direction of the enemy. Spend ammunition, spare lives. Marching fire "can be delivered from the shoulder, but it is just as effective if delivered with the butt of the rifle halfway between the belt and the armpit. One round should be fired every two or three paces. The whistle of the bullets, the scream of the ricochet, and the dust, twigs, and branches which are knocked from the ground and the trees have such an effect on the enemy that his small-arms fire becomes negligible. . . . Furthermore, the fact that you are shooting adds to your self-confidence, because you feel that you are doing something, and not sitting like a duck in a bathtub being shot at."

Violence drove Patton, but his genius lay in knowing how to use violence to save lives. Tactically, his goal was to erase the distinction between offense and defense. Offensive tactics were the most effective defensive tactics. Attack was the best protection. Like a balanced equation, offense and defense were completely equivalent and interchangeable—provided that you were fighting the right way. The right offensive tactics provided the best defense, and the best defensive tactics were invariably the tactics of attack.

Continuing on to Coutances, Patton encountered Major General Robert W. Grow, 6th Armored Division CO, sitting on the side of the road with his deputy, poring over a map. While he gazed at the map, his division was halted on the bank of a small river, where it had become the target of sporadic German fire.

"Grow was not showing any life so I built a fire under him," Patton wrote. He asked him what he was doing. Grow answered that his deputy "was in charge of the advance guard and that he, personally, was doing nothing." In Patton's conception of combat, there was no such thing as doing nothing. "I asked him whether he had been down to look at the river, and he said 'No.' So I told him that unless he did do something, he would be out of a job." Then Patton demonstrated what to do. He walked down to the river, waded in, and returned bearing two vital facts. First, although he could see "a few Germans on a hill," nobody fired on him. Second, the river "was not over a foot deep." Conclusion: There was no reason to wait. The division advanced.

It was at this point that Omar Bradley caught up with Patton and shared his expanded ambitions for what had been the "timid" Cobra. The fire in Patton's belly blazed up: "I think we can clear the Brest [Brittany] peninsula very fast," he wrote in his diary. "The thing to do is to rush them off their feet before they get set."

He scribbled a doggerel poem titled "Absolute War." He acknowledged that war confronts us

> *. . . with conditions which are strange*
> *If we accept them we will never win.*
> *Since by being realistic, as in mundane combats fistic*
> *We will get a bloody nose and that's a sin.*

We naturally exaggerate the bloody nose as a "fell disaster" and misinterpret it as "the result of fighting faster"; therefore, "We resort to fighting carefully and slow / We fill up terrestrial spaces with secure expensive bases / To keep our tax rate high and death rate low."

> *But with sadness and with sorrow we discover to our horror*
> *That while we build the enemy gets set.*
> *So despite our fine intentions to produce extensive pensions*
> *We haven't licked the dirty bastard yet.*

The great thing was to realize that, "in war just as in loving you must always keep on shoving / Or you'll never get your just reward."

> *For if you are dilatory in the search for lust or glory*
> *You are up shitcreek and that's the truth, Oh! Lord.*
> *So let us do real fighting, boring in and gouging, biting.*

Let's take a chance now that we have the ball.
Let's forget those fine firm bases in the dreary shell raked spaces,
Let's shoot the works and win! Yes win it all.

From his days at VMI and West Point, Patton had thought himself one of a "different class" of men. While the majority would dig in under fire (it was, after all, the natural thing to do), he would march into fire, while firing all the while himself. While just about everyone withdrew from a bloody nose, he would invite one, if that's what it took to bring the fight to the enemy, knowing that you could survive a bloody nose and keep on fighting. While others recoiled from battle as from death, he thrust himself into it, as a man thrusts himself into a lover. While others sought the apparent protection of "those fine firm bases," Patton saw only that they had been built "in the dreary shell raked spaces."

As dusk enfolded the Cotentin Peninsula, advance elements of the 4th Armored Division took Avranches and held it as more of the division rushed in. Now Patton had his springboard.

"Things are real[l]y moving this morning," he wrote to Beatrice on July 31, "and so am I at long last." He finished his letter then met with his staff to thank them "for their long endurance during non-employment." He told them that he "knew they would be just as good when the fighting started" and he added his customary injunction "to always be audacious."

In his morning letter to his wife, he had related that, even on the very verge of what he had long believed would be the fulfillment of his destiny, he had "spent a gloomy evening . . . arranging" Paddy Flint's personal papers and belongings. "It is strange how little of moment there is left to send [home]. I got the helmet, a few letters, and a map, that's about all."

In the diary entry written on the same day as the letter, Patton noted his visit to the VIII Corps command post after supper. Corps CO Troy Middleton greeted him, saying that "he was glad to see us as he did not know what to do next and could not get hold of Bradley." His orders, he explained, had been "to secure the line of the Sélune River, which he had done, but he did not cross it. I told him that throughout history it had always been fatal not to cross a river, and that while I did not officially take over until tomorrow noon, I had actually taken over on the 28th." Patton continued: "Therefore he was to get over now."

CHAPTER 4

FROM BREAKOUT TO BREAKTHROUGH

"We are having one of the loveliest battles you ever saw. It is a typical cavalry action in which, to quote the words of the old story, 'The soldier went out and charged in all directions at the same time, with a pistol in each hand, and a sabre in the other.'"

—PATTON, LETTER, AUGUST 6, 1944,
TO MAJOR GENERAL KENYON ASHE JOYCE,
CO, FORT MYER, VIRGINIA, 1933–1937

Speed was the hallmark of Patton's drive. You can't turn a battleship on a dime, and an army is much bigger than a battleship; but Patton handled it as if it were one of his cavalry ponies. No sooner did he order Troy Middleton to cross the Sélune River—it is fatal to halt on the near side, Patton had told him—than he received word that the 4th Armored Division under Major General John S. Wood had secured the critical river dams, thereby preventing the Germans from flooding the ground through which VIII Corps—and, soon, the entire Third Army—were to advance. Along with this came the welcome news that the bridge at Pontaubault, a few miles south of Avranches, had been captured before the Germans could blow it up.

As a horseman, Patton knew that a rider could not simply impose his will on his animal. There is a give and take between horse and man, the rider responding as much as commanding. When Patton learned that the bridge across the Sélune was intact, he responded by ordering Middleton to kick the 6th

Armored Division across it immediately. A general responds as well as commands, shaping his plan to the evolving situation on the ground—but without sacrificing or subordinating his intention. Patton intended to take Brittany and take it fast, so that the rear of his army would not be menaced and so that a secure route from Brest, the port town at the tip of the Brittany peninsula, would be assured to help feed the invasion. When circumstances presented an opportunity to achieve his objectives faster than even he had contemplated, he sent two divisions, one armored, one infantry, to Brest and another two—again one armored, the other infantry—to the central Brittany town of Rennes.

On the night of the 31st, Patton mustered his staff and delivered one of the pre-campaign speeches for which he was famous. Those who write about Patton typically call them pep talks but, in truth, they were statements of tactical theory bound up with sheer passion. "Forget this goddamn business of worrying about our flanks," Patton exhorted his officers. *That* was something you would never hear at West Point or at the Infantry School or even in the humblest of ROTC classes. The doctrine of deploying static forces to protect the flanks of an advance—to prevent the enemy's coming at you perpendicular to your line of march or, even worse, getting around behind you—was so elementary, so basic that it was never questioned. Repeatedly, through to the very end of the war in Europe, Bradley would fret about exposed flanks, even after he'd learned to put his full faith in Patton.

"Some goddamned fool once said that flanks must be secured," Patton continued his speech, "and since then sons of bitches all over the world have been going crazy guarding their flanks. We don't want any of that in the Third Army. Flanks are something for the enemy to worry about, not us."

The conventional, common-sense craft of modern war pre-scribed that any advance—the most aggressively offensive movement an army performs—had to include a defensive component dedicated to protecting the army's flanks. But Patton was loath to dilute an offensive operation with a defensive one. It was not that he was foolhardy (he was no such thing), but that he believed static conventions, such as the flank defense, furnished not security but the feeling of security. True safety lay in rapid movement, unimpeded by auxiliary operations, so that everything could be poured into the attack, which always advanced. If you kept moving and fighting, there was no need to protect your flanks, because your speed and violence made it impossible for an enemy to get into position to flank you.

"I don't want to get any messages saying that 'We are holding our position,'" Patton warned. "We're not holding anything! Let the Hun do that. We are advancing constantly and we're not interested in holding on to anything except the enemy."

Back in the Sicily campaign, Bradley—then serving under Patton—was appalled by what he regarded as his senior's childishly reckless need to beat Montgomery to Messina. The idea of running a race in the middle of a war disgusted Bradley. It is true that Patton took great pleasure in beating Montgomery, but the object of his "race" was to run as much as it was to win. Or, more accurately, as Patton saw it, to run *was* to win. Throughout virtually all of military history, up to and including World War I, the "great captains"—the commanders who excelled in the field—were those who out-positioned the enemy, as if war were the equivalent of a game of chess. The great lesson of blitzkrieg was the leading lesson of this *second* world war. Position had given way to movement, stasis to motion, defense to offense.

As for holding the enemy, even here Patton diverged sharply from long-accepted American military doctrine. Late in his career, the legendary Colonel John Boyd, Korean War fighter pilot, air combat tactician, pioneering champion of the fighter air force, became a major theorist of the art of war. He was a fierce critic of what he called the U.S. Army's pet tactic of "hi diddle diddle, straight up the middle," attacking the enemy head-on with main force. Several weeks after Saddam Hussein invaded Kuwait in August 1990, secretary of defense Dick Cheney summoned Boyd to his Pentagon office for a secret discussion of the war plans for Operation Desert Storm.

Robert Coram, in *Boyd: The Fighter Pilot Who Changed the Art of War,* explains that the theater commander, General H. Norman Schwarzkopf, had proposed "a head-to-head assault against the main strength of the Iraqi forces, the classic mindset of Army commanders imbued with the theory of attrition warfare. Slug it out *mano a mano,* toe-to-toe, force against force, and the last man standing wins." Cheney rejected the proposal, remarking to Army chief of staff General Colin Powell, "I can't let Norm do this high diddle up the middle plan," expressing himself in the very phrase John Boyd was known to use. Cheney ordered a new plan to be drawn up by other hands, and, in the end, what he accepted for Operation Desert Storm came straight out of Boyd's tactical playbook. Even Cheney later remarked that Boyd "clearly was a factor in my thinking" about Gulf War tactics.

The plan was this: A Marine unit would stage what looked to be a major amphibious assault at Kuwait, thereby drawing the attention of the Iraqi army. While the Iraqis positioned themselves for the Marines' next move, the main Coalition force, consisting of tanks and mechanized infantry, would swing at high speed in a great arc through the desert, enveloping the entire body of the Iraqi army on its left flank and rear.

Schwarzkopf was conventional army, Boyd the maverick. This was 1990. Forty-six years earlier, on the evening of July 31, 1944, George Patton told his officers that he was not interested in holding on to anything except the enemy. "We're going to hold him by the nose and we're going to kick him in the ass." It is easy to dismiss this as a Blood-and-Guts "pep talk." In reality, it was a tactical exposition worthy of John Boyd. Patton's imagery actually meant something. It meant that he was all for advancing aggressively and quickly, but also wittingly. When a major engagement came, he favored using infantry to pin the enemy down—hold it by the nose—while armor swung around like a boxer delivering a haymaker, a roundhouse punch to the side of the head. Of course, Patton's own image was far more colorful: While infantry held the enemy by the nose, armor—which had all the speed—would take the long way around to envelop the enemy, kicking him in the ass. Patton combined the drive of the *mano-a-mano* combat commander that was the army's ideal with a canny tactical wisdom that would not be widely seen until the 1980s and 1990s, the era of John Boyd and his intellectual progeny.

Once one nose-holding, ass-kicking contest had been won, another would commence. As Patton told his officers, "we're going to kick the hell out of him all the time and we're going to go through him like crap through a goose." To energy and wit in the advance and attack was added relentlessness. By tradition—and by the nature of warfare through World War I—wars had been regarded as a series of battles. But this was not the way Patton saw modern war. It was continuous, seamless, the victorious army kicking the hell out of the enemy "all the time."

Preparation, training, and discipline were valuable in this kind of warfare, but one quality above all was indispensable. "We have one motto, '*L'audace, l'audace, toujours l'audace!*' Remember that, gentlemen." Audacity, audacity, always audacity! In the great 1970 Franklin Schaffner biopic, *Patton*, George C. Scott (in the title role) attributes the quotation to Prussia's Frederick the Great—of whom Patton was indeed something of a student; actually, it was Georges Danton, a figure some historians identify as the driving force behind the eruption of the French Revolution, who said it.

On the eve of the Third Army's activation, Patton had overseen the opening of Brittany and the unambiguous defeat of many of the peninsula's German defenders. VII and VIII Corps converged on Avranches, at the corner where the Cotentin peninsula joins the neck of the Brittany peninsula. From here, it would be a grand drive into Brittany, from which the remains of the German Seventh Army would be swept away.

At noon of August 1, the Third Army was finally activated. Simultaneously, Omar Bradley stepped up from the First Army command to command of the 12th Army Group, which encompassed the First and Third armies, soon to be joined by the Ninth, and arrived at Patton's headquarters four hours later. It was Bradley's job to ensure coordination among the armies, and he allotted to the Third Army a narrow corridor between Avranches and St. Hilaire, about ten miles to the south of Avranches, through which the entire army had to pass, hemmed in by the Channel coast to the north. Bradley also fretted about the vulnerability of Avranches to attack from Mortain, a little less than twenty miles inland and southeast of the town. Chomping at the bit, Patton did "not give much credence" to the probability of an attack on what would be the exposed Third Army flank as it threaded its way through the passage between Avranches and St. Hilaire, but he figured out a way to address his boss's concerns while also maintaining the forward momentum into Brittany. By "moving the 90th Division," he wrote in his diary, "I can get it forward and also cover the exposed flank." As soon as this was clear to him, Patton "started this movement by truck at once."

Moving the 90th, which was still in the Third Army rear area, required "an operation which, at Leavenworth [the Command and General Staff School], would certainly give you an unsatisfactory mark." Throwing away the rule book, Patton cut "the 90th Division through the same town and on the same street being used by two armored and two other infantry divisions." The reason? "[T]here is no other way of doing it at this time."

The sentence, straightforward as it appears, says much about Patton's tactical consciousness. He did not simply declare that there was no other way of doing what had to be done, but that there was no other way of doing it *at this time*. Patton always conceived operations in terms of space and time, and time always trumped space and everything else, including the lessons instilled at the Command and General Staff School.

Patton was never content to make plans and let others execute them. To him, it was just as important to personally ensure the speed and accuracy of execution. If his army was always on the move, so was he. His aide-de-camp, Lieutenant Colonel Charles Codman, wrote in his diary on August 8, the end of Patton's first full week as Third Army CO, that he had raised "merry hell." Patton had the uncanny faculty of appearing everywhere, and everywhere he appeared he kicked "someone's ass." Having ordered Troy Middleton to send an infantry division with the 4th Armored Division in the advance on Brest, Patton discovered that the VIII Corps commander had instead sent the infantry to augment another unit, Task Force A, along the north coast of the Brittany peninsula. When Patton confronted him, Middleton explained that he had had reports of an enemy concentration at St. Malo, a town on the peninsula's north coast fronting the English Channel. Patton countered by ordering him to send the 8th Infantry Division behind the 4th Armored Division, along with a motorized combat team. The 79th Infantry Division would follow the 6th Armored in its advance on Rennes, while Task Force A would continue to move, unsupported, along the north road. Patton directed Middleton to assign the task force a very specific objective, "to secure the seventeen miles of trestle on the railway in the vicinity of [the coastal town of] Morlaix." Patton understood that "if this piece of trestle [were] destroyed, the capture of Brest will have little value" as a principal port of supply and reinforcement.

These were high-risk movements, as Middleton saw it. As for Patton, he remarked in his diary that he could not "make out why Middleton was so apathetic or dumb. I don't know what was the matter with him." Then he went on to explain precisely what was the matter with him: "Of course it is a little nerve-wracking to send troops straight into the middle of the enemy with front, flanks, and rear open." In fact, Patton found that he "had to keep repeating to [himself], 'Do not take counsel of your fears.'"

What drove Patton but failed to drive Middleton?

Call it strategic ambition. "Bradley simply wants a bridgehead over the Sélune River. What I want and intend to get is Brest and Angers." He acknowledged that the "truck movements of large numbers of infantry [were] very dangerous and might be almost fatal if" German aerial reconnaissance detected them. The greatest danger, Patton recognized, was a traffic jam. Not one to take counsel of his fears, Patton nevertheless exercised all prudence compatible with his strategic ambition. He stationed all available staff officers at critical points to ensure that the 90th Division got "through without a jam." Moreover, Patton resolved to go himself in the morning, "as I have a feeling something may happen."

Given his thirst for violent engagement, which was not easily slaked, Patton's nickname, "Old Blood and Guts," seems almost inevitable. No one is sure where it came from exactly. It is known that, between the wars, Patton frequently admonished subordinate officers to anticipate in combat being "up to their necks in blood and guts." He used the phrase so often, some say, that it stuck to him. But there are also other origin stories:

- Patton delivered a speech in which he said that the chief requisite for the men of an armored division was "blood and brains," a phrase reported in newspapers as "blood and guts."

- The nickname was invented by a reporter in 1942, when Patton commanded the Desert Training Center in California.

- It came from a lecture to division officers, in which Patton, expounding on leadership, suddenly ad-libbed: "War will be won by blood and guts alone."

If his nickname irritated him, Patton never let on. Actually, he seems to have relished it. And yet he knew that war was not in fact won by blood and guts alone. If Patton's driving energy was explosive, it was the explosion of a shaped charge, its force always directed precisely where he wanted it to be. This was the result of Patton's other great military passion: discipline.

"East of Avranches," he recorded in his diary on August 2, "we caught up with the 90th . . . The division is bad, the discipline poor, the men filthy, and the officers apathetic, many of them removing their insignia and covering the markings on helmets." Officers wore one thick vertical bar on the back of their helmets, and non-commissioned officers (NCOs) had a horizontal bar. In this way, the men in charge could be identified by the troops behind them—the assumption being that officers and NCOs would always be in the lead. "I saw one artillery lieutenant jump out of his peep [a common World War II synonym for jeep] and hide in a ditch when one plane flew over at a high altitude firing a little."

Patton's remedy for the situation was to correct "these acts on the spot." He got out of his jeep "and walked in the column for about two miles, talking to the men." Patton believed that a general had to make frequent trips to the front to assess for himself the situation on the ground and to encourage the troops. He believed that a general should be seen by the front-line soldiers, who had to know that a general could get shot at just as readily as a private. He talked with the men who were on foot, attempting to lift their morale. When he saw that some soldiers "were getting rides on guns and the others [on foot] made no comment," he loudly called the riders babies. That was sufficient to get them to dismount.

Correcting the situation "on the spot" sometimes meant empathizing and sometimes meant shaming, but Patton understood that the problem underlying these superficial manifestations was a lack of discipline. The men had not been trained well.

He had seen this before, most recently when Ike had called him in to replace Lloyd Fredendall as CO of II Corps in Tunisia. Patton recognized the problem as soon as he walked into II Corps headquarters. The soldiers were unsoldierly. Patton began to transform them from a mob into an army by issuing what became known as the "necktie order." He required that each soldier wear the regulation necktie, the universally unpopular lace-up leggings, and, at all times, a helmet—the steel helmet, not just the helmet liner. The necktie order provoked a lot of grumbling—What use is a necktie in a combat zone?—but Omar Bradley understood just what Patton was about: Each time a soldier knotted his necktie, threaded his leggings, and buckled on his heavy steel helmet, he was forcibly reminded that Patton had come to command the II Corps, that the pre-Kasserine days had ended, and that a tough new era had begun.

Patton did a lot of talking to officers and men, but he knew that no communication was more powerful than action. He had less than two weeks to instill discipline and morale into II Corps. There was no time to start with abstractions and pep talks. He forced the corps to focus on the details that made civilians feel like soldiers, reasoning that if they felt like soldiers, they would perform like soldiers.

Although the necktie order in Tunisia was made famous by the film *Patton*, it was not the first time the general had issued it. Months earlier, at the Desert Training Center near Indio, California, he addressed a staff meeting:

We have reached the stage in our desert training where there is no excuse for any soldier not to be clean and in proper uniform. . . . Army regulations will be enforced. No man, officer or enlisted man, leaves this post without being in proper uniform. And that uniform better be clean! He must be wearing the insignia of I Armored Corps on his arm below his left shoulder. Any man out of uniform or with long hair and dirt stays on the post. No man can have any pride if he looks as if he has to go to the bathroom or has just been there!

This initial order made no mention of neckties, but when Patton learned that soldiers enjoying a weekend pass removed their neckties and even their uniform blouses as soon as they got past the main gate guards, he added the necktie provision.

As Bradley would have understood, the order had symbolic value for each soldier who tied a tie or laced up leggings. But the order did much more. As Patton wrote it, the order directed any officer or non-commissioned officer who saw a soldier out of uniform to stop the offender and get his name and company—whether the sighting took place in camp or in town. Two men from the same company reported would mean that the company commander had to write a detailed letter explaining why the men were out of uniform. If three soldiers from the same company were caught out of uniform, orders would be cut for the company commander to resign or face court martial.

The symbolism of the order affected each soldier, but Patton applied the real pressure to the commanders, not to the men themselves. He made the captains responsible for the actions of their men, so that they were motivated to enforce discipline. In this way, discipline became an issue that not only forced the individual to be a soldier, but forced the soldiers to cohere into an army. Actions were assigned consequences.

Initially, the necktie orders, both in Indio and Tunisia, induced irritation, but this soon gave way to pride in an appearance so spit-and-polish that it set Patton's command apart from troops in other outfits. Soldiers began to speak of themselves as Patton's men. They looked sharper than the others, and they even saluted sharper. In the World War II Army, the expression "give a George Patton" meant rendering an especially smart hand salute. Not only did Patton's men begin to feel like the best soldiers in the U.S. Army, those who saw them believed they were as well.

"All human beings have an innate resistance to obedience," Patton wrote. "Discipline removes this resistance, and, by constant repetition, makes obedience habitual and subconscious. Where would an undisciplined football team get? The players react subconsciously to the signals. They must, because the split second required for thought would give the enemy the jump." So there it was, the connection between discipline and speed. For Patton, the speed of thought was fast, but the speed of obedience much faster—and that is what would give Patton's men the edge over any enemy.

In addition to the speed of obedience, discipline also created courage. "No sane man is unafraid in battle," Patton observed, "but discipline produces in him a form of vicarious courage which, with his manhood, makes for victory. Self-respect grows directly from discipline. The Army saying, 'Who ever saw a dirty soldier with a medal?' is largely true."

Instilling discipline in troops and subordinate officers was one thing, but fending off interference from above was quite another. Once he had succeeded in getting the elements of Middleton's VIII Corps rolling rapidly into Brittany, Patton, on August 2, turned to Wade Haislip's XV Corps, which he was anxious to get moving in the opposite direction, east, in preparation for the moment at which Brittany had been taken and the entire Third Army would break through in its grand advance across France and into the homeland of the enemy. The first step in this journey was to get Haislip marching toward the Mayenne River, which flows through the towns of Mayenne and Laval. This represented a southeastward advance of about forty miles from St. Hilaire, near which XV Corps was presently positioned. No sooner had he turned his attention from Middleton to Haislip, however, than Bradley showed up at Middleton's command post. Bradley and the VIII Corps commander huddled over a map. "I hate to attack with so much of the enemy at my rear," Bradley muttered to Middleton, "especially while it's so exposed. If the other fellow [i.e., the Germans] were to break through at Avranches to the coast, I'd be cut off way out here in Brittany."

The Third Army commander had sent VIII Corps deep into Brittany without protecting his rear or flanks. "Dammit," Bradley exclaimed to Middleton. "George seems more interested in making headlines with the capture of Brest than in using his head on tactics. I don't care if we get Brest tomorrow—or ten days later. Once we isolate the Brittany peninsula, we'll get it anyhow. But we can't take a chance on an open flank. That's why I ordered George to block the peninsula neck."

With this, Bradley drove out to Patton's command post and awaited the general's return from the field. Bradley recalled their meeting this way:

"For God's sake, George, what are you going to do about this open flank of Troy Middleton's? I just ordered the 79th down there [to protect the flank]. But I hate to by-pass an Army commander on orders to a corps."

He went on to explain that he had ordered the 79th Division to move east to a position near Fourgeres—that is, in the opposite direction from the rest of the corps. He said that he was still very much concerned about an attack from Mortain.

Bradley remembered that Patton "smiled sheepishly," then put his arm around his shoulder. "Fine, fine, Brad. That's just what I would have done. But enough of that—here, let me show you how we're getting on."

As Bradley told the story, the exchange is a telling one. Patton's failure to take conventional—and conventionally prudent—measures to protect his flank and rear was just the kind of headlong move that gave Bradley pause about Patton. At the same time, the sheer velocity with which Patton was accomplishing the breakout was evidence of just how much Bradley needed him. Patton was a loose cannon, but a very potent cannon. If his recoil packed a sharp kick, his impact on the enemy was proportionally that much greater. Had Bradley really been fed up with Patton, he would have cringed and bridled under his patronizing arm and his cooed assurance of "Fine, fine, Brad." He did no such thing, however. Instead, he let himself be charmed.

Interestingly, Patton recalled the encounter differently. He wrote that Bradley, after informing him that he had detached the 79th and sent it east, said that "he knew I would concur" in the order. Patton—according to Patton—responded that he would indeed concur, but went on to declare that he did not agree with him. He told Bradley that he "feared he was getting the British complex of over-caution." In his own thoughts was the "noteworthy" fact that a year earlier, when he was senior to Bradley, he "had to force him to conduct an attack in Sicily." At this point, Bradley's distrust of Patton was more than amply reciprocated by Patton. In any case, it was not that Patton was unconcerned about German strength in the vicinity of Mortain, but that he substituted the speed of his advance for static force protection. A counterattack takes time to organize, time to launch, and time to reach its target. Move fast enough, and you rob the enemy of time.

Patton had observed that the corridor through which his army was obliged to pass into Brittany was narrow, but he did not complain. Instead, he resolved to shove forty thousand vehicles and two hundred thousand men along a two-lane road, sacrificing the logistical principle of keeping units separate. It was like liquid through a funnel. Whoever and whatever was ready to move moved. There was no waiting. And when Patton, eager to see the movement personally, drove through Avranches only to discover a traffic jam at a crossroads, he leaped out of his jeep, ran to the intersection, and began personally directing traffic. The two armored divisions he had shoved into Brittany, the 4th and the 6th, moved so fast that Patton's headquarters frequently lost touch with them. To Patton, it hardly mattered. The divisions were moving fast because they encountered mostly light resistance. He wanted to take Rennes and Brest, so that he could turn everybody around and put them all into the advance into the east, "where the decisive battle of the European campaign would obviously be fought."

But before Brest could be taken, the German concentration at St. Malo on Brittany's northern coast had to be cleared out. It was a lingering threat to any force on the peninsula. On August 6, Patton went to VIII Corps headquarters "to see what is delaying the capture of St. Malo." The problem was that top-drawer German troops held the town, they were well dug in, and there were a lot more of them than Patton's G-2 had estimated. Battle here was not fast hit-and-run, but slow siege. Patton, however, refused to acknowledge that the enemy was the obstacle. Instead, the delay was due to "the fact that the people are so damn slow, mentally and physically, and lack self-confidence." The problem was neither more nor less than "human frailty," with which Patton confessed himself "disgusted." Fortunately, he recorded in his diary on August 6, "the lambent flame of my own self-confidence burns ever brighter." For him, war was ultimately a matter of will, and his will had to outbalance the will of the frail and all too human.

On August 7, the Germans near Mortain directly challenged Patton's will by overrunning Mortain itself then charging toward Avranches. It was just as Bradley had feared. Patton continued to believe it was "a German bluff to cover a withdrawal," but something nevertheless moved him to do what he most disdained to do. He halted three divisions, the 80th, 35th, and the Free French 2nd Armored, near St. Hilaire, "just in case something might happen."

What happened was a knock-down drag-out fight between the 30th Division and the German units. Unwilling to let this action halt the eastward portion of his advance, Patton asked Bradley for permission to pass Haislip's XV Corps around the right flank of the Allied position. Satisfied that three divisions were poised to pitch in against the attack from Mortain if needed, Bradley agreed.

Haislip had already taken his initial objective and was crossing the Mayenne River. Permitting him to swing round the Allied positions enabled him to attack Le Mans, on the Sarine River, on August 8. Le Mans was some ninety miles inland from the D-Day beaches. This was magnificent progress indeed, and

Patton's plan was to turn Haislip at a right angle here, sending him north from Le Mans to Alençon and thence to Argentan, twenty-five and fifty miles north of Le Mans, respectively. This would begin the envelopment of the German forces that were counterattacking from Mortain. To be sure, this was an important objective; but Patton had begun developing bigger ideas.

Supported by USAAF ground attacks, the 30th Division was performing well against the German counterattack. Why not go for more? Patton now proposed ordering Haislip to move farther northeast before executing his due north turn. Chartres, somewhat more than sixty miles northeast of Le Mans, and Dreux, about eighty miles, were the objectives he had in mind. This deeper advance, Patton argued, would allow him to envelop the bulk of the German forces in all Normandy, tying off their eastern escape routes and squeezing them between XV Corps and the Allied positions that backed onto the Cotentin and Brittany peninsulas.

Bradley thought this was biting off more than Haislip could chew, and he told Patton that the defeat of the Mortain counterattack was certainly an ambitious enough objective. With this, Bradley approved Patton's original plan, the ninety-degree turn to the north at Le Mans, and although Patton fumed at what he thought was too shallow a bag, he executed his mission. On August 8, he ordered Haislip to turn. The result was the defeat of the counterattack from Mortain and the closure of the so-called Argentan-Falaise pocket, in which fifty thousand Germans were trapped by August 21. It was rightly counted as one of the early Allied triumphs of the European campaign, but had Patton been permitted the deeper encirclement he wanted, the bag would have been much larger and many more of the enemy would have been killed or captured.

Patton's letters to Beatrice were filled with a mixture of joy and disappointment. "The Army had a big day," he wrote on the 8th, "I am quite tickled." Exuberantly, he declared that he was "the only one who realizes how little the enemy can do—he is finished. We may end this in ten days." But on the 9th, he confessed to Beatrice that if he were on his own, he would "take bigger chances than I am now permitted to take."

Counterpointed to Haislip's eastward advance and northern turn was Major General Robert C. Grow's approach to Brest, which lay far to the west, at the tip off the Brittany peninsula. Some historians have criticized Patton for splitting his forces and attacking in two directions at once. Patton believed that dividing his advance in this way divided the defenders— which was harder on the defenders than on the attackers. Moreover, he felt that it was essential to get the eastward advance moving as quickly as possible, since that was where the European campaign would be won. Much of the historical criticism of Patton's bifurcated strategy in August 1944 should rightly be directed at Omar Bradley, who in mid September granted Patton's request to advance to the Moselle River in northeastern France but also ordered a simultaneous attack on Brest, at the other end of France and the European theater of operations. Brest had refused to fall in the opening weeks of the Normandy breakout and was still in German hands in September, albeit very far to the rear of Allied lines. The German garrison in Brest was completely cut off, the rest of Brittany having been cleared by Patton. Surely, both Bradley and Patton understood that Brest was no longer of strategic importance. Despite this, it was Bradley who committed the eighty thousand men of Troy Middleton's VIII Corps to taking the city. More than a year earlier, in the Sicily campaign, Bradley had been appalled and outraged by what he condemned as Patton's monomaniacal obsession with getting to Messina before Montgomery, even after that port city had ceased to be a strategically critical objective. Now, in September 1944, it was Bradley who spent men prodigally—Middleton suffered ten thousand casualties in taking Brest—to obtain precisely what Bradley had called Messina, a "prestige objective." After the war, Bradley argued that capturing Brest was a matter of logistical necessity. This hardly seems the case, however. Once finally sprung from the bocage, the Allied advance had moved so fast that the port of Brest, remote from Allied lines, was of only marginal logistical value. To Patton, however, Bradley confidentially remarked, "I would not say this to anyone but you, and have given different excuses to my staff and higher echelons, but we must take Brest in order to maintain the illusion . . . that the U.S. Army cannot be beaten." It was a motive with which Patton fully concurred. "Anytime we put our hand to a job we must finish it," he replied to Bradley.

On August 9, Grow sent Patton Karl Spang, a German lieutenant general that his division had captured outside of Brest. Patton held a courteous interview with him, expressing his regret "that the General, who is a professional soldier, should feel obliged to continue a useless struggle." To Patton's satisfaction, Spang did not deny that it was useless, but replied that he was following the order of higher command, which was to continue fighting. "As between soldiers," Patton responded, "I have nothing but respect for your attitude."

Spang's remarks and the scattered character of resistance in Brittany (except for the Brest garrison) persuaded Patton that marching through Brittany was now certainly less important than getting out of Brittany and turning east to capitalize on everything Haislip was accomplishing. This is when Bradley insisted on the importance of taking Lorient (on the southern coast of the peninsula), mopping up St. Malo (on the northern coast), and capturing Brest (at the tip of the peninsula). He told Patton to remove no more units from Brittany until these objectives had been attained. Patton smothered his frustration by immersing himself in planning the complex movements of what resources he did have immediately available.

Ultimately, he persuaded Bradley to release some elements from Brittany. He threw all that Bradley would spare him into the eastward push, but then overplayed his hand by not scrupling to cross the boundary separating Bradley's 12th Army Group (of which the Third Army was a part) and Bernard Law Montgomery's 21st Army Group. In the northward leg of its advance, Haislip's XV Corps had begun operating in the zone reserved for the British and Canadian forces. Bradley's chief of staff, Leven C. Allen, telephoned Patton, conveying Bradley's order to halt. Patton replied by asking "if he had any orders to permit" an advance north, beyond Argentan, and farther into Montgomery territory. "I told him . . . it was perfectly feasible to continue the operation." Allen replied by repeating the order to halt and consolidate.

It was anathema to the commander who had admonished his officers that he wasn't interested in holding anything except the nose of the enemy just long enough to kick him in the ass. Patton believed the order came not from Ike or Bradley, but "emanated from the 21st Army Group, and was either due to [Montgomery's] jealousy of the Americans or to utter ignorance of the situation or to a combination of the two." Patton was certain that, had he been permitted to advance "on to Falaise and [make] contact with the Canadians northwest of that point," he could have "definitely and positively closed the escape gap," the so-called "Falaise-Argentan pocket," through which much of the German army was withdrawing to fight another day.

Patton believed that Bradley and Eisenhower would sooner sacrifice a speedy victory than international coalition courtesy. There may actually have been an element of this in Ike's decision. After all, Montgomery assured him that, coming down from the north, his Canadians could more readily close the gap than Patton could coming up from the south. (Montgomery was wrong.) As usual, Bradley was unwilling to accept the notion of substituting what Patton deemed the real safety of speed for the illusion of safety that conventional flank and troop consolidation tactics furnished. Bradley was worried that a gap of seventy-five miles separated Third Army's XV Corps from First Army's VII Corps and thereby exposed the flanks of both armies to attack. Additionally, it seemed to him that the Germans, who were withdrawing through the very Falaise-Argentan gap Patton wanted to close, would overrun the XV Corps troops holding at Argentan.

Thwarted—by higher command, not by the enemy—at Argentan, Patton responded not by yielding but by grabbing for even more in another direction. If he would not be allowed to push north of Argentan, he decided to get Bradley's consent to his earlier request for permission to move farther east in order to expand the Third Army's encirclement of the Germans in Normandy and northwestern France. He proposed moving his XX Corps toward Dreux on the Eure River, a Seine tributary, less than thirty miles due west of Paris, and his XII Corps toward Chartres, twenty miles south of Dreux, also on the Eure. His XV Corps would, as Bradley had ordered, consolidate where it already was, at Argentan. These positions, Patton recorded in his diary, would allow him to "turn from north to southeast without crossing columns" and would allow him the flexibility to "shift divisions between corps at will." He would have the greatest number of options for maneuver, putting him in an ideal position to choke off two full German armies. In effect, the combination of XX and XII Corps within thirty miles of Paris and XV Corps in Argentan constituted an encircle-ment within an encirclement, answering to Patton's own ever-grasping strategic ambition while at the same time satisfying the relative conservatism of Bradley.

To Beatrice he wrote on August 13, *"L'audace, l'audace, tou-jours l'audace."* Moreover (he continued to his wife), "I have stolen the show so far and the press is very mad that they can't write it." Patton's speed in Brittany had captured many col-umn inches in the tabloids, and Ike had put something of a gag order on any news about the Third Army's movements eastward. "This is probably the fastest and biggest pursuit in history," he wrote to Beatrice on August 13, dropping the "probably" in the diary entry he made on the following day: "In exactly two weeks the Third Army has advanced farther and faster than any Army in the history of war."

On August 14, Patton flew back to Bradley's 12th Army Group headquarters to "sell him the plan." To his immense surprise and relief, the 12th Army Group commander not only con-sented, but gave Patton even more than he asked for, permit-ting "me to change [the plan] so as to move the XX Corps on Chartres, the XV Corps on Dreux, and the XII on Orléans," on the River Loire, some forty miles southeast of Chartres. Thus the encirclement became even more ambitious than Patton had originally proposed. "It is really a great plan," he recorded in his diary, "wholly my own, and I made Bradley think he thought of it. 'Oh, what a tangled web we weave when first we practice to deceive.' I am very happy and elated." For added insurance, Patton "got all the corps moving by 2030 [8:30 p.m.] so that if Monty tries to be careful, it will be too late."

Leaving three XV Corps divisions to hold Argentan, Patton sent the rest east to their assigned objectives. If everyone moved quickly everywhere, the Falaise-Argentan gap would be closed, bagging the Germans west of that line, *and* the Paris-Orléans gap would be closed, bagging any of the enemy who had escaped east through Falaise-Argentan. Patton's boast that the expanded plan was "wholly" his own but that he had sold it to Bradley by making him think that the idea was really his was at once mean-spirited, inaccurate, and partially true. As Patton thought of him, Bradley was conservative and cautious; however, compared to most of the army's top field commanders, men blooded in battle by World War I trench warfare, Bradley appeared bold and forward looking. Nevertheless, in comparison with Patton, he *was* conventional and cautious. Conversely, Patton was audacious to the point of recklessness in comparison with Bradley.

What had actually happened was that, from the moment Patton had begun expanding Operation Cobra, transforming Bradley's "very modest plan" into an increasingly breathtaking and epoch-making breakout, the two very different commanders began catalyzing and stimulating one another. At first reluctant even to have Patton under his command, Bradley now used and exploited him. And Patton, though he continued in the privacy of his diary to berate and belittle Bradley—"His motto seems to be, 'In case of doubt, halt,'" he wrote on August 15—used and exploited Bradley's plans to build his own. Patton grew Operation Cobra exponentially, making of it the true commencement of the liberation of Europe. The seed, however, had been Bradley's.

CHAPTER 5

"I WISH I WERE SUPREME COMMANDER"

*"You had better send me a couple of bottles of pink medicin[e].
When I am not attacking I get bilious. . . ."*

—PATTON, LETTER TO BEATRICE PATTON,
OCTOBER 31, 1944

*PATTON THE THIRD ARMY'S CHIEF
SENATORS CONFIRM HIS PROMOTION*
*PLANNING TO SET THE TRAP FOR
GERMANS IN NORMANDY*

Under these headlines, the *New York Times* (August 16, 1944)
ran an Associated Press story identifying Patton as "the tactical genius who has driven the rampant United States Third
Army across Brittany, through Le Mans and then northward
through Alençon and Argentan, completing the southern jaw
of the trap on the Nazi Seventh Army."

It was typical of the press Patton was drawing by mid
August 1944. Radio announcers all over the country broadcast
a United Press wire story that claimed a "fiction writer couldn't
create" George S. Patton Jr. "History itself hasn't matched him.
. . . He's dynamite. On a battlefield, he's a warring, roaring
comet."

Astoundingly, Eisenhower was still trying to keep Patton
under wraps. As late as August 12, the *Washington Star* had run
an editorial commenting on a story released by "the Nazi news
agency Transocean" reporting that Patton was in France leading the Third Army. "General Eisenhower's headquarters has

made no such announcement and no Allied communiqué has even hinted about 'the Third American Army' or the where-abouts of General Patton." The editorial writer admitted that the Nazi news agency's speculations about Patton "may be all wrong," but concluded that a "great number of Americans would be happy" if Patton really were commanding an American army in France. It would be a vindication for "a man who may be short on diplomacy but whose qualities as a fighting officer are beyond dispute." The writer of the UP radio story that called Patton a "warring, roaring comet" did not hesitate to explain the army's refusal even to comment on the general's whereabouts as just so much professional jealousy: "No wonder the brass hats don't like Lieutenant General George Patton. When this war is ended . . . one of the vivid most human pages will be the saga of General Patton."

The truth was not so simple. Eisenhower really was making an effort to milk Operation Fortitude, the great campaign of deception surrounding the Normandy invasion, for all it was worth. But it was also undeniable that Patton was widely regarded as a showboat, and just as widely resented for it. For his part, Patton never denied his hunger for glory, but he sought always to justify it in the context of his military effectiveness. Wearing his beautifully tailored uniforms, shiny cavalry boots, and shinier helmet even in combat zones was not an example of vainglory, he would explain, but his attempt to emulate the greatest of history's commanders. Lord Nelson at Trafalgar, he more than once pointed out, dressed so as to make himself a target. It was an inspiring display of fearlessness in the face of the enemy and a demonstration of the top commander's willingness to share every danger to which his men were exposed. That Nelson was one of the few casualties the Royal Navy suffered at Trafalgar only served to underscore this point, Patton would somewhat irrelevantly assert.

Patton repeatedly dared and defied death, and he went out of his way to be seen doing so. When the Luftwaffe bombed his troops as they had approached Avranches, the general sat in a folding deck chair, watching his junior officers scurry for the hedgerows. Between puffs on his cigar, he sat as the bombs detonated nearby. "Those goddamned bastards, those rotten sons-of-bitches!" he shouted to no one in particular. "We'll get them!" It was indeed the stuff a fiction writer couldn't create—or wouldn't dare to. It was the stuff of legend, and Patton knew it.

Did he have a "death wish"? Maybe. Did he always look for opportunities to prove to himself that he was no coward? By his own admission, yes. But whatever the psychological drivers of his compulsive defiance of death, there was a practical, tactical motive as well. "An army," he said, "is like spaghetti. You can't push a piece of spaghetti, you've got to pull it." The only way to pull something, of course, is to get in front of it. "If you want an army to fight and risk death, you've got to get up there and lead it." For it was not only a general's verbal and written orders that were disseminated through his command; his very attitude also trickled down. Death is the stock in trade of a soldier. If the commander showed that he was unafraid of it, his army would be unafraid of it, too.

Patton could point to the high score of his Third Army as evidence that his "showboating" worked. As of August 26, 1944, his men had killed 16,000 Germans for a loss of 1,930 of their own—an eight-to-one kill ratio. In addition, the army wounded 55,500 of the enemy and captured 65,000. A little over 9,000 Third Army personnel had been wounded, and none captured.

At home, everyone expected Patton to lead his Third Army in the liberation of Paris. His sister, Nita, wrote a congratulatory letter to him on August 19, about how he was "surely getting . . . revenge on all the slimy jealous toads who tried to do you harm. . . . Lordy I wish I could see you going down by the Arc de Triumph in your tank. You are a modern knight in shining armour, and that is one trouble, the Toads do not like knights in shining armour, they like home town boys who sold papers on the street when the weather was cold, in other words newsmen do not LIKE GENTLEMEN."

But such was not to be. The honor of liberating Paris was accorded General Jacques LeClerc, leading the 2nd Free French Armored Division. At the time (the day of liberation was August 25, 1944), LeClerc's division was part of the First Army, having been transferred from the Third Army on August 17. Ladislas Farago, Patton's first biographer, reported that the general was "bitterly disappointed," and that his staff "was stunned." His officers "regarded the decision as the last straw in Eisenhower's increasingly apparent measures to exclude Patton from the glory road."

Actually, if Ike and Bradley had been given their way, the liberation of Paris would have been put on hold. Both defined their principal mission as killing Germans, not "liberating" cities. Much as Ulysses S. Grant had reasoned during the Civil War, a war is won as soon as the enemy army surrenders—or is killed. It is not won as a result of taking this or that city. But Franklin D. Roosevelt and Winston Churchill insisted on the importance of liberating the French capital, and that left Eisenhower no choice. Because Paris was no longer a key military objective, but rather a morale objective, Eisenhower believed it important that the maximum morale value be harvested from its liberation. This meant giving a Frenchman the honor of marching first into the capital. The reason for the transfer of LeClerc's division to the First Army was not some nefarious plot to rob Patton of glory, but the result of the change in the Allied strategy with regard to the Falaise-Argentan pocket, the very change—expansion of the encirclement—Patton himself had asked for.

Patton was surely disappointed that he was not riding by the Arc de Triomphe, but what he thought of LeClerc's being given that honor is not recorded. More than likely, he would have recognized the justice, the propaganda value, and the morale value of the gesture. That ceremony, glory, and accolades meant more to Patton than they did to Eisenhower is obvious. Less obvious is just what these things did mean to Patton. They were powerful psychological weapons and motivators. A modern military officer might call them "force multipliers," factors, intangible as they might be, that increase the effective strength of an army or other unit. Eisenhower and Bradley tended to discount the value of glory in modern war. Contemporaries said of them that they were businesslike in their approach to war—so businesslike, in fact, that Ike regarded devoting time and effort to liberating Paris, a glorious psychological prize, as an instance of misplaced priorities, something that took resources away from the *real* business of war, which was killing the enemy army. Patton defined the business of war differently. In his view, glory was at the heart of the business. It was no less essential than gasoline in maintaining the momentum of the Allied advance.

The picture the public had of the war in Europe in August of 1944—of Patton (in the words of secretary of war Henry Stimson) running his tanks throughout France "like bedbugs in a Georgetown kitchen"—was hardly the whole picture. Recall that Patton, when he was ordered to turn Haislip's XV Corps at Le Mans north from its eastward advance, sought permission to advance north beyond Argentan, his intention being to tie off the Falaise-Argentan pocket. When Haislip warned him that this would take him into Montgomery's territory, Patton told him on August 11 to "Pay no attention to Monty's goddamn boundaries"; however, on the next day, when Haislip had reached Argentan and Patton telephoned Bradley seeking permission to send Haislip farther north, all the way to Falaise, Bradley ordered Patton to halt him at Argentan, so as not to trespass on Montgomery's turf. He told Patton that Montgomery had promised that the Canadians would easily take Falaise from the north, thereby closing the gap and cutting off the avenue of German retreat from Normandy.

But the Canadians' progress proved desperately slow, and Germans continued to pour through the gap. Alarmed by this failure, Bradley showed up at Patton's command post on August 15. He ordered him to stop his eastward advance at the line of Chartres, Dreux, and Chateaudun, just short of the Seine. The problem, Bradley explained, was that if XV Corps were unable to stop the flow of Germans through the Falaise-Argentan gap, the other Third Army units would be needed to intercept the German retreat.

Patton's response is not recorded. Did he point out the obvious: that Bradley had ordered XV Corps to halt its northward advance at Argentan in anticipation of the southward advance of the Canadians, and that the failure of the Canadians to close the gap was now causing all the trouble? We don't know. But now, after thwarting him at Argentan, Bradley wanted his eastward-moving troops to hold themselves available for cleaning up the mess that he (Bradley) and Montgomery had made. In his diary entry for the day, Patton scoffed that his CO was "suffering from nerves." To Bradley himself, he replied that the Third Army was already at the Seine River—that, as a matter of fact, in the manner of the ancient conquerors, he "had pissed in the river that morning." *What do you want me to do*, he asked Bradley, "pull back?" To his diary, he muttered: "I wish I were Supreme Commander."

Some among two or three generations of armchair generals come and gone since the end of World War II have expressed the very same wish.

It is often said that the history of any war is written by the winners. From the Allied point of view, the Normandy campaign has been almost universally portrayed as a story of triumph, and, from a distance in time, it is difficult to view the campaign in any other way. Once the Allies had fought their way inland from the beaches at Normandy, the war was lost for the Germans. Yet the Normandy campaign, victorious though it was, was hardly a masterpiece. Although some fifty thousand Germans were captured or killed within the Falaise-Argentan pocket, as many as forty thousand escaped through the gap in the pocket Bradley and Montgomery had failed to close—or, more to the point, had not permitted Patton to close. Patton sought compensation for this disappointment by securing permission for a longer envelopment east of the Le Mans-Alençon-Argentan line, only to be asked a short time later to halt that advance in order to repair at Argentan what never should have been allowed to break.

The history of a war may be written by the winners rather than the losers, but, in this case, there was potentially a third option: the history of the war as written by George S. Patton Jr. That possibility ended with his death on December 21, 1945, as a result of injuries sustained in an automobile accident thirteen days before. Eisenhower and Bradley were both far more fortunate. They lived to write their histories, and both argued that Patton's plan had risked too much. Penetrating from Le Mans far into Montgomery's territory would have invited a catastrophic collision with the Canadians, Bradley claimed. "I much preferred a solid shoulder at Argentan," he wrote in his postwar memoir, *A Soldier's Story*, "than a broken neck at Falaise." In all of their postwar writings, both Eisenhower and Bradley, after expressing due admiration of Patton, explained that they always had to restrain him, that the chances he took were almost always too great, and that he persistently refused to protect his flanks. True, they admitted, if Patton had been turned loose, the Normandy campaign might have moved faster, might have achieved even more than it did, and therefore might have brought a faster end to the war in Europe; however, had he failed, the Allied armies would have suffered far greater casualties than they did, and the war might have been prolonged.

This is how the assessment of the Normandy campaign must stand. We cannot know what Patton would have written, had he lived to write it, but we can speculate that he would have answered Bradley and Eisenhower the same way that he answered all commanders who were more conventional than he. A speedy advance and attack, whether one is talking about platoons or about armies, is both bolder and safer than giving the enemy time to counterattack by slowing down to protect your flanks against the possibility of counterattack. It is better to avoid counterattack in the first place than to defend against a counterattack once it has been launched.

Still, the public view, all those headlines trumpeting fifty-mile single-day advances in which tens of thousands of Germans were killed or captured, had their effect not only on the civilian home front but on top Allied military commanders, who should have known better. Blitzkrieg was intoxicating, whether you were German high command in 1939–1940 or Allied high command in 1944. Without doubt, the German army was hemorrhaging, but it still had a lot of blood to lose. Patton liked victory, which he thought was very good for the morale of an army, but he also understood that it could easily breed complacency. Eisenhower intuited this as well, and began frequently speaking of "victory fever," by which he meant potentially fatal overconfidence. But even he seemed to take ultimate triumph for granted.

As it turned out, the Canadians finally managed to take Falaise, leaving Patton free to continue in full force to the Seine and beyond. "I could have had it a week ago," he grumbled to Beatrice on August 18, but modesty [his nickname for Bradley] via destiny [Eisenhower] made me stop." "Omar is O.K.," he wearily remarked to Beatrice, "but not dashing. All that I have to do [I do] over protest." In fact, Patton "just pushed on a lot" without even consulting Bradley. He wrote to Beatrice that the phone lines between his command post and Bradley's HQ were down, and that he had arranged with his staff to warn him "over [the] extension when the phone works," because that would mean that Bradley could call with orders to stop. "Luckily [the phone] is out for the time."

Patton had drawn up a plan he labeled "Plan A," which called for an advance across the Seine followed by a sharp hook to the north as far as the town of Beauvais, about fifty miles due north of Paris. Executed quickly, this would, Patton believed, encircle most of the German troops in France. Pending approval of Plan A, Patton pursued the plan by pushing his army east. On August 20, a combat team of the 79th Division crossed the Seine at Mantes. These were the first Allied soldiers to cross that river.

On this same day, Patton called in his XX Corps and XII Corps commanders, Walton H. Walker and Manton Eddy. He told them to get ready to move out at daylight; XX Corps would advance toward Melun, on the east bank of the Seine, about twenty-five miles southeast of Paris, and XII Corps would aim for Sens, some twenty-five miles southeast of Melun, from which it would continue east another twenty-five miles to Troyes, farther east along the Seine. "I gave them one code word," Patton recorded in his diary, "'Proset,' which means 'halt in place,' to be used in case Bradley loses his nerve at the last moment." Having just written this sentence, he started a new paragraph about the state of his own "nerve": "I always have a funny reaction before a show like this. I think of the plan and am all for it, and then just as I give the order, I get nervous and must say to myself, 'Do not take counsel of your fears,' and then go ahead." To him it seemed just like a steeplechase: "You want to ride in it and then when the saddling bugle goes, you are scared, but when the flag drops, all is well."

Patton knew fear. He experienced it perhaps even more keenly than most other men. Whereas most tried to ignore, suppress, deny, or run away from fear, Patton embraced it. By understanding it, he could deal with it. Fear before combat was no different than fear before a steeplechase. There was initial excitement, followed by being "scared"—he used the childish word rather than the more adult "fear" or "anxiety." This emotion was displaced by a feeling of well-being once "the show" actually began. He had to remind himself of this familiar sequence and use the thought of it not as a means of ignoring his fears, but as a way to avoid taking "counsel" of them.

In a letter to his wife, he did admit that the plan looked "very risky" on paper, but he went on to say that he didn't think it really was. Looking at the plan, General Eddy asked him: "How much shall I have to worry about my flank?" Patton answered that it depended on how nervous he was. Eddy went on to suggest a rate of advance of about a mile a day. Patton "told him to go fifty and he turned pale." To his son George, in a letter of August 21, Patton wrote that he had but "one principle in these operations," then quoted from Rudyard Kipling's "If." His "one principle" was to

> *Fill the unforgiving minute*
> *With sixty seconds worth of distance run.*

Kipling had put this in the quatrain that concludes the poem:

> *If you can fill the unforgiving minute*
> *With sixty seconds' worth of distance run,*
> *Yours is the Earth and everything that's in it,*
> *And—which is more—you'll be a Man, my son!*

A fitting enough message from father to son, but Patton followed the quoted lines with a fatherly admonition even more sharply focused: "That is the whole art of war, and when you get to be a general, remember it!"

Just as speed rendered unnecessary any concern about defending your flanks, so speed meant not having to worry about the enemy's intentions. "I have never given a damn what the enemy was going to do or where he was," Patton continued to son George. "What I have known is what I have intended to do and then have done it. By acting in this manner I have always gotten to the place he [the enemy] expected me to come about three days before he got there."

From writing to his son, Patton turned to his diary: "We have, at this time, the greatest chance to win the war ever presented." All that could interfere was a stop order. "If they will let me move on with three corps . . . we can be in Germany in ten days." He saw "plenty of roads and railroads to support the operation," which could be accomplished with three armored divisions and six of infantry. "It is," he concluded, "such a sure thing that I fear these blind moles don't see it."

In his August 20 letter to Beatrice, Patton turned from writing about the planned advance and encirclement to describe how the people of the French villages and countryside had all quit work to "stand along the roads cheering, throwing kisses or apples and offering wine, all as presents." The adulation gratified and cheered him, then suddenly forced him to glimpse what he truly feared: peace. "It will be pretty grim after the war to drive ones self and not be cheered. . . ."

On the evening of the 21st, Patton was able to write to Beatrice that his army had not advanced fifty miles in a day, but seventy, taking Sens, Montereau, and Melun, and doing this so quickly that the Germans had no time to blow up the Seine bridges. "We are going so fast that I am quite safe," he assured Beatrice, and observed that his "only worries are my relations not my enemies." He decided, therefore, to take up his Bible before going to bed, so as to "be ready to have celestial help in my argument tomorrow to keep moving."

At midday of the 22nd, he flew to 12th Army Group headquarters to present his plan to Bradley, only to find that he was away, meeting with Ike and Montgomery. He left the plan with Leven Allen but was gratified to learn from him that Bradley already had "an almost identical plan." Reasonably confident that Bradley would give him everything he wanted, Patton continued to push east. At the southern flank of his advance, XII Corps reached the outskirts of Troyes—southeast of Paris— by August 25, the farthest Allied penetration to date. At the northern flank, XV Corps was participating with units of 21st Army Group in an encirclement of those enemy soldiers who had escaped through the Falaise-Argentan gap.

On the 25th, Bradley summoned Patton to 12th Army Group headquarters, now at Chartres. Patton made a stop at the town's famed cathedral and was relieved that it had not been damaged. The stained glass had been removed for safekeeping, and the cathedral was flooded with light. After saying a "prayer for continued success," he met with Bradley, who issued a new directive based on his meeting with Eisenhower and Montgomery.

Montgomery, it seems, had objected to the Americans' crossing the Seine because pre-invasion plans had had his 21st Army Group invading Germany north of the Ardennes, supported by the 12th Army Group going in on the south end of the Ardennes. The original plan thus gave the British (and Canadians) the leading role in the invasion of Germany. While

Montgomery conceded that the breakthrough had proceeded faster than expected in the American sectors, he still believed that the penetration of the German border should be along a concentrated front. He bolstered this argument by pointing out that the V-1 and V-2 launch sites were located in the north, and that the Allies owed it to the people of England to take these out as soon as possible and stop the rain of ruin on London and other cities. Finally, Monty asserted, the principal English Channel ports, chief among which was Antwerp, were all in the north.

Eisenhower listened, but objected to Montgomery's "narrow-front" plan and proposed instead a broad-front strategy, arguing that this would force the Germans to spread out their defenses to the point of disintegration. His additional, unspoken, motive was a desire to distribute more evenly between the British and the Americans the glory of invading Germany. After listening to Ike's objection to Montgomery's plan, Bradley proposed penetrating Germany at the so-called Frankfurt gap. This meant that the First Army would advance north of the Third Army, which would break through both the Maginot and Siegfried lines in the Saar. But Eisenhower objected to Bradley's plan for the same reason that he had rejected Montgomery's. Its front was still too narrow. He wanted 12th Army Group to advance through the Frankfurt gap as well as the Saar while Montgomery's 21st Army Group, after first securing Antwerp as a major invasion supply port, would enter Germany via the Ruhr.

On August 25, Bradley told Patton and First Army commander Courtney Hodges that the First Army would cross the Seine at Melun and Mantes, two towns captured by the Third Army. From here, Hodges was to drive toward Lille. At the same time, the Third Army would advance to the Metz-Strasbourg line. Patton was pleased because the direction of his advance was part of his Plan A, and on August 28, he wrote to son George that "We are really having a swell time and have just captured Chateau Thierry," famous as a World War I battleground, about forty-five miles east of Paris on the Marne. His "chief difficulty," he wrote, was "not the Germans but gasoline. If they would give me enough gas, I could go anywhere. . . ."

Plenty of gasoline was actually coming into the western ports, but overland logistics could not keep pace with the speed of Patton's advance. Getting the gas from the ports inland to where it was needed became a greater and greater problem with each mile of advance. On August 28, Patton complained to his diary that he had to beg Bradley "like a beggar for permission to keep [advancing] on to the line of the Meuse. What a life." Bradley yielded, but cautioned that gasoline was in short supply and that Ike had decided to give Monty priority in receiving it, partly on the assumption that, if the British and Canadians could take Antwerp, many of the current logistical problems would be solved. On the 29th, Patton discovered that the Third Army had been shorted 140,000 gallons of its gasoline allotment, meager as it now was. He resolved to discuss the problem with Bradley, prudently restraining himself from making a radio call, lest the enemy overhear—"and I do not wish him to know we are short of gasoline."

Patton met with Bradley and Harold "Pinky" Bull, Ike's G-3 (logistics chief), as well as Eisenhower's chief of staff Leven Allen. Patton pleaded his case for launching an immediate advance against the Siegfried Line, Germany's so-called "West Wall" defenses. Patton and the others well knew that, in many places, the Siegfried Line was so thinly manned as to be virtually undefended. This situation would not last long, and it was therefore critically important to seize opportunity before it evaporated. Although Bradley "was sympathetic," Ike's representatives persisted in giving Montgomery top priority. "The British have put it over again," Patton complained to his diary. "We got no gas because, to suit Monty, the First Army"—now under Montgomery's control—"must get most of it."

It is terrible to halt, even on the Meuse. We should cross the Rhine in the vicinity of Worms, and the faster we do it, the less lives and munitions it will take. No one realizes the terrible value of the "unforgiving minute" except me. Some way I will get on yet.

He left the conference with Bradley and Ike's men, resolved to continue at least as far as the Meuse. "I have to battle for every yard," he wrote to Beatrice on August 30, "but it is not the enemy who is trying to stop me, it is 'They.'"

On the eve of war, during the massive Texas and Louisiana maneuvers of September 1941, Patton won a standout victory that drew a chorus of accolades as well as cries of foul. Using his tanks, he made a brilliant end-run dash around the opposing army, briefly straying from the allotted maneuver area and running out of gas. His solution was to pay for fuel—out of his own pocket—at local filling stations. He silenced his opponents' grumbling about his "breaking the rules" by proclaiming *victory* as the only real *rule* in war. Now, with his vanguard at the Meuse, he wrote to Beatrice, "If I could only steal some gas, I could win this war," and he went on to say that "a colored truck company did steal some for me by careful accident." He also managed to capture approximately a million gallons of German gasoline, which was of poor quality but could run American tank engines, provided they were already hot.

Having expanded Operation Cobra into a spectacular break-out leading to a breathtaking breakthrough encompassing virtually the entire French theater, liberating within the space of a month most of France north of the Loire, Patton ran out of gas on the banks of the Meuse, within spitting distance of the West Wall of Germany itself.

Patton believed (as he recorded in his diary on August 30) that the decision to give Montgomery priority in supplies was a "terrible mistake" destined to "cause much argument" when it came out "in after years." Patton was a soldier, however, and he knew he had to reconcile himself to much that he found disagreeable, infuriating, and even tragic. But on September 1, he noted in his diary what seemed very nearly the last straw. "At 0800 we heard on the radio that Ike said Monty was the greatest living soldier and is now [promoted to] Field Marshal." To diffuse the pain of this broadcast, which he took as a slap in the face from Ike, Patton flew up to his command post and immersed himself in "administrative papers for the rest of the day."

Stalled at the Meuse, unappreciated, even denigrated, by the supreme Allied commander, Patton felt the exhilaration slipping away from him. Painful enough that Montgomery had been elevated over him, but even worse was the loss of momentum of a drive—*his* drive—which had brought final victory within the grasp of the Allies.

In 1856, the Victorian essayist and critic John Ruskin coined the phrase "pathetic fallacy" to describe the treatment, in painting and literature, of inanimate objects and of nature itself as if they had human feelings. Thus, in cheap fiction, the sun shines when the hero triumphs, and the skies darken with storm clouds when he is defeated. Life seemed now to imitate art, as the gorgeous, clear, dry weather of summer, weather custom made for an attack, suddenly yielded to unseasonably early rains, ice storms, and snow in the fall of 1944. The changed weather was a perfect reflection of Patton's changed mood. As he had feared, the interruption of his drive conceded to the enemy the most valuable of gifts in war: time. The Germans scurried to man the Siegfried Line, the West Wall, the final bastion guarding the Fatherland.

The general struggled to put the best face on the situation when he granted an interview to Third Army correspondents on September 7. Mindful of what the press could and had done to him, he warned: "I am not quotable, and if you want to get me sent home, quote me, goddamn it."

He remarked that crossing the Moselle River was "a very historic event . . . and I am very proud of the troops of this Army for getting across the goddamn river. I like it because I like that kind of wine, but I am not quotable, goddamn it. I don't drink anything but lemonade, when I can't get anything else." As the laughter subsided, he said that he hoped he would "go through the Siegfried line like shit through a goose," adding, "That is not quotable." At this, a scoop-hungry reporter asked Patton point blank about the gas shortage. "We mustn't talk about that," Patton snapped, but then continued: "Off the record and not to be quoted . . . had we had the gas, which was a physical impossibility to get because we had gone much faster than we were supposed to, had we hit the Moselle four days earlier, it would have been like pissing to the wind. We would have gone on over." As if he instantly regretted this frank outburst, he shifted back to a tone of bantering optimism: "We *are* over now, so it doesn't make much difference . . . I never cared where I killed the bastards. . . ." But then he let slip the most soberly revealing remark of all: "Whenever you slow anything down, you waste human lives."

By the second week in September, the Third Army had been substantially resupplied, and Patton renewed his drive, but, given the turning weather and the German consolidation of defenses, he knew that the going would be slower, harder, and bloodier from now on. He took Nancy on September 15, but the formidable fortress town of Metz proved more stubborn. It was greatly reduced by mid November, but the last defenders of this fortress complex held out until just days before Christmas.

Taking these strong points was big news, but it was Hodges's First Army, not Patton's Third, that crossed into Germany first, on September 12. Everyone was itching to breach the Rhine now. As important as that great river was strategically, it mattered even more to the morale of both sides. The Rhine was to Germans what the Mississippi was to Americans, a mythic heartland river, the physical and spiritual guardian of the nation and its people. To cross it was to signal the beginning of the finality of total defeat.

Field Marshal Montgomery pushed through Operation Market-Garden, a bold but fatally flawed bid to cross the lower Rhine via Holland for what Monty called a "dagger-thrust into Germany." Launched September 17, 1944, it collapsed by the 25th. The American units involved in the operation—all part of the ad hoc First Allied Airborne Army, which was attached to Montgomery's 21st Army Group and included the 82nd and 101st Airborne Divisions—attained their initial objectives, but the British airborne contingents were "misdropped," land-ing too far from their targeted Rhine crossing to efficiently penetrate German defenses and seize the bridgehead at Arn-hem, Netherlands. On the 25th, some 2,300 British and Polish Legion paratroops managed to withdraw from Arnhem, hav-ing left more than 6,000 of their comrades, about half of them wounded, to a POW's fate.

As fiercely competitive as he was with Montgomery, and despite his rage over the galling adulation Ike had accorded him, Patton took no satisfaction in the failure of Market-Garden. If anything, it added to the depression and fatigue that had set in when he was halted at the Meuse.

The Third Army was finally under way again by mid Sep-tember, but the summer of fifty- and seventy-five-mile single-day advances was over and done. Patton continued to advance, but slowly and at a much heavier cost in blood. Strategically, Germany was finished. Tactically, however, its military still had options, and resistance grew fiercer the more the Allies menaced the West Wall.

Then, toward the end of September, the supply tap was again reduced to a trickle, and Patton was forced to accept what higher command called the "October pause." Once more, it seemed to him, the needs of Bernard Law Montgom-ery constituted the choke point. Ike wanted the entire invasion force to conserve ammunition, gasoline, and other supplies until Montgomery finally opened the port of Antwerp. Pat-ton understood that possessing Antwerp meant that supplies would be unloaded far closer to the advancing Allied armies, but he faulted Montgomery for his inability to gain timely con-trol of his assigned objective. Now with ammo as well as gas rationed, Patton had no choice but to accept the only kind of war he hated: defending in place.

He projected his own profound dejection on the Third Army as a whole and was fearful that enforced inaction would do to his men what it was doing to him. Just because his army was no longer on the move didn't mean he had to sit still, however. Patton toured throughout the Third Army area, assembling units for morale-lifting speeches and talking one-on-one with small, informal groups of soldiers. To unit commanders, he preached the critical necessity of maintaining morale. This required getting the soldiers the best food available, including as many hot meals as possible, and, even more important, ensuring that mail from home reached every soldier rapidly and regularly. Just as Patton had demanded the utmost of all unit commanders in combat, now he called on them to move heaven and earth to get fresh food when, supposedly, only C and K rations were available, and to prod their G-3s into giving mail the highest priority.

Or, more accurately, the second-highest. Patton became obsessed with preaching the gospel of dry socks. Trenchfoot, an infection that thrived in a moist, dirty environment, was as disabling as any serious wound. Recovery from a bad case could take weeks, and, in too many instances, the infection left a man permanently disabled. Since dry socks were the only sovereign defense against trenchfoot, Patton made obtaining them the business of every one of his commanders. The soldier, Patton often said, *is* the army, and he did not want his idled troops to suffer and his stalled army to rot. Besides, mightily frustrated by higher command, he turned to whatever he knew he could get his arms around, whatever situation he could control or at least improve. During this period, a reporter asked him if he still thought "the corporal is the most important man in the army." Patton shook his head "no." "The private first class," he said.

Early in November, Bradley announced the end of the "October pause" and gave Patton the supplies and authorization he needed to resume attacking. But now there was a new enemy. Rain, ceaseless and heavy, churned the roads to mud, which seemed to swallow tanks and other heavy vehicles. Crawling, wallowing, Patton and his Third Army could only listen to the reports of elements of the newly formed Sixth Army Group crossing the Rhine north of Patton's position. As had happened during his long Sicilian exile following the "slapping incidents," Patton was falling out of the headlines. From November 8 to December 15, the Third U.S. Army advanced a paltry forty miles, every yard of it paid for in blood.

The general did his best to look forward to his big breakthrough attack against the West Wall and his advance to the Rhine. Once across, his objective would be Frankfurt, a most significant prize. Yet as he prepared to move his headquarters east, he felt not the customary exhilaration that had always accompanied the contemplation of a great attack. Instead, he was worried. It was not a feeling to which he was accustomed, not, at least, when he was assured of battle. He had often spoken about possessing a "sixth sense" when it came to combat, but rarely did that intuition create anything other than eager anticipation, and certainly not worry. As November came to a close, he was able to put into words the source of his concern, noting in his diary that "First Army is making a terrible mistake in leaving [Troy Middleton's] VIII Corps static" on the western border of Luxembourg, "as it is highly probable that the Germans are building up east of them."

Middleton's corps was positioned just to the southeast of a Belgian town called Bastogne. Everyone in Allied command could see this. They all worked from the same maps. Yet Patton, who strove never to take counsel of his fears, seems to have been alone in recognizing the hazard of a line so thinly held there. Always concerned about the welfare, condition, and "seasoning" of the men, Omar Bradley had marked out the area around Bastogne as what in World War I had been called a "quiet sector." It was a place for as-yet unblooded out-fits to be eased into relatively low-intensity combat and for war-weary veteran units to rest and recover. Besides, although the weather was miserable and the earth muddy, the German army, for all the fight it kept up, was obviously finished. Stub-born defense against the Allied advance was one thing, but mounting a counteroffensive? Well, it was out of the question.

Patton was not so sure. He had spent the past month and a half slogging through the hardest, most unforgiving fight-ing of his war. With every inch gained, he had seen and felt the intensity of resistance this "beaten" army could still offer. When he had been advancing fifty or seventy-five miles in a day, attacking at every opportunity, he cared little (he had told his son George) about what the enemy was thinking or doing. Reduced to a bloody crawl, however, it became urgently nec-essary to care about what the enemy was thinking, and Patton thought he knew what was on the German mind. Visualizing the Bastogne "quiet sector" through the eyes of the enemy commanders, he could see the sum of it all. The Germans were in full retreat. The Germans were short on men, gaso-line, ammunition, equipment, everything. The German nation was being crushed in an Allied vise. The situation for Hitler's armies was as grim as it could possibly get. The reasonable thing, the "right" thing to do would be to continue retreating and consolidating. But the reasonable and right thing, Patton felt, was precisely *not* what the Germans intended to do. With every circumstance crying out to them to fold, to give up, he reasoned that they would instead attack.

CHAPTER 6

"DON'T BE FATUOUS, GEORGE!"

"I have it—but I'll be damned if I can define it."

—PATTON, LETTER TO HIS SON
GEORGE S. PATTON III, JANUARY 16, 1945

Maps were to Patton what sheet music is to a virtuoso. As a musician hears the notes he sees, so Patton envisioned combat in all its dimensions from studying contours and lines on a page. When he wasn't in the field, he was in front of a map. Toward the end of November, the maps he read spoke to him of danger, of the "terrible mistake" of leaving Troy Middleton's undermanned VIII Corps "static" on the border of Luxembourg and Belgium. He saw in the maps what he believed the Allies' German counterparts must also have seen: the opportunity for a counteroffensive. It is "highly probable," he wrote in his diary, "that the Germans are building up east of" Middleton's corps.

There was nothing for Patton to do about it, of course. Middleton was now Bradley's concern, and Patton was slogging it out a hundred or so miles to the south. On December 13, the last fort at Metz, in Lorraine, surrendered to him, and on the 14th, he toured the Saar River town of Saarlautern (Saarlouis), where fighting was still hot. "Nearly all the houses I inspected . . . are really forts." He noted in his diary that the rifle strength in his army's infantry battalions was now "very low, poor devils, but they are killing large numbers of Germans." Patton drove his soldiers hard, doing so in the belief that only maximum effort brings victory and that American troops are at their best when they are pushed beyond the limit.

As usual, the Germans weren't Patton's only enemy. Montgomery, he knew, was "bitterly opposed" to the Third Army's operations, wanting "all available forces massed on the north" under his command. Contrary to Eisenhower's insistence on a broad-front advance into Germany, Montgomery persisted in maintaining "that the Rhine can be crossed at one place . . . Cologne, and that this must be done under one Army Group commander," namely himself.

Patton did his best to ignore Montgomery's demands, resolving to continue his own attack "with its present short means," knowing that if it failed to break through, he would have to go on the defensive pending the arrival of reinforcements. But his other enemy, the weather, could not be ignored. The rain, cold, icy rain, was incessant. He appealed to God— for he felt that he and God were on intimate speaking terms, that perhaps God even owed him something—for the rain to let up, and on December 14 he observed, more hopefully than not, that it "has certainly rained less since my prayer."

On the 15th, rain gave way to a damp, heavy fog. "This is one of the days when every one but me has lost faith," he wrote to Beatrice. "I still have to push them over but it does not seem to bother me."

Up north, the fog was even thicker than in Patton's sector. The Ardennes, which enveloped Middleton's men, was smothered in it, and what had fallen as rain along Patton's front came here as snow, accumulating to five inches by the predawn hours of December 16. In the bitter cold, the fog began to thin and was replaced by a shimmering ground haze rising from the blanket of white. It was very beautiful, gentling the craggy, twisted old-growth forest that climbed and descended the hills and low mountains of Belgium, Luxembourg, northeastern France, and Germany's Eifel. In places, the mountains became rolling hills, and the hills dropped suddenly into boggy moors, frozen solid now; elsewhere, the mountains backed up against steep-sided valleys that had been scooped out by millennia of river flow. The snow almost made one forget just how formidable the Ardennes topography was. Before the war, the French had ended their Maginot Line where the Ardennes began, certain that no invader would ever choose to come through these woods, these valleys, these mountains. Of course, the blitzkrieg on the Western Front had begun in just that way, when General "Schneller Heinz" (Hurry-Up Heinz) Guderian ran around the northern end of the Maginot, crashing his panzers through the Ardennes and into France. Had Omar Bradley forgotten this cruelest of surprises when he deployed the First Army's two weakest, least experienced divisions, together with veterans worn out and recuperating from continuous battle, in this very place?

What happened in the white-blanketed, mist-white dawn of December 16, 1944, must be remembered the way Pearl Harbor is remembered: as the devastating surprise attack that should have come as no surprise at all. On orders from Hitler himself, nearly 600,000 troops—the very best the Wehrmacht and SS could still muster—assembled along the eastern edge of the Ardennes. They built up and they trained for weeks. The Allies had long commanded the skies and could fly reconnaissance virtually every day of the week without meeting opposition from the all-but-depleted Luftwaffe—though the weather had lately held flights to a minimum. The "bright boys" in Bletchley Park, not far from London, had learned long ago the secrets of Germany's military ciphers, and U.S. G-2 and British military intelligence were extensively plugged into an array of intelligence networks. Yet still it came without warning, without even an inkling—but for the suspicions born of Patton's map reading. Montgomery believed that a major offensive was an impossibility for the battered German armies. And Eisenhower, although he was always wary of Allied complacency, what he called "victory fever," joined Bradley in his belief that a breakthrough in the Ardennes sector was a very remote possibility indeed. High command was effectively blinded by December fog and its own assumption that, by any meaningful measure, the Germans had already lost the war.

In the days before what the German generals called, even more aptly than they knew, Operation Autumn Fog, the artillery fire that sometimes hit the American position fell away, as did the stream of V-1s that tore across the sky above the neophyte GIs and their war-weary comrades. Everyone assumed that the enemy was running low on ammo, and that most artillery emplacements had been bombed out along with V-1 launch sites. The sudden silence, the accumulating snow, and the milky ground fog combined with the unremitting cold to lull the troops into a stupor that was surreal in a war zone but nevertheless irresistible.

Well before dawn on the morning of December 16 the somnolence was shattered by a titanic resumption of the artillery barrage, this time targeted directly against the weakest section of the generally weak eighty-mile front that was held by just five understrength, green, or exhausted divisions: the 99th and 106th from Courtney Hodges's V Corps, the 28th and 4th from VIII Corps, and the 9th Armored. The pounding came down hardest near the picturesque German border town of Monschau, which had been chosen, in orthodox blitzkrieg fashion, as the *Schwerpunkt*—the main thrust—of an overwhelming attack led by Sepp Dietrich, one of Hitler's most trusted SS commanders. Against this area, the Germans threw everything they had: bombs, mortar fire, artillery rockets, conventional artillery, and even V-1 buzz bombs, which, hitherto directed exclusively against civilian targets, had never been used before as a battlefield weapon. Even more bewildering to the Americans under fire were the bizarre five-foot-long dartlike projectiles that sometimes drilled into their lines. These were fired from another weapon that had been designed to terrorize English cities, the *Hochdruckpumpe* ("High-pressure Pump"), which used a series of propellant charges spaced at intervals in side-chambers along its otherwise conventional gun barrel to augment the initial charge, thereby providing phenomenal muzzle velocity—enough (such was Hitler's plan for the weapon he intended to christen the V-3) to propel barrages across the English Channel and into the heart of London. Now the Hochdruckpumpe was turned with everything else against the weak American line in the Ardennes.

At 5:30 in the morning, the leaden clouds above the Americans were suddenly illuminated by hundreds of antiaircraft searchlights. The cusp-of-dawn gloom of a cloudy winter day brightened unnaturally, allowing the German infantry and tanks to see all that lay before them. The attack was overwhelming. Everywhere, the American lines buckled and broke, bulging back westward like an aneurism filling with blood, the vital membrane stretching thinner and thinner. To the Germans, it would be the Ardennes Offensive; to the Americans, the Battle of the Bulge.

Adolf Hitler had begun planning Autumn Fog in the late summer. The idea was all his. He—not his generals—had detected the vulnerability of the Ardennes sector feebly held by no more than eighty thousand Americans. As usual, he became obsessed with his strategic brainchild and strangled virtually the entire Western Front in order to horde men, equipment, ammunition, and fuel for this single dagger thrust with which, he believed, the fortunes of his war could suddenly be turned. He ordered absolute radio silence; all orders and other messages went out by landline telephone or messenger. This in part accounts for the utter failure of Allied intelligence, which had long been based on intercepting and decoding radio traffic. Add to this the almost unbroken succession of overcast days—which severely restricted aerial reconnaissance—and the complacency bred of victory fever, and the Anglo-American armies were deaf and blind.

Hitler's intention was that overwhelming victory in the Ardennes would demoralize the Allies and prompt a favorably negotiated end to the war. If demoralization alone was not sufficient to bring the Allies to the conference table, breaching the Ardennes would make a hole through which the German armies—what was left of them—would flow, thrusting north and west across the Meuse, into and through Belgium and to the Dutch port-city prize that was Antwerp, now the principal supply source for the Allied invasion. In the process, the breakthrough would split the British and Canadian forces from the Americans, allowing the Wehrmacht and SS to crush the Brits once and for all, thereby forcing the Americans to seek terms.

The plan, of course, was as bold and simple as it was ultimately delusional in its ambition. But delusional or not, it was destined to explode into the single biggest and costliest land battle of the European campaign.

Precisely because the plan was unrealistic, Ike, Monty, and Bradley could never have imagined it. Moreover, the artillery barrage that preceded the panzer and infantry attack had knocked out most communications from the Ardennes, rendering that sector, so far as First Army headquarters was concerned, "quiet" indeed. When the reports started trickling in, they were sketchy, low-key, and oddly colorless. They did not much disturb First Army commander Courtney Hodges or his guest, 12th Army Group commander Omar Bradley, who, having just enjoyed a gentlemanly breakfast at First Army headquarters, the Hotel Britannique in the town of Spa, were being custom fitted for bespoke shotguns that had been crafted in Liège. As a Monsieur Francotte measured the officers in efficiently tailorlike fashion, more notes drifted in from the Ardennes. The incoming reports soon assumed the pattern of crescendo, each note louder than the one before, indicating a bigger attack, a greater penetration, a lengthening litany of villages falling to enemy occupation, and, finally most alarming of all, the encirclement of one unit after another. Hodges began to transmit orders to the five beleaguered divisions of his army, and Bradley drove off to 12th Army Group headquarters in Luxembourg. The shotgun "tailoring" would have to wait.

While Middleton's corps fell under barrage and panzer attack, General Eisenhower, in SHAEF headquarters, Paris, far from the developing battle, was reading a letter from Field Marshal Montgomery, soliciting leave to "hop over" to England for Christmas. It was Montgomery's assessment, as he had written the day before in his 21st Army Group Situation Report, that the "enemy is at present fighting a defensive campaign on all fronts; his situation is such that he cannot stage major offensive operations. . . . The enemy is in a bad way."

Indeed, in his letter to Eisenhower, he reminded the supreme Allied commander of the five-pound wager they had made fourteen months earlier, on October 11, 1943, Monty betting the war would end by Christmas 1944, Ike betting it would not. Enclosing a wager marker in his note, the field marshal scrawled across it: "For payment I think at Christmas." "Dear Monty," Eisenhower wrote in reply, "I am delighted that you can find opportunity to spend Christmas with your son. I envy you." He continued: "The data contained in your memorandum respecting the bet is exactly correct according to my own note. However, I still have nine days, and while it seems almost certain that you will have an extra five pounds for Christmas, you will not get it until that day." After completing his letter to Montgomery and letters to other correspondents, Eisenhower, with most of his staff, drove to the Louis XIV Chapel at Versailles, to attend the wedding of Ike's faithful valet, Mickey McKeogh, to Pearlie Hargrave, a WAC sergeant from Queens, New York. Ike was fond of the couple and entertained them and the rest of the wedding party at his personal billet in Saint-Germain. The supreme commander was in a very good mood, the Senate having just approved his elevation to General of the Army, adding a fifth star to the four he already wore.

Throughout the 16th, Hodges and Bradley believed they were both fully on top of the situation. Despite the increasingly dire, even frantic, messages that reached Hodges at Spa, the tempo of command did not quicken. Hodges's reports to Bradley reinforced the 12th Army Group commander's belief that the Ardennes sector was experiencing a strictly local "spoiling attack" and nothing more. Toward evening, Bradley drove to Eisenhower's Paris headquarters to discuss routine matters. By this time, German radio silence had been broken, and Allied intelligence was once again intercepting and decrypting messages, messages that should have created considerable alarm because they indicated that Hodges's 80,000 men were under attack by nothing less than two full panzer armies—about 250,000 men. Yet even this was not enough to dispel the prevailing torpor enveloping high command. More astoundingly, early on the 17th, Allied intelligence decrypted a broadcast message from Gerd von Rundstedt, overall commander of Autumn Fog: "The hour of destiny has struck. Mighty offensive armies face the Allies. Everything is at stake. More than mortal deeds are required as a holy duty to the Fatherland."

Still, neither Hodges, nor Bradley, nor Eisenhower stirred— not, at least, until it became clear that the entire Sixth SS Panzer Army was now fully committed to battle. After the war, conflicting accounts emerged among Hodges, Bradley, and Eisenhower as to who was really the first to conclude that more than a local spoiling attack was in progress. Ultimately, Eisenhower's claim that it was he who urged (not ordered) Bradley to reinforce the Ardennes became the most widely accepted version. What is certain is that Bradley, who was still at Eisenhower's Paris headquarters, telephoned Patton with an order that he detach the 10th Armored Division from Third Army XX Corps and send it north to Middleton's VIII. Bradley spoke blandly of the need "to help repulse a rather strong German attack," and despite his earlier intuition about danger lurking in the Ardennes, Patton responded to Bradley in kneejerk fashion, assuming that the order, which would force him to interrupt his own eastward-moving offensive (already weakened and imperiled by the incessant manpower demands of Montgomery), flowed from the same overabundance of caution that perpetually afflicted the 12th Army Group commander. Over the phone, he complained to Bradley that the Third Army had paid heavily "in blood in the hope of a break through at Saarlautern and Saarbrucken" and that losing an armored division would invite the Germans to attack precisely at the areas where he intended to break through. Bradley, Patton recorded in his diary, "admitted my logic but took counsel of his fears and ordered" the transfer. This left Patton no choice, except to growl out (in the privacy of his diary) a wish that the army group commander "were less timid."

Sometime after hanging up the telephone and after recording his initial disgust with Bradley's timidity, Patton's original intuition seems to have kicked back in. "He probably knows more of the situation than he can say over the telephone," Patton wrote more thoughtfully, and, later in the day, he recorded that the German attack was taking place on "a wide front and moving fast." It was possibly "a feint," he allowed, but "at the moment it looks like the real thing." His analysis of the situation was as simple as it was characteristic. First Army's V and VIII Corps should have been "more aggressive" all along. Had they been, "the Germans could not have prepared this attack; one must never sit still."

The observation cannot be dismissed as a mere I-told-you-so. In fact, there is no rancor or pettiness in it. Nor is it an idle criticism. Rather, it is evidence of Patton's unflagging determination to learn from what happened on the field. The point here was not that Troy Middleton or his boss, Courtney Hodges, or Hodges's CO, Omar Bradley, was inept, but that they had all violated a principle of warfare indispensable in the era of mobile combat. They had allowed a force to "sit still." Advance was the key. It was the object of modern combat, and it was also (despite natural urges to self-preservation and the dictates of apparent common sense) where one's greatest security lay. Take cover, sit still, and you invite attack. Move, and you make attack more difficult. Move *forward*—into the enemy—and you make it even harder. As Patton more than once observed, the enemy is always reluctant to launch an attack close to his own lines.

Major General Fox Conner (1874–1951) occupies no place in the American public's pantheon of World War II generals, but Dwight Eisenhower spoke for his own generation of commanders—Bradley and Patton included—when he called him "the ablest man I ever knew." A "tall easygoing Mississippian—practical—down to earth—as open and honest as any man I have known," Eisenhower judged him "a natural leader and something of a philosopher," who possessed "an extraordinary library, especially in military affairs." After U.S. entry into World War I, Conner was appointed to Pershing's staff as chief of G-3, charged with directing strategy and tactics, the essence of which he defined as solving the problem of how to inflict more damage more quickly on the enemy than he could inflict on you. The public heard all about Black Jack Pershing, but army insiders knew that Fox Conner was the intellectual engine driving American Expeditionary Force operations in the "Great War."

After that conflict, from 1921 to 1925, Conner commanded a brigade in Panama and took under his wing a still-young Ike Eisenhower, for whom the experience "was a sort of graduate school in military affairs and the humanities, leavened by the comments and discourses of a man who was experienced in his knowledge of men and their conduct."

On December 17, 1944, as the magnitude of the crisis in the Ardennes was becoming clear to him, Patton wrote to Fox Conner, retired to Hendersonville, North Carolina, since 1938. It is telling that he chose to communicate with this particular man at this particular time. "Yesterday morning the Germans attacked to my north in front of the VIII Corps of the First Army," he wrote. "It reminds me very much of March 25, 1918"—when the Allies, including the AEF, were faced with one of German generalissimo Erich Ludendorff's massive offensives; Patton continued: "and I think will have the same results." Those results, both Patton and Conner well knew, included the defeat of Germany. While others were just beginning to take alarm and worry that the surprise counteroffensive in the Ardennes could bring about a terrible Allied setback, Patton calmly elaborated to Conner on his analogy to 1918. "I am convinced that this attack by the Germans will be thoroughly smashed, and they will have nothing left." Where others saw menace, Patton conceived opportunity.

He did not seek from Conner counsel or advice, but historical confirmation, using the masterfully studious military mentor in much the same way that he had used the experience of William the Conqueror, as related in Edward A. Freeman's 1879 *History of the Norman Conquest*: to provide a precedent on which to base present action and to predict the outcome of that action.

At mid morning on the following day, Bradley summoned Patton and his staff officers to his headquarters in Luxembourg. When Patton arrived, Bradley spoke to him with almost as much trepidation as if he were the enemy. "I feel you won't like what we are going to do, but I fear it is necessary."

With this, he showed Patton to the map. Even the Third Army commander was taken aback by what he saw. The "German penetration is much greater than I thought," he recorded in his diary account of the meeting. The source of Bradley's reluctance to tell Patton what he wanted was now clear. Bradley needed more of the Third Army diverted to the north from its eastward drive. But he gave no order. Instead, he *asked* Patton what he could do.

The question reveals the reason many believe Bradley to have been a brilliant and canny commander, despite his strategic shortcomings and absence of Pattonesque audacity. He knew his man. If he had simply told Patton what to do, Patton would have followed orders, no more and no less. By instead asking him what he *could* do, Bradley understood that Patton would more than rise to the challenge. No one could set the bar higher than Patton himself. Bradley's question was a brilliant stroke of leadership.

Barely taking a beat, Patton declared that he would halt the eastward advance of his 4th Armored Division at a position where it would be ready to turn north. He would start the 80th Division on its march toward Luxembourg (just twelve miles from the battle) and would alert the 26th Division to be prepared to begin marching north on twenty-four hours' notice, if need be.

Bradley was clearly satisfied; Patton instantly put all the necessary wheels into motion, then headed out to confer with Major General Walton Walker, commanding the XX Corps. Before leaving, he phoned his chief of staff, Hobart "Hap" Gay, to let him know, among other things, that "It will probably be late when I come home." It was a dark winter night when Patton drove back to his headquarters. In blackout conditions and over treacherous, shell-damaged roads, it seemed to him "a very dangerous operation, which I hate." No sooner did he arrive at his desk than Gay passed on a request from Bradley that he phone the 12th Army Group commander at 8:00 p.m. Bradley told him that the situation had become much worse than when they had conferred just hours earlier. He asked Patton to put the promised units into motion right away and summoned him, together with one staff officer, to meet him at Eisenhower's Verdun headquarters at 11:00 the next morning.

"I understand from General Eisenhower that you are to take over VIII Corps as well as the offensive to be launched by the new troops coming into the area," Bradley informed Patton. The intent of this message was clear. Bradley wanted Patton to know that Ike had tapped him as just the man to turn around a desperate situation. But Ike's choice of words, as conveyed by Bradley, was especially significant. He wasn't asking Patton merely to rescue forces under siege, but to launch an offensive against the Germans. *This* was why Ike called on him. He understood that attack was congenial to Patton's nature, and he further understood that, having been forced to slow down and even to assume the defense for long stretches since the end of summer, Patton would be all the more hungry for a fight.

Fifteen minutes after the start of this phone call, Patton convened a meeting with his staff officers and III Corps commander John Millikin and his staff. Together, they quickly planned the routes of march for the 4th Armored and 80th Infantry. XII Corps, which was about to begin an offensive push against the Siegfried Line following an aerial bombardment, would have to hold its position and instead go on the defense. The planned bombardment was called off.

Even as he arranged these movements and the temporary sacrifice of his eastward push, Patton refused to think that he was embarking on a rescue mission. Back in July and August, during his expansion of Operation Cobra, he had unsuccessfully tried to persuade Bradley and Montgomery to let him penetrate as far east as possible before turning to the north, so that his Third Army could bag the entire German army north of the River Loire. Now he saw a similar opportunity—but, this time, the Germans, not his own Third Army, were doing the pushing. Where others feared the great bulge growing in the American lines, with miles of real estate changing hands and Antwerp threatened, Patton saw a big bag stuffed full with Germans. Why not let the bag get bigger, then attack from the north (Monty's turf) and the south (Patton country), tying off the bag at the German rear? As Patton understood war, the object was to kill the enemy, not defend territory, and here was a golden opportunity to trade territory for the slaughter of the German army. Once the enemy armies were killed or captured, the territory would return to its rightful owners because the war would be over and won. This was the great lesson of World War II in Russia, was it not? The German juggernaut had rolled deep into that country, apparently unstoppable, only to be swallowed up, cut off, millions killed, wounded, or captured.

Of course, this vision of victory tested even Patton's formidable nerve. Some 250,000 German combat troops, excellent soldiers freshly trained, participated in the initial advance against the 80,000 soldiers of VIII Corps, most of them either green or assigned to the sector to recuperate after months of uninterrupted combat. Little wonder that the Americans were being driven back through Luxembourg and Belgium. By the 19th, the "bulge" was fifty miles deep, the backs of some VIII Corps soldiers uncomfortably close to the Meuse. Months ago, Patton had goaded a hesitant Troy Middleton into crossing the Sélune River by reminding him that "throughout history it had always been fatal not to cross a river." Patton had no reason to believe that the Germans were any less knowledgeable about military history than he. He assumed that they would do anything to get across the Meuse and, once across, they would be hard to stop before they threatened Antwerp. For the time being, therefore, he kept his vision of the big bag to himself and instead plowed ahead with plans for coordinating VIII and III Corps in a counter-counteroffensive intended to stop the German advance as soon as possible.

Patton rapidly sketched out three alternative plans, each intended to meet a particular contingency. With these in hand, at 9:15 on the morning of the 19th, he and Paul Harkins of his staff left for Verdun, reaching Ike's headquarters ninety minutes later.

The conference at Verdun included Patton, Bradley, British air marshal Arthur Tedder, and Jacob Devers, commander of the 6th Army Group, which had been created in July out of a dozen U.S. and a dozen French divisions. Ike began by yielding the floor to his G-2 (intelligence officer), who solemnly traced a pointer over a map and painted the situation in the Ardennes in the darkest possible shades.

Such a grim presentation would have invited several moments of sullen silence had Eisenhower not risen from his chair before the echo of the officer's final sentence had even died.

"The present situation," he peremptorily declared, "is to be regarded as one of opportunity to us and not of disaster. There will be only cheerful faces at this conference table."

At first blush, this was precisely the kind of response Patton heartily welcomed. As Eisenhower recalled in his postwar memoir, *Crusade in Europe*, "True to his impulsive nature, General Patton broke out with, 'Hell, let's have the guts to let the ___ _ ___ go all the way to Paris. Then we'll really cut 'em off and chew 'em up.' Everyone, including Patton, smiled at this one, but I replied that the enemy would never be allowed to cross the Meuse."

Yet as enthusiastically as he welcomed Ike's will to exploit opportunity, Patton was appalled by what he regarded as his remarkable failure to grasp the full reality of what was happening in the field. Major Allied losses were being inflicted by the hour. Ike, according to Patton's diary, said "he wanted me to get to Luxembourg and take command of the battle and make a strong counterattack with at least six divisions. The fact that three of these divisions exist only on paper did not enter his head." Patton exaggerated—but not by much. Three divisions had been badly mauled and greatly reduced by the Germans. For all practical purposes, they were little more than lines on a map.

Ike turned next to Devers, asking him how much of the line south of Saarlauten he could take responsibility for. By way of response, as Patton recalled it, "Devers made a long speech on strictly selfish grounds and said nothing." As for Bradley, he "said little," and Patton himself "kept still, except that I said we needed replacements."

Eisenhower must have been disappointed by the responses and nonresponses of his top commanders when he turned eagerly to Patton.

"When can you attack?" he demanded.

"On the morning of December 21, with three divisions."

"Don't be fatuous, George!" he scolded. "If you try to go that early, you won't have all three divisions ready and you'll go piecemeal. You will start on the twenty-second and I want your initial blow to be a strong one! I'd even settle for the twenty-third if it takes that long to get three full divisions."

In his diary, Patton noted that his pledge to move three divisions nearly a hundred miles north and attack within forty-eight hours created a "commotion," leaving some at the conference table seemingly "surprised and others pleased—however, I believe it can be done." Eisenhower, Patton recorded, "said he was afraid that this was not strong enough, but I insisted I could beat the Germans with three divisions, and if I waited [for more troops], I would lose surprise."

"*Don't Delay*," Patton wrote in a set of comments titled "Reflections and Suggestions" and collected in his posthumously edited and published *War as I Knew It*. "The best is the enemy of the good. By this I mean that a good plan violently executed *now* is better than a perfect plan next week. War," he insisted, "is a very simple thing, and the determining characteristics are self-confidence, speed, and audacity. None of these things can ever be perfect, but they can be good."

Even so, the technical and logistical demands appeared overwhelming. Since the beginning of Operation Cobra in the early summer, the orientation of the Third Army had been to the east along a fairly broad front. To turn any army ninety degrees to the north required extraordinary measures just to prevent units from piling up on one another. Beyond this, changing the line quickly from its eastward-facing north-south orientation to one facing the north and arrayed along an east-west axis required finding a multitude of roads for the advance and providing the logistical mechanism to ensure an uninterrupted flow of supplies, which had, after all, been allocated in dumps placed specifically to accommodate a line advancing east.

But, with the proviso that he take an extra day—even two extra days—Eisenhower approved of the plan to turn tens of thousands of men and machines on the tactical equivalent of a dime. Patton sensed that his moment of greatness was at hand. Maybe he was grateful that Ike didn't have enough sense to tell paper divisions from real ones. Maybe that's what it took for the top commander to approve of what he proposed. Patton refrained from telling Ike and everyone else that his promise was not the product of impulse. He had been sketching plans ever since his meeting with Bradley. At Verdun, he carried three in his briefcase, and he had already alerted key units to prepare for a move.

As the meeting broke up, Ike, having just received his fifth star, good-naturedly observed to Patton: "Every time I get a new star I get attacked." And Patton, with at least the appearance of good nature, replied, "And every time you get attacked, I pull you out."

The Third Army's pivot was unprecedented in this war—or so it seemed to everyone but Patton himself. True, turning a quarter-million men and thousands of vehicles ninety degrees in a matter of hours had never been done. But sharply turning a single corps—some sixty thousand men—from east to north *had* been, and it was Patton who had done it, when he turned Haislip's XV Corps at Le Mans to Argentan during the assault on the Falaise-Argentan Pocket. For Patton, it was now a matter of applying that experience but magnifying its scale.

Not that Patton left anything to chance. He set about doing what he had long been famous for doing: materializing, as if by magic, in every corner of the Third Army. He drove to every division headquarters to explain to his commanders as much as he could in person, to feel them out, to answer their questions, to build their morale, and to fire them up. He thoroughly appreciated that the technical demands of the movement were complex, but even more daunting was the fact that most of the army had been engaged in three months of continuous combat, much of it in brutally cold, wet, nasty weather. Nevertheless, they were now being asked to march into fiercer combat and uglier weather—some traveling as much as a hundred miles to reach it.

They were tired. They had a right to be tired. Patton knew this, but he also knew that the last three months had hardened the men and had redefined the limits of their endurance. He had trained them, and he was confident that, far from having depleted his soldiers, the experience they had gained ever since they left the lodgments at Normandy had made them better soldiers, giving each of them a personal stake in the outcome of the Battle of the Bulge.

Accounts of the relief of Bastogne, in which the 101st Airborne and the 10th Armored Division were surrounded, and of the entire Battle of the Bulge are legion. We will do no more than outline this vast and complex battle here—for the Allies, the biggest and costliest of the entire European campaign.

Patton's initial attack, by III Corps, was set for 0400, December 22. "On the twenty-first," he recalled in a manuscript published posthumously in *War as I Knew It*, "I received quite a few telephone calls from various higher echelons, expressing solicitude as to my ability to attack successfully with only three divisions. I maintained my contention that it is better to attack with a small force at once, and attain surprise, than it is to wait and lose it." Before he had left the Verdun conference, Patton drew Bradley back to the map that had been the focus of Ike's doleful G-2. Punching it with his fist, he ground his knuckles with a twist into the outline of the bulge.

"Brad, the Kraut's stuck his head in a meat grinder. And this time I've got hold of the handle."

His original ambition reemerged, but now the bag had become a meat grinder. He wanted to let the German forces jam themselves another forty, even fifty miles into the bulge. He would direct his attack as far to the northeast as feasible in order to close off what was both the funnel into the bulge and the only avenue of retreat out of it. Attacking the offensive from the rear, he would drive the enemy against the main Allied strength to the west.

To Patton's dismay, Bradley responded just as he had to his earlier proposal to encircle every German north of the Loire. Bradley's chief concern was for the imperiled 101st Airborne and other troops holding Bastogne. Moreover, because Bastogne was a crossroads—the portal to all points west—he ordered Patton to direct his attack there. He wanted Bastogne relieved, the embattled Americans rescued, and a key junction once again under Allied control. If this meant thrusting fewer Germans into the meat grinder, so be it.

As usual, Patton sought a means of having it both ways—of relieving Bastogne while realizing as much of his more aggressive plan as possible. He ordered Millikin, with three divisions, to Bastogne; then, once he was confident that the Bastogne relief was going well, he would send Manton Eddy's divisions, when they arrived from the south, east of Bastogne, to the base of the bulge—the handle of the meat grinder.

As he had promised, Patton launched the attack of III Corps early on the morning of December 22, personally orchestrating the complex movements over the phone, the receiver glued to his ear hour after hour. The weather, strong ally of the Germans, having provided the snow-and-fog cover that had made complete surprise possible, worsened during Millikin's attack.

III Corps was forced to advance on a twenty-mile-wide front in heavy snow and temperatures as brutal as any that had been felt in these parts for a generation. As hard as the going was on the ground, it was impossible in the air. Aerial bombardment, reconnaissance, and ground attack—the entire air component of American blitzkrieg—were unavailable, a circumstance that threatened to severely compromise the effectiveness of this first strike.

As the enemy commanders in the field saw it, the Americans could no longer hold Bastogne. Early in the morning of the 22nd, two German officers and a pair of noncoms, one of whom bore a white flag, approached the town with a piece of paper. It was a surrender ultimatum. A somewhat bewildered American officer carried the message to Brigadier General Anthony McAuliffe, acting commander of the 101st Airborne Division. As an airborne officer, McAuliffe believed that it was the business of paratroopers to drop behind enemy lines and fight from a position of encirclement. Desperate as conditions at Bastogne were, they were nevertheless his usual stock in trade, and he assumed the officer was bringing him a *German* offer of surrender. When the messenger corrected this assumption, telling the general that it was the Germans who were demanding the surrender of the 101st, McAuliffe spat out something like a laugh.

"Us surrender? Aw, nuts!"

And so it was that this richly American monosyllable of outrage, contempt, defiance, and rejection was conveyed to the German envoys as the commander's reply to the demand for capitulation.

McAuliffe's aides saw to it that news of the response— "Nuts!"—reached the outside world, where it rapidly spread throughout the Third Army and was broadcast across the

European theater and to the American home front. In the midst of the greatest Allied crisis of the European campaign, a thrill of optimism and confidence in victory suddenly blossomed. Patton was delighted with what he called McAuliffe's eloquence, but he also knew that it would take more than a splendid stroke of vernacular audacity to save Bastogne and to convert the German offensive into a German defeat—especially with the weather so thoroughly and consistently favoring the enemy. Air support, not performance on the ground, had become the choke point. Without it, there was virtually no hope of breaking through the German lines, of converting defense and relief into a genuine offensive. It is at this point that the 1970 film *Patton* has the general order up a "weather prayer" from Third Army's chaplain. This is not quite the way it actually happened. Patton had ordered the prayer back in November, during an earlier bout of bad weather. Monsignor (Colonel) James H. O'Neill complied:

> *Almighty and most merciful Father, we humbly beseech Thee, of Thy great goodness, to restrain these immoderate rains with which we have had to contend. Grant us fair weather for battle. Graciously hearken to us as soldiers who call upon Thee that, armed with Thy power, we may advance from victory to victory, and crush the oppression and wickedness of our enemies, and establish Thy justice among men and nations. Amen.*

Patton was so pleased with the prayer that he now took it out of his drawer again and ordered it to be printed on 250,000 wallet-sized cards to be distributed to the officers and men of the Third Army. For the occasion, O'Neill did add a new composition, a Christmas greeting on the general's behalf:

To each officer and soldier in the Third United States Army, I wish a Merry Christmas. I have full confidence in your courage, devotion to duty, and skill in battle. We march in our might to complete victory. May God's blessing rest upon each of you on this Christmas Day.

G. S. Patton, Jr.
Lieutenant General
Commanding, Third United States Army

It was no mere charade of public relations or cheerleading. Patton told O'Neill that he was "a strong believer in prayer," explaining there were "three ways that men get what they want; by planning, by working, and by praying." He said that any "great military operation takes careful planning or thinking" as well as well-trained troops to carry it all out. Nevertheless, "between the plan and the operation there is always an unknown. That unknown spells defeat or victory, success or failure. It is the reaction of the actors to the ordeal when it actually comes. Some people call that getting the breaks; I call it God." The lord, he concluded, had "His part, or margin in everything. That's where prayer comes in."

On Christmas Day, the overcast cleared just barely, but it was enough to launch at long last massive air operations coordinated with Millikin's closing on Bastogne. If Patton was surprised that the prayer had actually worked, he didn't show it. On the 23rd, he had purportedly written a prayer of his own—authorship has never been definitively ascertained—which began, "Sir, this is Patton talking" and went on to complain about two weeks of "straight hell" in the form of "snow, more rain, more snow," so much bad weather, in fact, that "I am beginning to wonder what's going on in your headquarters.

Whose side are You on anyway." This was followed by another prayer on December 27, in which Patton (or an author claiming to be Patton) confessed to God that He had, after all, "been much better informed about the situation than I was, because it was that awful weather which I cursed so much which made it possible for the German army to commit suicide." The prayer congratulated God on His "brilliant military move," calling it the work of "a supreme military genius."

The day before this second prayer was purportedly written, December 26, Hugh Gaffey, commanding one of Millikin's divisions, phoned Patton to report that he was now in position to break through to Bastogne, but that it would certainly be hazardous to do so. Unsurprisingly, Patton recorded in his diary, "I told him to try it." He went on to note that "At 1845 they made contact, and Bastogne was liberated." Patton was not complacent. He acknowledged, "Of course they may be cut off," but he doubted that would happen because the "speed of our movements is amazing, even to me, and must be a constant source of surprise to the Germans."

The fighting did grind on, the enemy simultaneously continuing to pound against Bastogne while successfully slipping out of each Third Army attempt at encirclement. Nevertheless, by December 29, it was clear to Patton (as he wrote to Beatrice) that the "relief of Bastogne is the most brilliant operation we have thus far performed and is in my opinion the outstanding achievement of this war. Now the enemy must dance to our tune, not we to his."

Feeling confident that Bastogne had been saved, Patton wanted to bite into a bigger piece of the German army by refusing to let up, thereby cutting off any retreat from the bulge. Ike and Bradley saw Patton's mission as pushing back the bulge; Patton saw it as using the bulge to grind up the enemy.

Both the supreme allied commander and 12th Army Group commander were satisfied that Patton was accomplishing his assigned mission, and they fretted (not unreasonably) that the ninety-degree turn, the long northward march to Bastogne, and the battle for its relief had driven the men of Third Army beyond their endurance. They needed to ease up. Patton countered that war was precisely about driving men beyond their endurance. He believed that the collective emotion produced by a sustained maximum effort, in which rest would come only after absolute victory had been achieved, compelled men to draw on reserves of personal strength in the knowledge that doing so would hasten victory and thus make their own relief possible. In short, properly managed and experienced among well-trained troops, the extremity of exhaustion was a source of momentum rather than a drag on progress. Patton protested that failure to keep up the pressure against the Germans at the base of the bulge would allow many to escape, which meant that there would be just that many more of the enemy to fight against tomorrow, next week, next month.

Patton's army had executed its mission only too well, it seemed. Once the menace to Bastogne, the 101st, the 10th Armored, and the roads to Antwerp had been neutralized, Eisenhower and Bradley as well as most of the commanders in the field lost the motive that crisis furnishes. Patton was not permitted to continue his attack, and, even worse, Eisenhower ordered in February 1945 a shift in the main effort of the Allied offensive from the American army to Montgomery's British. "I feel pretty low to be ending the war on the defensive," he wrote to Beatrice on February 4, 1945. He went on to complain that "too many 'safety first' people" were pulling all the strings, and he confessed that he didn't "see much future for [himself] in this war."

As had so often happened before, Patton felt that he was of a breed apart from virtually everyone else. "I have it," he had written to his son George little more than two weeks earlier, "but I'll be damned if I can define it." After all this time, after months of continual combat in Europe and a lifetime in the army, the naturally eloquent Patton could come up with no word more descriptive than "it" to describe his own nature. The compact monosyllable was irreducible, an atom rather than a molecule, the alpha and the omega of his being. As far as Patton himself could tell, it was susceptible to no deeper analysis.

CHAPTER 7

"I BELONG TO A DIFFERENT CLASS"

"The best end for an old campaigner is a bullet at the last minute of the last battle."

—PATTON, TO AN AIDE, QUOTED IN ROBERT S. ALLEN,
LUCKY FORWARD, PP. 401–402

Early in February 1945, the Third Army resumed its eastward advance. On the tenth, Bradley telephoned to convey a question from Eisenhower: How soon could the Third Army go on the defensive so as to send more troops to aid Montgomery's offensive?

Patton snapped back to Bradley that he would resign before he gave away the offensive with victory so near. By this time, Omar Bradley had been thoroughly converted from the long-suffering army group commander forced to tolerate a mercurial prima donna to Patton's stealthy coconspirator against what seemed to both men Eisenhower's determination to hand the honor of victory in Europe to Bernard Law Montgomery. He told Patton that remaining in command was something he owed his men, and he promised to make it crystal clear to Ike just how things stood.

The Allies' chief maker of war in Europe, a career soldier, Dwight Eisenhower was at heart a peacemaker. Ever since the North African campaign, he had struggled mightily to hold together an Anglo-American alliance so contentious that British historian David Irving titled his controversial 1981 study of it *The War between the Generals.* Ike knew now that if he enforced his order that 12th Army Group, including Patton's

Third Army, assume the defensive, he might well lose Patton and dishearten in so doing some 1.2 million American GIs. On the other hand, if he yielded to Patton by giving permission for the resumption of his offensive, he would just as surely outrage Montgomery and, through him, Churchill, Parliament, and the British people. It would seem, however, that there was no middle course; an army either plays defense or offense. But, by this time, Ike Eisenhower had become accustomed to finding the middle way between any number of apparently irreconcilable, mutually exclusive alternatives. He directed Bradley to assume a posture of "aggressive defense."

It was just the exquisitely military oxymoron Patton needed. With it, Eisenhower secretly subscribed his name to the unspoken pro-American, anti-Montgomery conspiracy between Bradley and his Third Army commander.

"I chose to view ["aggressive defense"] as an order to 'keep moving' toward the Rhine with a low profile," Patton wrote in his diary on February 26. And when he used the expression "low profile" what he meant was attacking and advancing such that "the gentlemen up north" would learn about it only "when they [saw the results] on their maps."

Patton's low-profile approach required personal guerrilla action behind "enemy" lines. Patton cordially infiltrated the inner sanctum of SHAEF (Supreme Headquarters Allied Expeditionary Force), inviting Eisenhower's chief of staff, the notoriously brusque and impenetrable Walter Bedell ("Beetle") Smith, to accompany him in a relaxing afternoon of hunting. Between them, they bagged three ducks, one pheasant, and three hares—and Patton came home with something more valuable: Smith's endorsement of his bid for more Third Army troops.

Shortly after the hunting expedition, Patton asked Bradley

to return to the Third Army the 10th Armored Division, which had been attached to the First Army during the Battle of the Bulge. There was a time, and not so very long ago, when Bradley would have turned him down flat by invoking Eisenhower's orders. Now, however, he not only agreed to send him 10th Armored, but instructed Patton to keep away from telephones for the next several days until it was too late for Ike or anyone else to recall the division. Naturally, Bradley could not order Patton to disobey an order, but he could advise him to make certain he was unavailable to receive *any* orders. On March 1, once again under Third Army command, the 10th Armored and an infantry division captured Trier, chief city of Germany's Eifel region. With this trophy on his mantel, Patton started answering the phone again, and it was not long before the order came from SHAEF to bypass Trier. In reply, Patton sent a message: "Have taken Trier with two divisions. Do you want me to give it back?"

Trier was a handsome prize, but the news that Brigadier General William Hoge had led elements of the 9th Armored Division—part of Jake Devers's 6th Army Group—across the Rhine at Remagen on March 7 caused Patton more than a twinge of disappointment. He had long assumed that it was his destiny to be the first across this richly symbolic German river. Hoge had had the good fortune to find a bridge intact. Patton, whose Third Army reached the Rhine, at Coblenz, on the very day 9th Armored had crossed it at Remagen, grumbled to his diary that "All the Rhine bridges in my sector are out. . . ."

With the knowledge that, up north, Montgomery had been making extravagantly elaborate and time-consuming preparations to cross the Rhine with many divisions, Patton decided not even to take time building a proper bridge, but instead ordered his engineers to throw a pontoon bridge across the river right away. It was ready by March 22, and, after nightfall, Patton sent Third Army's 5th Division quietly across.

"God be praised," he wrote in his diary on March 23—the day Montgomery finally crossed as well. He had beaten Monty to Messina in Sicily, and now he had beaten him across the Rhine by a single day. On the twenty-fourth he drove to the river, crossed to the middle of the pontoon, and stopped "to take a piss in the Rhine." He then drove the rest of the way across to "pick up some dirt on the far side . . . in emulation of William the Conqueror."

Southern Germany, Patton's slice of the Allied conquest, was crumbling like an old cheese. Third Army elements harvested prisoners of war, taking more than a million by the end of April—far exceeding the number captured by any other single Allied army, the Russians included. On April 12, Patton took Eisenhower and Bradley to see the Ohrdruf concentration camp, which his 4th Armored Division had liberated on April 4; it was a forced-labor sub-camp of Buchenwald, the major camp liberated by Third Army troops on April 11. In *War as I Knew It*, Patton called it "the most appalling sight imaginable," but pointedly avoided putting his emotions into words. U.S. diplomat Robert Murphy, who was present at Patton's subsequent visit to the Buchenwald main camp, recalled that the general "went off to a corner thoroughly sick."

There can be little doubt that Patton's experience at Ohrdruf and Buchenwald brought him down low, and his depression only deepened when Eisenhower, having decided to leave Berlin to the Soviet Red Army, ordered the Third Army to break off its march to the German capital—which, like Rome and Tokyo, was universally regarded as one of the greatest prizes of the war—and head instead toward Czechoslovakia via Bavaria, which, Allied high command mistakenly believed, harbored extremist Nazi holdouts determined to make a last stand. His mood brightened briefly when, during a brief visit to Paris on April 18, Everett Hughes, one of Ike's staff, handed Patton a copy of *Stars and Stripes* as the two breakfasted together.

"He read the headlines and threw the paper back on the table," Hughes wrote to Beatrice Patton. Hughes passed the paper to him again, and again Patton glanced at it then tossed it aside. Amused and exasperated, Hughes "picked it up [a] third time and said 'read that,' pointing to the announcement" that President Truman had nominated George S. Patton Jr. for the fourth star of a full general. Leaning back in his chair, Patton sputtered "Well, I'll be —," apparently with such verve that all "who had been hovering in the vicinity" were vastly amused. Yet in the privacy of his diary that day, Patton remarked that while he was "glad to be a full General, I would have appreciated it more had I been in the initial group" of those promoted, which included Bradley and Devers as well as Mark Clark.

The much-discussed, much-anticipated, and much-feared "National Redoubt"—the supposed south German diehard Nazi stronghold—proved nonexistent, and Third Army's V Corps passed quickly through Bavaria and pressed on to Czechoslovakia, reaching Pilsen on May 5. Patton phoned Bradley with the news and sought permission to continue all the way to Prague. After consulting Eisenhower, Bradley returned Patton's call. Ike's answer was no. Pilsen was to be the end of Patton's drive across Europe. Two days later, at 2:41

in the morning of May 7, 1945, a delegation of German officers signed an unconditional surrender at Eisenhower's headquarters in Reims, France. At the paranoid insistence of Joseph Stalin, the surrender was repeated the next day in Berlin. The war in Europe was over.

Naturally, Patton wanted to be sent to the Pacific, where the war was far from over, but he was pretty certain that high command would deem no hemisphere big enough to hold both him and Douglas MacArthur. So the end of the European war meant that Patton's war was over. He didn't want it to be. The Japanese, as he saw it, were not the only enemy left standing. On May 7, Patton bluntly told undersecretary of war Robert P. Patterson, who was touring the theater, that it was a grave error to break up the army and send it home. He advised that the Americans in Europe be allowed to keep their "boots polished, bayonets sharpened," so as to present to the Russians "a picture of force and strength," which is the "only language they understand and respect." Failing this, he told the undersecretary, "I would . . . say . . . that we have had a victory over the Germans and have disarmed them, but have lost the war." He urged Patterson to resist the call for headlong demobilization, hold the American army in Europe, and "have your State Department, or the people in charge" tell the ever-advancing Russians "where their border is, and give them a limited time to get back across. Warn them that if they fail to do so, we will push them back across it."

Incredulous, Patterson pointed out the might of Soviet arms. Patton replied that their supply system was "inadequate to maintain them in a serious action such as I could put to them." He declared that it "would make no difference how

1897: Young warrior as young fisher-man—"Georgie" Patton is pictured (left) with his pal, Hancock Banning, in San Marino, California. **(Virginia Military Institute Archives)**

1903–1904: Not quite ready for West Point, Patton spent a year as a Virginia Military Institute cadet before he gained entry in the United States Military Academy. **(Virginia Military Institute Archives)**

1909: Patton realizes his first dream of martial glory—appointment as Cadet Adjutant of the class of 1909, West Point. **(Patton Museum of Cavalry and Armor, Fort Knox, Kentucky)**

1910: The groom is Second Lieutenant George S. Patton Jr., the bride Beatrice Ayer. (**Virginia Military Institute Archives**)

About 1930: Patton had dreamed of making general before he was out of his twenties. By 1930, he was a forty-five-year-old colonel deeply discontented in an army mired between wars. (**Virginia Military Institute Archives**)

1918: Lieutenant Colonel Patton, number two man in the brand-new U.S. Tank Corps, poses in front of an FT-17 Renault light tank, one of the "dogs of war" he led in the St. Mihiel and Meuse-Argonne offensives. (**Patton Museum of Cavalry and Armor, Fort Knox, Kentucky**)

1930s: Languishing in the peace he
dreaded, Patton sought to beguile the
dull hours with fierce polo matches,
reckless steeplechase races, and
savagely genteel fox hunts; this one,
in company with General Henry E.
Mitchell, took place at Middleburg,
Virginia. **(Virginia Military Institute
Archives)**

1940: Horse-drawn grandeur on
the eve of war—Colonel George
S. Patton Jr. and Brigadier General
Maxwell Murray review the troops
of 16th Field Artillery at Ft. Myer,
Virginia, as part of a ceremony in
Murray's honor. **(Virginia Military
Institute Archives)**

May 1941: Tank commander
in riding boots—Major
General Patton addresses a
rally of the 4th Division at
Fort Benning, Georgia. **(Patton
Museum of Cavalry and Armor,
Fort Knox, Kentucky)**

1941: Patton (left) huddles with Colonel Harry A. ("Paddy") Flint during war games in Louisiana. Patton wears the football-style helmet and coverall uniform of a hands-on tanker. **(Patton Museum of Cavalry and Armor, Fort Knox, Kentucky)**

January 17, 1943: General Patton hosts President Franklin D. Roosevelt, who had come to Casablanca, North Africa, to meet with Churchill. **(Patton Museum of Cavalry and Armor, Fort Knox, Kentucky)**

July 11, 1943: Patton, whose helmet now sports the three stars of a lieutenant general, begins the conquest of Sicily. Note the landing craft in the background and the steel mesh carpet engineers have laid to facilitate vehicle transport across the loose beach sand. Contrast the tailored splendor of Patton's field uniform with the ordinary-issue dress of the men who accompany him. **(Patton Museum of Cavalry and Armor, Fort Knox, Kentucky)**

July 11, 1943: Field glasses at the ready, Patton scans the village of Gela, immediately after his landing on Sicily. In obedience to Patton's standing orders, the soldier seated at the left with his rifle wears the regulation leggings cordially despised by all enlisted men. **(Patton Museum of Cavalry and Armor, Fort Knox, Kentucky)**

July 23, 1943: Maps were to Patton what a sheet music score is to a symphony conductor. Here he lays out plans for the capture of Palermo with his field command-ers. **(Patton Museum of Cavalry and Armor, Fort Knox, Kentucky)**

August 1943: Caesar with field glasses and swagger stick—Sicily conquered. **(Virginia Military Institute Archives)**

April 1, 1944: In Europe at last, Patton inspects 2nd Division soldiers newly arrived at Armagh, Northern Ireland. **(Patton Museum of Cavalry and Armor, Fort Knox, Kentucky)**

August 26, 1944: At the triumphant conclusion of the Normandy Campaign, Patton (center) lays out Third Army's next moves with General Hugh J. Gaffey (seated) and Colonel M. C. Helfers of the 5th Division. **(Virginia Military Institute Archives)**

September 30, 1944: Patton assembles with his staff, key field commanders, and the bull terrier he named Willie (in honor of William the Conqueror) outside of his headquarters in Etain, France, awaiting a visit by Supreme Allied Commander Dwight David Eisenhower. Ike once confessed to imagining that Patton made a habit of wearing his trademark high-gloss helmet to bed. **(Patton Museum of Cavalry and Armor, Fort Knox, Kentucky)**

October 25, 1944: Patton loved the literal nuts and bolts of mechanized warfare. Here, Staff Sergeant Woodrow W. Smith explains to the general the function of a new type of valve grinder suited to making field repairs to Third Army Sherman tanks. Patton was notorious for showing up anywhere, anytime on the front lines. **(Patton Museum of Cavalry and Armor, Fort Knox, Kentucky)**

1944: The top U.S. command in Europe assembles in Belgium to welcome England's George VI on one of his tours of the front. To Patton's left is 12th Army Group commander Omar Bradley, and to his left, Dwight D. Eisenhower, Supreme Allied Commander, Europe. First Army commander Courtney H. Hodges stands to Ike's left, and Fifth Army's Mark Clark—the tall, handsome general Churchill affectionately called his "American Eagle"—is at the far right of the photograph. **(Patton Museum of Cavalry and Armor, Fort Knox, Kentucky)**

November 27, 1944: Patton takes Averill Harriman (standing, middle), U.S. ambassador to the Soviet Union, on a tour of the front lines. The vehicle they ride in is an armored reconnaissance car that the general fitted with the biggest and loudest pair of klaxon horns (lower middle of the photograph) he could find. It was his custom to descend on his troops at high speed, klaxons blaring—the mechanized warfare equivalent of ancient heralds' trumpets or the horn gallant Roland blew at Roncevalles. **(Patton Museum of Cavalry and Armor, Fort Knox, Kentucky)**

February 20, 1945: Patton pays a visit to a bridge the 1303rd Engineers threw across the Sauer River and named in honor of their Third Army commander. **(Patton Museum of Cavalry and Armor, Fort Knox, Kentucky)**

February 20, 1945: Patton thanks the engineers who built the Sauer River bridge and many more. Though legendary as a combat commander, Patton never neglected his logistical troops. **(Patton Museum of Cavalry and Armor, Fort Knox, Kentucky)**

May 1945: Awarded his fourth star, Patton improvised a way to add it to the three already on his helmet—up top, surmounting all. He still wears his much-practiced "war face," but the eyes betray the profound weariness that set in at war's end. **(Patton Museum of Cavalry and Armor, Fort Knox, Kentucky)**

General George S. Patton Jr. Oil portrait by Boleslaw Czedekowski, 1945. The painting is housed at the Virginia Military Institute. **(Virginia Military Institute Archives)**

many millions of men they have, and if you wanted Moscow, I could give it to you."

This talk was alarming enough, but, after telling Patterson that he wanted to make war on Russia, Patton, a general in the army of the world's greatest democracy, disclaimed democracy itself. "There is nothing democratic about war," he said. "It's a straight dictatorship. . . . We the Armed Forces of the U.S.A. have put our government in the position to dictate the peace." He continued by explaining that, backed by force, the United States could impose a peace that would give back to the nations of Europe the "right to govern themselves." In effect, Patton was advocating violent dictatorship for the purpose of restoring democratic governments.

Patton was not alone in envisioning what would become a half-century of cold war. His prescription for preventing this, however, was extreme. He urged the continuation of the current *hot* war, only against a new enemy.

Of course, no one in power wanted to hear such a proposal. Thus, on the very day the Germans surrendered, Patton was already entering into the social, political, spiritual, and emotional exile reserved for born warriors in times of peace. He could not go to the Pacific to fight the Japanese, and nobody wanted to continue the European war. General George S. Patton Jr. was now a man without a place in the world.

The conversation with Patterson took place on May 7. On May 8, in a farewell press conference with Third Army correspondents, some of whom were doubtless aware that Patton had privately remarked to military colleagues that Britain and America should recruit the Germans in a war against the

Soviets, he fielded a reporter's question about whether captured SS should be treated differently from regular-army POWs. Creator of the war's Buchenwalds, the SS was the embodiment of the very evil the Allies had fought and died to vanquish. Patton's response was therefore stunning.

"No," he answered without hesitation, the SS should not be treated differently. "SS means no more in Germany than being a Democrat in America," he explained; then, thinking better of this, he added, "that is not to be quoted. I mean by that initially the SS people were special sons-of-bitches, but as the war progressed, they ran out of sons-of-bitches and then they put anybody in there. Some of the top SS men will be treated as criminals, but there is no reason for trying someone who was drafted into this outfit. . . ."

Patton's tongue had yet again betrayed him, but amid the joyous public tumult that accompanied V-E Day, his comments failed to ignite the usual firestorm—at least not right away. After an interval of stateside leave with his family, Patton returned to Europe in July 1945 as military governor of Bavaria. The next month, two atomic bombs ended the war in Japan. On August 10, he wrote Beatrice from his headquarters at Bad Tolz: "Well the war is over. We just heard that Japan had quit. Now the horrors of peace, pacafism, and unions will have unlimited sway. I wish I were young enough to fight in the next one . . . killing Mongols," using his habitual code word for Russians. On the same day, he wrote in his diary: "Another war has ended and with it my usefulness to the world." What he wrote next is rich with meaning: "It is for me personally a very sad thought," the redundant word "personally" revealing his understanding that few people would or could appreciate—let alone empathize with—his sentiments. He belonged, after all, to a different class.

Giving himself over to self-pity, he wrote on: "Now all that is left to do is to sit around and await the arrival of the undertaker and posthumous immortality," but then he remembered that he still did have a mission: "Fortunately, I also have to occupy myself with the de-Nazification and government of Bavaria." It was the mission that would effectively end his career.

All around him, U.S. and British officials were zealously purging Germany of Nazis and Nazism—and doing so at blitzkrieg pace. But not in Patton's sector. Not in Bavaria. The issue was raised in a press conference held at his headquarters on September 22. Why, a correspondent asked, were Nazis still occupying key Bavarian administrative posts?

Patton's aide Hobart "Hap" Gay tried to rescue his boss by violently shaking his head in an almost comically mimed signal to dodge the question. Patton must have seen him. Perhaps he took the warning as a goad.

"In supervising the functioning of the Bavarian government, which is my mission, the first thing that happened was that the outs accused the ins of being Nazis. Now, more than half the German people were Nazis and we would be in a hell of a fix if we removed all Nazi party members from office." Incredibly, he went on to repeat the earlier analogy, which had largely escaped public notice: "The way I see it, this Nazi question is very much like a Democratic and Republican election fight." Only after dropping this bombshell did he finally state a reasonable justification of his policy: "We had no alternative but to turn to the people who knew what to do and how to do it. So, for the time being we are compromising with the devil

. . . for lack of anyone better until we can get better people."
But neither the press nor the politicians got as far as this justification. They could not see—or chose not to see—beyond the
equation of Nazis with American political parties. Once again,
Patton had made himself the target of righteous outrage.

Seeking damage control, Eisenhower ordered Patton to
convene another press conference for the purpose of retracting
the offending remark and assuring the people of the United
States and the Allied nations that de-Nazification would
proceed as quickly as possible in his sector. Patton accepted
the order and convened the press conference. Doubtless, he
intended to fix the problem he had created. He even prepared a
written statement, so that he wouldn't stray into trouble again.
But then, when he actually stood before the reporters, he suddenly departed from his script and essentially repeated what
he had said earlier, that everyone who knew how to do anything had been a Nazi and so unreconstructed Nazis would
have to remain in office until adequate replacements could be
found. Worse, his tone became unmistakably petulant, as if to
say *This is reality. Like it or lump it.*

In response, Eisenhower resisted the urge to send Patton
home. He did, however, remove him as military governor of
Bavaria and, far worse, took the Third Army from him. Eisenhower reassigned Patton as CO of the Fifteenth Army, an
administrative organization of perhaps 1,500 personnel, a mere
"paper army," whose only mission was to begin compiling an
official history of the war in Europe. Ike insisted that it was an
important assignment, but Patton took it for what it undoubt-
edly was, an invitation to retire. Nevertheless, whether out of
spite or a genuine sense of duty, he accepted the assignment,
apparently figuring that it would give him some time to contemplate his next move.

In a quiet ceremony on October 7, Patton turned over command of the Third Army to Lucian Truscott, who had served under him in Sicily. This done, he addressed his staff: "All good things must come to an end. The best thing that has ever happened to me thus far is the honor and privilege of having commanded the Third Army."

Patton endured his new job through the rest of October, November, and into December, finally deciding to go home for Christmas. Looking ahead, he did not plan to return to the Fifteenth Army. Perhaps some stateside assignment would hold appeal, but maybe it was finally time to retire and write about the war as he knew it. Assuming Ike, Bradley, and Montgomery gave the possibility of a Patton memoir much thought, they might well have been unnerved by the prospect. If Patton could not help but speak his mind—or his id—when he was in uniform and under orders, what horrors would escape his mouth and his pen when he became a *former* general?

Anxious to leave, Patton was scheduled to take Eisenhower's personal aircraft to Southampton, England, from which he would sail to New York on December 10. Thoughts of imminent escape failed to dispel Patton's melancholy, and just two days before he was set to leave Europe, Hap Gay, eager to lift his chief's spirits, suggested a leisurely drive into the countryside west of Speyer to hunt pheasant. As Gay hoped he would, Patton brightened at the idea, and the two set out from Bad Nauheim, where the Fifteenth Army was headquartered, at 9:00 on Sunday morning, December 9.

Shortly before noon, driver PFC Horace L. Woodring eased the big Cadillac staff car to a stop at a rail crossing just outside of

Mannheim. After the train passed, he started across the tracks. Approaching just ahead was a two-and-a-half-ton truck—the ubiquitous army "deuce-and-a-half."

It was 11:45, local time, when TSgt Robert L. Thompson spun the truck's steering wheel to the left, intending to turn into the quartermaster depot. In the Cadillac, Patton gazed out his window at the derelict German vehicles that had been pushed to the shoulder of the road.

"How awful war is," he said. "Think of the waste."

Coming from "Old Blood and Guts," it was a remarkable statement—sufficiently so, apparently, to have momentarily drawn Woodring's attention from the road. Suddenly, the side of Thompson's truck filled the windshield, Woodring slammed on the brakes, and yanked the steering wheel hard left.

Seated in the back beside the general, Gay managed just two monosyllables—"Sit tight"—and stiffened in preparation for impact. Patton, head and body turned toward the window, was lost in thoughts of the waste of war.

It could have been much worse. By turning and braking, Woodring had reduced a potentially major collision to the status of a fender bender. Gay, it is true, was slightly banged up—a few bruises—but neither driver was hurt.

Gay looked to his side. General Patton no longer occupied the seat. He had slid to the ample floor of the limousine, blood oozing from an ugly gash made by the diamond-shaped dome light mounted on the head liner. He was fully conscious and asked Gay and Woodring if they were all right. After both had responded that they were, Patton stated as blandly as one states any matter of fact, "I believe I am paralyzed. I am having trouble breathing." Then he became more insistent. "Work my fingers for me," he asked Gay. "Take and rub my arms and shoulders and rub them hard." Feeling nothing, he raised his voice for the first time—"Damn it, rub them"—then returned to his former matter-of-fact tone.

"This is a helluva way to die," he said. Patton was a quadriplegic.

In a Heidelberg hospital, he was placed in traction that called to mind the rack of the medieval dungeon. The hope was that this would promote healing and restore—well, restore something. The general lived like this for thirteen days without complaint and with nothing but polite requests and kind words for his doctors and nurses and for Beatrice, who had arrived in the airplane Eisenhower had put at her disposal.

On December 21, as she had for almost two weeks, Beatrice Patton read to her husband until he drifted into sleep. It was about four in the afternoon, and she lingered by his bedside. When his somnolent breathing turned from rhythmical to irregular, she summoned the physician she had brought with her from the States, Dr. Glen Spurling, a respected neurosurgeon. The crisis, however, seemed to pass, and by 4:45, Patton was breathing and sleeping normally. Dr. Spurling suggested to Mrs. Patton that now was a good time to get dinner.

At 6:00, Dr. William Duane Jr. entered the hospital mess, located Beatrice Patton and Dr. Spurling, and asked them both to return with him to Patton's room. By the time they reached his bedside, he was dead.

The Patton mythology, partly self-created, was well developed even while the general lived, but his death allowed it to flower without any interference from Bradley, Ike, Montgomery, or the press and the politicians of the rational American democracy Patton both served and threatened.

Many outranked him, but Patton became and remains the most famous general of World War II. Fame and legend cry out to be shattered or at least diminished. But what the Third United States Army achieved under Patton's command is fact, cannot be diminished, and only adds to the lore surrounding the man.

The Third Army's After Action Report is the official record. "In nine months and eight days of campaigning," it begins, "Third U.S. Army compiled a record of offensive operations that could only be measured in superlatives, for not only did the Army's achievements astonish the world but its deeds in terms of figures challenged the imagination." The report notes that

> *Third Army liberated or gained 81,522 square miles in France, 1,010 in Luxembourg, 156 in Belgium, 29,940 in Germany, 3,485 in Czechoslovakia, and 2,103 in Austria. Patton's army liberated or captured an estimated 12,000 cities, towns, and villages; 27 of these had populations exceeding 50,000. The Third Army captured 1,280,688 prisoners of war between August 1, 1944 and May 13, 1945. Its soldiers killed 47,500 of the enemy and wounded 115,700—inflicting a total of 1,443,888 casualties while incurring 160,692, including 27,104 killed, 86,267 wounded, 18,957 injured, and 28,237 missing (of whom many were later reported captured). By the numbers, Patton's Third Army marched farther and faster, winning more, killing more, and capturing more than any other single army in World War II and, measured against the relatively brief span of its activity, more than any other army in the history of warfare.*

Patton was proud of this record, but not astonished by it. He believed that the achievement of it was nothing other than his destiny. From West Point, Plebe Patton wrote to his father on July 3, 1904, of a Fourth of July oration delivered by another cadet. "It was good," he allowed, "and described what the modern soldier was and what he stood for. Every one clapped and I believe they all agreed with the speaker. I didn't." From this self-observation, the young man found that he could draw but one conclusion: "I belong to a different class a class perhaps almost extinct or one which may have never existed yet as far removed from these lazy, patriotic, or peace soldiers as heaven is from hell." He confessed to his father his understanding that his "ambition is selfish and cold," but then contradicted himself: "yet it is not a selfishness for instead of sparing me, it makes me exert myself to the utter most to attain an end which will do neither me nor any one else any good."

He was a young man driven by whatever it was—for it seemed at once intimate and alien—that possessed him. Throughout his career, Patton would be criticized for a super-abundance of ego, but what he described to his father, the force driving him, was not selfish because it was not the self, the ego. It was something other, intimate yet alien, existing, it seemed, for its own ends and purposes (doing "neither me nor any one else any good"). Call it, perhaps, an id—an *it*—but not the sexually hungry entity Sigmund Freud famously described. Patton's was a distinctly martial id, which craved the glory of organized violence that results when one general wields men and machines such that *his* will triumphs over that of his enemy.

This *id* that existed to satisfy only itself tantalized young Patton, thrilled him, drove him, but it gave him neither comfort nor contentment. "Of course," he wrote his father, "I may be a dreamer"—could this be self-delusion after all?—"but I have a firm conviction that I am not. . . ." The fact was that neither

153

the possibility of delusion nor the conviction that he was not
a deluded dreamer mattered. "In any case," he continued both
affirmatively and uncomfortably, "I will do my best to attain
what I consider—wrongly perhaps—my destiny."

As a child growing up on the family vineyard in Southern California, "Georgie" Patton—that's what everybody called him,
except when his father proudly referred to him simply as "the
Boy"—reveled in the tales of his military ancestors from the
American Revolution and the Civil War. Among his very earliest childhood memories was "playing soldiers" with Anne,
the sister whom everyone called Nita, who gave herself the
rank of major while Georgie "claimed to be a private which I
thought was superior." (This misunderstanding he corrected
not long afterward, when he began styling himself "Georgie S.
Patton, Jr., Lieutenant General.") He took to horses early in life,
and his father—himself a graduate of Virginia Military Institute, though a lifelong civilian—encouraged his developing
martial interests by building forts with the Boy and fashioning
wooden swords for him to play with. Doting though George S.
Patton Sr. was, even he found it impossible to keep up with the
Boy's nonstop activity, fueled by what seemed inexhaustible
reserves of energy.

The single disappointment in Georgie's young life was the
great difficulty he had learning to read and write. His modern
biographers have diagnosed dyslexia, and it is true that idiosyncratic spelling characterized all of Patton's writings, even
into adulthood, and that he always either improvised speeches
or delivered them from memory rather than attempting to read
from a prepared script. His parents protected him as well as

they could by hiring tutors to educate him at home and then, when he turned eleven, sending him to an exclusive private school in Pasadena, where his favorite subject, not surprisingly, was history, especially military history. From his earliest memories through his school years, Georgie Patton bathed himself in stories of conquest and martial glory. In 1908, when he felt compelled to justify to his prospective father-in-law, Frederic Ayer, his intention of pursuing a military career, he acknowledged that the soldier's life was indeed financially unrewarding (an echo of what he had written to his father in 1904: "an end which will do neither me nor any one else any good"), but that it was nevertheless "as natural for me to be a soldier as it is to breathe" and that it "would be as hard to give up all thought of it as it would to stop breathing."

Throughout his life, Patton would speak of his "destiny" as a soldier. Whether it was this destiny that shaped his childhood absorption in things military or the total immersion that created the "destiny" is a matter for conjecture. Beyond speculation is the indisputable fact that he never considered a life other than that of a soldier and a leader of soldiers. Indeed, his martial visions were far too grand to be contained within a single life. The adult Patton became notorious for his candid and repeated admissions of his belief in reincarnation, which included descriptions of his own past lives. Just before the commencement of Operation Husky, the invasion of Sicily in 1943, British field marshal Sir Harold Alexander remarked to him that he "would have made a great marshal for Napoleon," qualifying his observation with "if you had lived in the 19th century." Patton parried the qualification by responding, "But I did." At various times, he expressed the belief that he had marched with Napoleon, that he had fought the fourteenth-century Turks in the army of John the Blind of Bohemia, and that he had been a Roman legionnaire. In a poem—for Patton was given to writing verse—he even speculated, "Perhaps I stabbed our Savior / In His sacred helpless side."

Though persuaded of his destiny, Patton did not passively await its coming to pass. He knew that an appointment to West Point was a prerequisite for the kind of military life he wanted, but he also knew that his learning disability made it unlikely that he would even pass the required entrance exams. Beginning in the fall of 1902, however, his father brought to bear his considerable political influence in a campaign to persuade Senator Thomas R. Bard of California to nominate Georgie as a West Point cadet. While recruiting supporters and maintaining a stream of letters to Bard's office, Mr. Patton hedged his bet by looking into the military program offered by the University of Arizona (the corps of cadets there was commanded by a cousin), and ROTC programs at Cornell and Princeton, as well as securing a slot at his alma mater, VMI, which had also educated his own father and two uncles. When Bard failed to reply with a definitive yea or nay, Mr. Patton enrolled Georgie in VMI, reasoning that a year there might be sufficient to get the Boy into West Point without the necessity of an entrance exam.

Cadet Patton thrived at VMI, but neither he nor his father ever let themselves forget that the goal was West Point. Throughout the school year, the senior Patton prevailed upon a throng of powerful Californians—his friends—to write to Senator Bard, who at long last nominated Georgie early in 1904. In a warmly congratulatory telegram, Mr. Patton assured his son that he had in him "good soldier blood," as if he needed to be reminded. He left VMI near the top of his class, entered West Point as a plebe (freshman), and immediately set as his ultimate goal graduating as cadet adjutant, the summa cum laude of the academy. As his first-year objective, he settled on promotion to cadet corporal.

But even as he sincerely felt himself superior to his fellow cadets, Patton was stunned by how much more demanding West Point academics were than those at VMI. By November of his plebe year, he despaired of achieving his initial objective, plaintively writing his father, "I actually think that if I don't get a corp I will die." What actually happened was much worse. Failing to pass his final exam in French, he was required to take it over, along with a math exam. (Why failure in one subject should trigger a test in another was the first of the many mysteries of army life to which Patton would be introduced.) It was failing the math exam that forced him to repeat his entire plebe year.

During the repeated year Patton took up football. The army intended that cadets should play the game like soldiers in combat. Patton, however, approached even practice this way and, as a result, injured his arm so severely that he was dumped off the squad. Undaunted, he took up track and fencing, ultimately becoming an Olympic-grade athlete, who would represent the United States in the pentathlon in the 1912 Olympics held in Stockholm. He also managed a sufficiently passable academic record to achieve appointment as *second* corporal for the upcoming second-year class. Second best was better than failure, he told himself, but not very much better.

As second corporal, Patton was assigned to "break in" plebes who attended a preparatory summer camp. The company of cadets over which he had charge learned to drill like veterans, but they also learned to hate their martinet of a commanding officer. Instead of praising, let alone promoting, Second Corporal Patton for producing the best-drilled company of the incoming class, the tactical officer who supervised him broke him from second to sixth corporal. Patton believed he knew the reason why. He was "too d— military": a man who belonged to a different class.

Though his was of a "different class," Sixth Corporal Patton nevertheless craved the praise conferred by others. He tried out for football again, and again practiced so furiously that he sustained sidelining injuries, but he earned the acclaim and admiration of the entire corps of cadets for his spectacular horsemanship and even more accomplished swordsmanship. This validation was absolutely necessary to him, yet not in itself sufficient to satisfy him. His father had once told him that the test of real courage was the ability to "face death from weapons with a smile." One day, he pulled duty as a target spotter on the rifle range. His job was to crouch below the lip of a trench that had been dug in front of the targets and to raise the targets for shooting, then lower them for scoring. It suddenly occurred to him that he had been presented with an opportunity and a challenge—a demand, really—to find out if he had the military-grade courage his father had defined. Amid the crack-crack-crack of the rifles and, overhead, the zing of the bullets followed by the thwack of their impact on the targets, Patton impulsively sprang to attention to face the firing squad, as it were, completely exposed from the chest up. There was no cessation of fire, and, to his infinite satisfaction, he was unafraid as the bullets continued to pass him left and right. It is not known what effect this self-administered ordeal had on others at the academy, and there is no record of any official notice or sanction.

By the spring of his sophomore year, Cadet Patton had clawed his way back to the rank of second corporal and was promoted to cadet sergeant major for his junior year. Then, as a senior, he was named cadet adjutant.

That from so inauspicious a beginning he had achieved his highest goal—becoming the cadet who every day received the orders of the day, marched to the center of the parade ground, and read out those orders to the assembled corps of cadets, whose attention was for a brief span day in and day out exclusively his—must have seemed to him irrefutable affirmation of his destiny. Yet he never forgot how hard it had been to alter the odds against him. "Do your damndest always," he wrote in the notebook he carried to capture passing fragments of thought that seemed important to him. Burned into memory was the bitter and debilitating sting of disappointment, failure, and even humiliation, and in his very muscles he would always feel the lingering burn that had come with the struggle to will his destiny into fulfillment.

CHAPTER 8

SIERRA BLANCA

"It is the call of ones ancestors and the glory of combat. It seems to me that at the head of a regiment of cavalry any thing would be possible."

—PATTON, LETTER TO BEATRICE,
SEPTEMBER 28, 1915

Patton graduated from West Point on June 11, 1909, ranked 46th out of 103. It was the last time in his military career that he would ever allow himself to fall in the middle of the pack. He had made no real friends during his five years at the academy, but a few classmates who were on good terms with him called him "Georgie," an incongruous sobriquet for a cadet many of the others called "Quill." In the vernacular of the early-twentieth-century United States Military Academy, the word functioned both as verb and noun. To *quill* a fellow cadet was to report him for an infraction, especially one the majority would either have failed to notice or have purposely overlooked. A cadet who routinely quilled other cadets was duly branded with the noun *quill.*

It would be easy to characterize Cadet Patton as a martinet, but that would also be an oversimplification. More accurate was his own earlier self-characterization as "too damn military," and if he made excessive demands on underclassmen, he was always obviously much harder on himself. Those who recognized this tended to forgive his unsparing attitude toward others. His ideal of soldiering was lofty, even stratospheric. In February of his final year at West Point, he wrote to Beatrice that the profession of arms "is the oldest and at one time was the only business that was proper. . . . Only . . . long peace has blinded people to its value. When danger comes it at once assumes its old proportions and is all. Nothing else counts." Patton was destined, of course, to experience this phenomenon in World War II. When danger stalked them, the American people were desperate for a fierce warrior, but when Patton showed too much ferocity, the popular reaction ranged from moral squeamishness to outrage. In any event, Patton revealed in his letter that his true martial motive was less a patriotic zeal to defend his country than it was a personal passion to make his mark and thereby escape being swept away by the relentless tide of history. "I dare say," he wrote, "that for every man remembered for acts of peace there are fifteen made immortal by war and since in my mind all life is a struggle to perpetuate your name war is naturally my choice." In the end, Patton's desire was not so much to be a soldier as it was to go to war—and that for the purpose of achieving at least a measure of immortality.

From the beginning, George S. Patton Jr. was steeped in the romance of warfare, and yet he was never blinded by this vision. In the very same letter to Beatrice in which he wrote of the matchless opportunities for glory war offered, he acknowledged "that there is nothing particularly heroic in drilling a troop." His willingness to accept the routine aspects of army life was sorely tested in his first assignment fresh out of the academy. Posted to Fort Sheridan in 1909, some twenty miles up the Lake Michigan shore from Chicago, Patton described the bachelor quarters assigned to him, a junior officer, as "pretty bad . . . empty and very dirty," the sum total of its furniture a desk and iron-frame bed.

The room, bleak and mean, was emblematic of an army that, in 1909, struggled to maintain its meager 80,672 men commanded by 4,299 officers. Only the tiniest of European armies were of comparable size. Until the Battle of Wounded Knee brought the epoch of the Indian Wars to an end in December 1890, the post–Civil War army had been little more than a frontier police force tasked with confining Native Americans to their assigned reservations. The regular army had been entirely unprepared to fight the Spanish-American War in 1898, despite a patriotic flood of enlistments, and most of the fighting was done by short-term U.S. Volunteers, not regulars. After the "splendid little war" was over (to use the phrase President McKinley's secretary of state John Hay applied to the fight with Spain), the army was rapidly demobilized, becoming a skeleton force by the time Patton entered it.

In the peacetime turn-of-the-century American military, practically all of a young officer's hours were devoted to the mundane tasks essential simply to maintaining the army. As a cavalryman, Patton pulled stable duty daily beginning at 4:30 p.m. and alternated with other second lieutenants in supervising the Fort Sheridan stockade, a mission that consisted mainly of going "into the cage" to count the inmates. "I felt like a convict my self before I had finished." His only hope for liberation from such drudgery was promotion to high rank, and because peacetime promotion proceeded on a time scale of years, even decades, Patton, having graduated dead in the middle of his West Point class, knew that he had to make himself stand out. This meant embracing rather than scorning all the dreary routines, performing each chore better than it had ever been performed before. Second Lieutenant Patton's objective was to impress his CO, Captain Francis C. Marshall, by means of exceptional performance combined with deft reminders that he came from a line of officers that stretched back to the Revolution.

As he saw it, distinguishing himself also meant taking the risk of yet again being judged "too damn military" by driving his men harder than any other officer dared drive them. Predictably, the privates and noncoms in his charge grumbled. Patton turned a deaf ear, but, one afternoon, even he acknowledged a line that never should have been crossed.

While working stable duty, he discovered that one horse had been left untied in its stall. Turning on his heel, Patton searched out the man responsible and, finding him at the far end of the stable block, he upbraided him. Next, by way of punishment, he ordered him to run to the animal's stall, tie the horse properly, then return to him, also at a run. The private's definition of *run* apparently failed to coincide with Patton's. As far as the second lieutenant was concerned, the man merely trotted.

"Run, damn you, run!" Patton roared, whereupon the soldier double-timed it.

The lesson in discipline finished, Patton turned away—but then turned back. He could not simply wipe the episode from his mind. *Damn it* would have been a perfectly acceptable thing for an officer to say to a soldier, he thought, but *damn you* was just plain wrong.

After the private had run back to him, Patton summoned all within earshot. The poor soldier braced himself for a public humiliation. Instead, at full voice, Patton apologized, not for having sworn, but for having cursed him, a soldier of the United States Army.

Second lieutenants chew out enlisted men a hundred times a day every day, but they rarely apologize, and they never do so publicly. Patton realized he had crossed the line from being "too damn military" (which he deemed perfectly fine) to being insulting and tyrannical (which he could not abide). The public apology was a sincere act of contrition, but it was also a scene of Pattonesque military theater. It became the talk of the barracks, and it not only set Patton apart from the other young officers, it set him on a path toward legend.

Those who served with Patton, as subordinates, colleagues, and seniors, were often put off—sometimes appalled—by his conduct. Most disturbing of all was the impossibility of separating his theatrics from sincerity; moreover, everyone had the impression that Patton himself could not tell where the one ended and the other began. Was he *born* a legend? Did scenes like the apology at the stables just come naturally to him? Or were they all part of an act, a self-conscious effort to build command presence by continually weaving a legend about himself?

Most likely, the Patton legend was a synthesis of the naturally inevitable and the carefully contrived. While serving at Fort Sheridan, he complained that "for so fierce a warrior, I have a damned mild expression," and he began cultivating what he would call throughout his career his "war face," the sidelong, hard-set, frowning mask that is visible in the vast majority of his photographs from World War II. The war face was both Patton's face yet also the face of an actor, and he rehearsed it in front of the mirror for long stretches at a time.

When the unplanned and unforeseen occurred, Patton was

quick to pounce on it if he scented the stuff from which his legend might be grown. At drill one afternoon, his horse bucked him off—in front of the men he was training. With neither a show of embarrassment nor an apology, he remounted. The animal, thoroughly spooked as horses often are, reared. Patton refused to be thrown a second time, but now it was the horse that fell and, as it came down, it pinned Patton's leg beneath its side. Playing through the pain, Patton pulled his leg out from under and scrambled to his feet—just in time to take, full in the face, the impact of the horse's head, which the animal tossed back as it also struggled to rise. A wide gash opened up just above the second lieutenant's eyebrow, and blood streamed down his face, dripping off at the jaw and dropping onto his sleeve. Without explanation, without pausing to wipe away the blood, fighting the urge to put his fingers to the wound, Patton continued the drill until precisely its scheduled end twenty minutes later. Dismissing the men without comment, he walked to the latrine to wash his face, then strode to the noncom school and taught his regular class there. After this, he attended, punctually, a scheduled class for junior officers. Only after his assignments had been completed did he drop by the office of the fort surgeon, who cleaned away the gouts of dried blood and stitched the wound closed. Like the apology, the day Second Lieutenant Patton was thrown, kicked, and bloodied without apparent effect on him became the stuff of Fort Sheridan lore.

His legendary toughness did not, apparently, extend to proposing to Beatrice Ayer when he visited her at Beverly Farms, the Massachusetts home of her parents, during Christmas 1909. Only after he had returned to distant Fort Sheridan did he write her, on February 28, 1910, and even now he stammered in his proposal: "If you marry [me] in June—please do."

They were actually married a bit earlier, on May 26, 1910, and spent a monthlong honeymoon in Europe before settling into half of a two-family house Patton rented outside of Fort Sheridan. Beatrice was pregnant by fall 1910 and threw herself into helping her husband translate a French military article into English. Patton became an avid contributor to all the professional army journals, far less out of a scholarly interest in military theory than as a means of opening up another front in his never-ending campaign to draw notice to himself. But this did not mean that he wrote just for the sake of being heard. Most of his early essays and articles expostulated on the mantra of *advance, attack, advance, and attack again.* Violence and motion were the qualities Patton wanted others to associate with him, even in the peacetime army.

Beatrice gave birth to a daughter, likewise named Beatrice, on March 11, 1911, an event that spurred the new father to accelerate his advancement all the faster. Up to this time, he had avoided asking his father to exercise his influence on his behalf, but now he did ask, and the senior Patton quickly identified a few strings to pull. As a result, the Pattons found themselves leaving Fort Sheridan, Illinois, for Fort Myer, Virginia, just outside of Washington. It was the army's plum posting; as headquarters of the Army Chief of Staff, it was the heart of the nation's professional army and the ideal springboard for any serious military career. As if conveyed by a whirlwind, the Pattons left their suburban Chicago house (or, rather, the half of it they rented) for elegant accommodations on post and a life punctuated by luncheons at Washington's elite military and political clubs followed by soirees attended by the capital's resident power brokers. Everywhere, it seemed, one encountered a figure of influence, including no less than the courtly Henry L. Stimson, President William Howard Taft's secretary of war. A retired army colonel, Stimson was an avid rider, who naturally took to the many equestrian trails Fort Myer offered. It was on one of these that Patton, among the most junior of the army's officers, struck up an acquaintance with the most senior civilian military official, save the president himself. It would blossom into a friendship that ended only with Patton's death.

More immediately, Stimson recruited Patton to serve as his uniformed aide for official social occasions, and this appointment, in turn, prompted his CO to make him squadron quartermaster. The new job lifted Patton above petty troop details and delivered to him as much time as he wanted to sufficiently refine his already prodigious riding skills to the point of becoming a champion steeplechase competitor and a savage polo warrior. The combination of his horsemanship, now frequently on display at Fort Myer, and his expertise in fencing led to his being tapped as the army's entry in the Modern Pentathlon, an event slated to debut in 1912 at the Olympic games to be held in Stockholm. Patton saw the pentathlon as the nearest thing to war that could be found in a world mostly at peace. The five events included a 5,000-meter steeplechase, pistol competition on a 25-meter range, fencing, a 300-meter swim, and a 4,000-meter foot race. Collectively, these events comprised a military pantomime intended to suggest the efforts of an officer who must convey a vital message on horseback, fight off an enemy along the way (the shooting and the fencing), then evade capture by means of a swim and a cross-country run.

Predictably, Patton pushed himself hard in training and harder still in the competition itself, defeating twenty of twenty-nine opponents in the fencing portion and finishing an impressive third in the steeplechase, though he came in a disappointing twenty-first of forty-two pistol shooters. Still, survival to the final event was a signal achievement. Fewer than half of the competitors, fifteen out of forty-two, ran the four thousand meter cross-country event, and Patton, who did not regard himself as a runner, crossed the finish line in third place. This done, and amid the tumultuous cheers of the spectators, he collapsed, unconscious.

His father (who, with sister Nita and their mother, had sailed to Stockholm with Patton, Beatrice, and little Beatrice) knelt beside his son. "Will the boy live?" he asked Patton's trainer.

The reply was hardly reassuring. "I think he will but can't tell."

The boy lived. He placed fifth overall in the Modern Pentathlon and earned plaudits from the Swedish press, which praised his energy as "incredible" and his swordsmanship as "calm," "unusual," and "calculated." Most noteworthy, in reporters' eyes, was his skill "in exploiting his opponent's every weakness." Inspired by his own performance, Patton and Beatrice made a journey to Saumur, site of the French army's cavalry school, where the renowned Adjutant Cléry gave him two weeks of private fencing lessons.

Second Lieutenant Patton returned to Fort Myer a celebrity of sufficient stature to merit a dinner invitation from none other than Army chief of staff General Leonard Wood. He also threw himself into the steeplechase, which he ran as if he actually intended to get hurt—which, not infrequently, he did. All of it was, as he himself said, "Advertising." And so was, at least to a degree, the report he wrote of his two weeks with Adjutant Cléry. Yet Patton did not simply trumpet the perfection of his own swordsmanship. He wrote a serious, thoughtful, analytical report, which stressed the fact that the French believed in thrusting with the saber when they attacked, using the point of the sword, whereas the Americans slashed with the weapon, using the blade instead of the point. In his report, Patton argued that a thrust came nearer to the spirit of the attack than a slash because it brought the cavalryman into faster, more intimate, and more efficient contact with the enemy. He advocated adopting the French approach, but, recognizing that the standard U.S. Army saber was designed for slashing and not thrusting—it was curved—he also proposed that the army adopt a new, straight design, which was better suited to the thrust.

Patton's report was published in the *Cavalry Journal*, where it excited a good deal of comment. Assigned to temporary duty in the Office of the Chief of Staff, he used the opportunity to advocate his ideas on saber combat and saber design among the army's most senior officers, and early in 1913, Secretary of War Stimson directed the chief of staff to order the chief of ordnance to manufacture 20,000 new cavalry swords following the pattern Patton had presented. To this day, the "Patton sword" (U.S. Army Saber, M-1913) is the army standard.

As with so much else Patton said and did, it is impossible to finally assess the depth of sincerity with which he advocated the sword in actual combat. In the *Cavalry Journal* in 1913, he wrote a concise but comprehensive article on the history of the sword in warfare and concluded by asserting that the weapon still had a role to play. Nevertheless, it seems likely that Patton was less wedded to the sword as a still-viable weapon than to the weapon as a means of building his reputation. It was an instance of branding. *Oh, yes,* Patton could imagine the conversation among senior officers, *he's the young second lieutenant who's so keen on swordsmanship.* But to fully exploit his brand, Patton understood that he needed to enshrine *his* conception of the sword within the *institution* of the army, and so he secured permission to study with Cléry at Saumur for six full weeks and to bring back to the U.S. Army's Mounted Service School at Fort Riley, Kansas, the Cléry method. This meant leaving the cosmopolitan luxury of Fort Myer for the Midwestern grit of Fort Riley, but Patton saw it as the next step up—especially after the army assigned him to the school as a fencing instructor and conferred upon him the well-nigh magical title of "Master of the Sword," which was created exclusively for him.

Patton reported to the Mounted Service School, Fort Riley, Kansas, on September 23, 1913. He was there both as a student and as a teacher—Master of the Sword—imparting to the other cavalrymen his French-inspired revision of traditional U.S. Army saber tactics, designed to promote thrusting attack rather than slashing defense. The dual role as student and teacher did much to focus Patton's attention, which was all to the good, since the social life and living accommodations at Fort Riley were a long step down from those at Fort Myer. He added to his learning and teaching duties completion of an assignment to write a manual of regulations for his M-1913 sword.

If he felt the petty pace of peacetime service creeping up on him, he could always turn to the newspapers, which, by April 1914, were filled with accounts of the U.S. occupation of the Mexican port city of Veracruz. Before he became New Jersey's governor and then president of the United States, Woodrow Wilson had been president of Princeton University and a political science professor. He came to office with the firm conviction that he could teach other nations how to govern, much as he had taught political science to his Princeton undergraduates. Mexico was in a state of revolutionary turmoil, and Wilson was convinced that the corrupt martial dictator General Victoriano Huerta, who had moved into office following the assassination of Francisco Madero in 1913, was incapable of building an American-style democracy, which, as Wilson saw things, was the only valid form of republican government. Until a well-intentioned and competent democrat became Mexico's president, Wilson believed, friendly relations between Mexico and the United States were impossible. He was contemplating various means of forcing Huerta out of office when, on April 9, 1914, a minor incident pushed his hand—ever so slightly, but sufficiently.

The commander of USS *Dolphin*, patrolling the waters off Veracruz, sent nine U.S. sailors in a U.S.-flagged whaleboat up a canal to pick up oil from a Tampico warehouse in the state of Tamaulipas. The warehouse building happened to be located near the Iturbide Bridge, which Mexican government soldiers were guarding against capture or sabotage by revolutionary insurgents. The whaleboat tied up alongside the warehouse, and seven of the nine sailors left to fetch the oil barrels and load them onto the boat. Assuming that the sailors' activity somehow represented a danger to the bridge, the Mexican soldiers confronted them. They spoke no English, and the sailors no Spanish. Language failing, the soldiers pointed their rifles toward the seven sailors, herding them, together with the two who had been waiting in the whaleboat, to the nearby regimental headquarters. Here the matter was very quickly cleared up, and the sailors sent on their way with the oil.

That, of course, is where the matter should have ended, but the commanding officer of the U.S. Atlantic Fleet, Admiral

Henry T. Mayo, was outraged by what he deemed an international insult. He handed the Mexican commander of the Tampico area an imperious demand for a full and formal apology from the Huerta government. The local officer instantly complied—in writing, no less—but he drew the line at Mayo's humiliating (not to say ridiculous) demand that he raise the Stars and Stripes over Mexican soil and render to it the honor of a twenty-one-gun salute.

Wilson saw in this refusal an opportunity for decisive action against Huerta. He secured from Congress approval to invade Veracruz, which took place on April 21, when a small amphibious force seized the port. The rationale for the invasion had by now shifted from redressing a national insult to preventing the landing of arms and other equipment that were being conveyed to Huerta's forces aboard a German cargo ship. When the landing party was met with substantial resistance by Huerta's forces, Wilson authorized more troops and a full-scale occupation of the city.

Through all of this, most of the citizens of the United States were anxious to avoid a major war. Patton practically prayed for one—"a good big one," as he wrote to his father on April 19, 1914. The problem with a short war, he explained, was that there would "be no chance for a man of my rank to make any reputation as a leader of men," although even a short war, he conceded, was better than no war at all, since it still "might afford an opportunity to make a personal record on which to base something in the future." Nevertheless, if the war lasted "a long time and attain[ed] any proportions a man with a reputation for personal ability ought to get a good volunteer or malatia [militia] command. Hence should I succeed in becoming notorious you must try to get me a place as a major at least of state cavalry as I think infantry will not have so good a chance in Mexico as mounted troops." He cautioned his father to make sure that, before bringing to bear his influence, he first ascertain where the prospective "regiment is to go as it would be very unglorious to command a regiment guarding a railroad."

Three points are significant in this letter. First there was Patton's unquestioned assumption that the chief good of war was his own advancement. Second was Patton's expressly stated motive, not to *perform well* or to *do his duty* or to *serve his country*, but to become "notorious." His ambition was personal, sensational, dashing, and romantic. Finally: Patton was less interested in serving with the regular army than with whatever volunteer or state militia force would instantly snag him a field-grade rank (he eyed major) and get him into Mexico right away.

Patton acknowledged in the letter to his father that "in all probability we will make up as peaceful as possible." To his chagrin, this soon proved to be the case. Huerta stepped down as president on July 15, 1914, the crisis abated, and, with this, Patton's visions of imminent war faded and vanished.

But not for long.

On June 28, 1914, the chauffeur driving Archduke Franz Ferdinand of Austria and his wife, the Grand Duchess Sophie, made a wrong turn up a blind lane in the obscure Bosnian capital of Sarajevo. Gavrilo Princip, a pale, frail consumptive Bosnian nationalist, had been given a Browning revolver by the "Black Hand," a Serbian secret society dedicated to the dissolution of the Austro-Hungarian Empire. The archduke's automobile pulled up in front of the outdoor café table at which Princip disconsolately nursed a cup of coffee. The chauffeur, anxious to correct his error of navigation, stopped the car and laboriously shifted it into reverse. As the gears clashed, Princip rose from his table, reached into the pocket of his outsized overcoat, felt for the revolver's handle, withdrew the weapon, leveled it, and squeezed off—point blank—three rounds, two of which found their marks in the archduke and the grand duchess. In the prevailing climate of mutual international suspicion and universal European malevolence, the assassination was sufficient to set into motion a series of acts entirely determined by a tangled web of treaties and secret agreements. Within a month, the result was a war that would engulf much of the world.

For the overwhelming majority of Americans, the "European War" was little more than a drama in which they, the audience, had not the slightest dream of acting. When it broke out, Omar Bradley and Dwight Eisenhower were West Point cadets in the class of 1915. As Bradley recalled in *A General's Life*, his posthumously published autobiography, World War I "seemed remote from our cloistered world" at the academy. "We received no official documents or reports on the war. Everything we knew about it—and that was very little—came from newspapers and periodicals." The new tactics and technologies employed overseas did not prompt "the slightest change in the curriculum at West Point. We continued to study the men and campaigns of the Civil War. . . ."

The indifference to the Great War was not peculiar to the academy; it pervaded the regular army. Patton was exceptional in his belief—or was it more a hope?—that the United States would eventually be forced to get into the conflict. For him, that eventuality couldn't come soon enough. In a letter to his father on November 11, 1914—Patton's birthday—he complained that he had "fixed twenty-seven as the age when I should be a brigadier and now I am twenty-nine and not a first Lieutenant." He was frequently heard to rail against President Wilson and his craven determination to "keep us out of war." True, the birth of a second daughter, Ruth Ellen, on February 28, 1915, lifted his spirits for a time, but as the June date of his graduation from the Mounted Service School loomed, he returned to the gloom that surrounds a warrior without a war. He would rejoin his regiment, which he heard was going to be sent to the Philippines. There was nothing unusual about an army officer serving a tour in this troublesome prize from the Spanish-American War. If anything, such service was virtually required. What worried Patton was that Philippine service was hardly a stepping stone to bigger and better things. Too often, it was the long, drawn-out end to a career.

Just as he was not above using his father's influence to get the postings he wanted, so he was more than willing to pull every available string he could find on his own to secure something more promising than an assignment in the Philippines. He wrangled eleven days' leave to travel to Washington, where he called on all the highly placed friends he had made during his Fort Myer tour. Through one connection, he was able to arrange transfer to Fort Bliss, in El Paso, Texas, on the Mexican border. Many another young officer would have scratched his head at this move. Border duty was hardly seen as desirable. Patton, however, believed that the border region was a hot zone, that U.S.-Mexican relations were so volatile that a very real conflict was likely to break out—again. He calculated that U.S. involvement in the European war was inevitable, but, chances were, that a war with Mexico would come first. Gain experience fighting in that conflict, he reasoned, and a young officer would become an instant veteran—high on the list for a command in the world war, whenever it was that America joined it.

In July 1915, Patton parted company with the 15th Cavalry, which departed for the Philippines, and joined the 8th Cavalry, which was scheduled to be domiciled at Fort Bliss, a post under the command of Brigadier General John J. Pershing. There was little enough action there at the moment, Patton knew, but it was a lot closer to a potential war than the Philippines were. As it turned out, Patton found himself in the odd position of arriving at Fort Bliss *before* the 8th Regiment did. This fact put him in the even odder position of finding no one who could tell him what he was expected to do. The old army saying, "Stay out of the orderly room"—don't ask questions and don't volunteer—never sat well with Patton. He kept trying to latch on to an assignment. Finally, he was told that, pending the arrival of his regiment, there really was nothing at all for him to do. He decided, therefore, to use his down time to bone up for the exam that would qualify him for promotion to first lieutenant, and to give himself every advantage, he succeeded in getting the exam date pushed back, so that he would have more time to study.

That is not all he did with the extra weeks. Learning that the president of the promotion was an aspiring polo player, Patton volunteered to help him train his string of polo ponies. As if this weren't sufficient brown-nosing, Patton soon found out that Captain—now Major—Francis Marshall, his former Fort Sheridan commander, had arrived at Fort Bliss for an official visit and, more important, was staying with a member of the promotion board. The army of 1915 was a small organization, and the officer corps even smaller; so Patton's good fortune was not all that remarkable. Nevertheless, he made the most of it by paying a social visit to his ex-CO *and* his promotion board member host. He had no doubt that "Maj. M" would "blow [his] horn."

Patton had gotten the date of his qualifying exam pushed back to October 20, but, in the meantime, he drew another assignment prior to the anticipated arrival of the 8th Cavalry. He would be sent with A and D Troops to relieve elements of the 13th Cavalry, which had been posted at Sierra Blanca. Located some ninety miles from El Paso in Hudspeth County, at the far western end of the Texas Panhandle and not many miles from the Mexican border, Sierra Blanca was populated by a few hundred souls. In Patton's eyes, its great advantage as a posting was its nearly mile-high location in grass country, which made for a cooler and less dusty climate than El Paso. As remote as the one-horse town was, Patton was even more thrilled by the prospect of being assigned to a detached post far outside of Sierra Blanca, which would give him an independent command. To be sure, he would hold sway over very few troopers, but they would be his and his alone.

Before departing Fort Bliss, Patton, quartermaster of Troop D, was "busy as a bird dog" arranging logistics in preparation for the four-day march from El Paso to Sierra Blanca. On day three of that journey, the troopers reached Finlay, "one house and a station in the middle of the desert." Sierra Blanca, at which they arrived the following day, was precisely twenty times bigger, consisting of twenty houses—plus a saloon; however, Patton was instantly delighted by it. He wrote to Beatrice on October 20 that it was the "funniest place" he had ever seen, "very tough and at least half the men wear boots and spurs and carry guns." Patton had arrived in the Wild West.

On the nineteenth, Patton met Dave Allison, "a very quiet looking old man with a sweet face and white hair," who happened to be "the most noted gun man here in Texas and just at present is marshall." He does not appear to have been related to Robert A. "Clay" Allison (1840–1887), the notorious Pecos gunfighter who killed four men in as many shootouts, but the name alone had magic in west Texas. In a letter to Beatrice, Patton remarked that Marshal Allison had "killed all the Orasco outfit," as if he expected her to be familiar with Pascual Orozco, the leader of a regional Mexican gang. He noted further that Allison "kills several mexicans each month." Particularly admirable, Patton thought, was the fact that Allison had shot Orozco and each of his four henchmen in the head at sixty yards, clean through.

Sierra Blanca overflowed with frontier testosterone. Besides Allison, Patton met a Mr. English, aged sixty-two and employed as a "hired fighter for the T.O. ranch across the border." His two grown daughters were "Cow girls who are very dashing ladies." In addition to meeting Allison and English on the nineteenth, Patton reported to Beatrice that a "ranger" had "jokingly threatened" to shoot him for not accepting his invitation to a drink. To forestall this eventuality, Patton bought him a bottle a beer and drank one himself. "Don't get worried," he assured Beatrice. "He was only trying to be hospitable according to his view. . . ."

Within a few days, two officers rode out from El Paso to administer the first lieutenant's exam to Patton, which he easily passed. He then rode out in company with one of the officers on a three-day, hundred-mile tour of inspection of the most remote army outposts. He punctuated the desolate ride by shooting jackrabbits from the saddle at a smart trot.

Patton reveled in the atmosphere of Sierra Blanca and accepted Marshal Allison's invitation to pistol practice, western style. He took the man seriously, learning a good deal from him, and particularly taking to heart his admonition always to aim for the animal when shooting at a mounted man. The shot was more likely to hit the bigger target—and more likely to bring the man down with the horse.

As October drew to an end, U.S.-Mexican relations continued to deteriorate. The Wilson government had originally favored what seemed to be shaping up as the populist democracy of the revolutionary bandit Pancho Villa, but, increasingly, the government of Venustiano Carranza appeared to offer greater moderation and greater stability. Wilson therefore turned from Villa and instead backed Carranza against all comers. The president even authorized Carranza to move his troops via American railroad trains, and, on October 30, Patton found himself in charge of three privates assigned to guard a railway bridge. At about four in the morning, the weather turned so cold that Patton ordered his men to dismount and lead their horses. The private who had taken the point, some two hundred yards ahead of Patton and the two other men, suddenly galloped back, warning of Mexicans on the bridge. Patton ordered his men to remount, draw their pistols, and trot to the bridge on the double.

Seeing no one once they got there, Patton called out "Who is there?"

A voice, which sounded "foreign" to him, replied, "Friend." But at that very instant, "six heads with rifles stuck over the bank" of the wash over which the bridge passed. Patton reported to Beatrice that, "Strange to say I did not think of running but wondered if I could get one before I was gotten."

Experience would prove this a typical Patton response to imminent danger. Where others have difficulty precisely recalling the sensations accompanying a life-threatening situation, Patton was always keenly aware of his feelings, as if he were outside of himself, merely observing his own behavior in extremity. Typically, he was also pleasantly astonished to discover that he was not afraid, that he was not a coward, and that he did not think of running away (even if he did think of *not* thinking of running away). It was as if courage did not come naturally to him; certainly, he did not take the quality for granted in himself. Finally, he was never so removed from the immediacy of the experience that he neglected to weigh his practical options. In this case, his overriding thought was whether he could kill one of the enemy before the enemy killed him. As it turned out, however, the "enemy" was a 13th Cavalry patrol.

Most of the days counting off toward Thanksgiving were spent in patrols that were uneventful save for the desultory thrill of hunting. But as Thanksgiving neared, the captain and first lieutenant of Troop D returned to Fort Bliss for the holiday, leaving Patton in command. On November 24th, he received a telegram from Fort Bliss warning that "200 Mexicans were going to rade" Sierra Blanca. He wrote his father that he did not "believe it at all" but nevertheless ordered the men to put their guns beside their beds. He also instructed them as to where to form up if the alarm was sounded. "I wish they would come," he confessed. "I have about a hundred men or more and could give them a nice welcome." But he dismissed the likelihood as a "baseless rumor" and closed his letter by complaining that "if this is the eve of battle it is not at all interesting nor so exciting as a polo game."

Patton's assumption that nothing would happen proved correct, but, on Thanksgiving Day, he received two more telegrams ordering him to advance against some eighty of Carranza's men whom Pancho Villa's raiders had chased across the border into the United States. The Wilson government's backing of Carranza had rapidly become half-hearted and certainly did not extend to allowing his forces to wander freely north of the Rio Grande. Patton's orders were either to drive the eighty back across the border or to take them prisoner.

He would have loved nothing more than to lead the attack himself, but General Pershing had sent another telegram warning that the Mexican bandit Chico Cano had been spotted headed toward Sierra Blanca. Once again, Patton did not believe this intelligence, but, once again, he ordered his men to sleep with their rifles at the ready. Because he was now the senior officer at Sierra Blanca, it was his duty to remain at the post and oversee its defense. He therefore assigned three patrols to look for the eighty Carranzistas, sending one to Finlay, one to Calduan—where the Mexicans had reportedly crossed the river—and the third to Fort Quitman, near which they had also been sighted. Early on Thanksgiving morning, at five, he sent all of Troop A to Quitman as well.

Troop A and the initial patrol returned to Sierra Blanca from Fort Quitman on Thanksgiving afternoon. No one in the patrol had actually seen the Carranzistas, but they had heard from others that they were on the U.S. side of the border, having fled an ambush in Mexico by two hundred Villa troops. Patton responded by sending another patrol to the vicinity of Fort Quitman, and on November 26, after receiving orders from the regimental colonel to act against the Carranzistas "with vigor," he summoned D Troop's first sergeant and told him that he would lead the men out of Sierra Blanca at four in the morning of the twenty-seventh, so as to reach Fort Quitman—and, he hoped, the Mexicans nearby at dawn. Because he knew that his men "think they have to eat breakfast"—a belief he scorned— Patton ordered the first sergeant to get them up at 2:30, but to wake him up an hour later. "I prefer sleep to food," he wrote to his father.

As he lay in bed contemplating the morning's likely action, Patton did what he would always do when ordered to attack. He interpreted the orders as violently as possible. "I went to bed," he wrote to his father, "and decided that to act with vigor meant to attack first and ask questions next." He intended to make a saber charge against the enemy's camp. "I thought I had a medal of honor sewed up and laid awake planning my report until one a.m."

Unfortunately for Patton, his captain and first lieutenant returned from Fort Bliss at about one in the morning, obliging him to "get up and explain the situation to them." Worse, this meant that he would not command the attack. Worse still, although First Lieutenant Tompkins was sick with dysentery, "he decided to go and being a d— f— [damn fool] he dicided to leave the sabers" at home. To attack without them was a profound disappointment for the master of the sword.

A swordless Patton led his swordless contingent, a patrol of ten men, out of the fort at 4:30 and, giving his troopers orders to fire at any armed men they met, rode under a fine full moon toward Fort Quitman. After thirty-two miles in four and a half hours, they "met nothing. There was nothing to meet." Probing in the vicinity of Fort Quitman eventually turned up fourteen ragged Mexicans, who, Patton believed, were in fact Carranzistas, "but there was no way to prove it though we violated law by searching the house for arms." On the way back to Sierra Blanca, the ailing Tompkins "gave out," and thus Second

Lieutenant Patton—on the verge of promotion—had the honor of leading the men home, albeit through "dust . . . so thick that you could not see the fence at the side of the road." It almost didn't matter. The mere prospect, the mere thought of battle had been intoxicating to him, especially in this remote and rugged country. "I had a good sleep," he assured his father, "and feel fine."

CHAPTER 9

THE PUNITIVE EXPEDITION

"I was much less scared than I thought I would be, in fact all that worried me was the fear they would get away."

—PATTON, LETTER TO HIS FATHER,
MAY 15, 1916

The modern U.S. military has a special name for the deep indigo to purple to pale blue that marks the prelude to sunrise. They call it the BMNT, Beginning of Morning Nautical Twilight. Doroteo Arango Arámbula, who called himself Francisco Villa and whom the world called Pancho Villa, knew these hours well and cherished them as the deadliest part of the day, the time for the predawn attack, the attack he always favored. Like the modern soldier, Villa understood that the eerie interval separating profound slumber from the first stirrings of consciousness was the ideal span in which to hit an enemy more numerous yet less fierce than oneself. For him, the ghostly minutes on the cusp of dawn were made for striking against the arrogant, the more powerful, the wicked.

Of arrogance, power, and wickedness Villa had much experience. He was born in 1878, according to the most popular story of his life (indisputable fact has always been and remains hard to come by where Villa is concerned) to an impoverished field worker. When his parents died early in his life, he went to work for the owners of the estate on which his father and mother had labored. About the time Villa turned sixteen, the *patron*'s son raped—or tried to—for the facts are fluid here as well—his sister. For this, Villa shot and killed him.

Pursued as a murderer, he fled into the mountains and lived the remainder of his teenage years as a bandit. At some point in the course of this fugitive life, Villa discovered that he possessed a power the wealthy, the arrogant, and the wicked—men of the class who attacked his sister and victimized the masses from which he came—could not buy. The common word for it is *charisma*, but Patton might have called it "command presence," and he would have recognized it in Villa as very much the same "lambent flame" he felt burning within himself. Around Villa, partisans of the revolutionary leader Francisco Madero coalesced, and by 1909 he was named commander of the División del Norte, the Northern Division of Madero's guerrilla army, which sought to overthrow Porfirio Díaz, whose long dictatorship was propped up by the nation's wealthy merchants and even wealthier landlords.

As Villa's "lambent flame" blazed up, it began to shine too brilliantly to suit Victoriano Huerta, at the time an ambitious Madero underling. Many years later, General Patton would likewise feel the consequences of a flame that burned too brightly, but, for him, the consequences, though wrenching, were hardly as extreme as those Villa faced. In 1912, Huerta accused him of horse theft and insubordination, both crimes that, under revolutionary guerrilla discipline, warranted the death penalty. Fortunately for Villa, Madero intervened, saved him from the firing squad, and instead packed him off to prison, where he would be out of the public eye as well as out of Huerta's reach. Villa soon escaped, however, and fled to the United States, living north of the border until word reached him of Madero's assassination. Returning to Mexico in 1913,

Villa quickly assembled a guerrilla band several thousand strong and offered his services to Venustiano Carranza, a man with a plan to topple Huerta, who had usurped the presidency in February 1913.

Most of Carranza's revolution went badly during 1913, except for the victories achieved by Pancho Villa. For these, Carranza was most grateful, even though Villa's ruthlessly unconventional tactics created one diplomatic crisis after another. In the course of Villa's campaign, his troops murdered a prominent Englishman and a prominent American, and Villa himself highhandedly arrested the governor of Chihuahua. But by the summer of 1914, thanks in large part to Villa and to pressure from the United States—culminating in the occupation of Veracruz—Huerta's forces formally surrendered on August 15, 1914, and, five days later, a triumphant Carranza entered Mexico City.

Carranza had spurned Villa's request to accompany him on his victory lap into the capital. This affront widened the growing breach between the two men. Villa and fellow guerrilla Emiliano Zapata had been instrumental in the defeat of Huerta, but Carranza disavowed them now as too radical. Villa and Zapata in turn repudiated Carranza because he was unwilling to embrace the sweeping social reforms Zapata articulated and Villa endorsed. Zapata formally broke with Carranza on September 5, 1914, and Villa followed suit on the twenty-third.

During his campaign against Díaz and then against Huerta, Villa had been widely regarded as a popular champion of democracy against oppression. He became world famous and, outside of Mexico itself, nowhere more so than in the United States. Hollywood came calling with a lucrative offer to film him in action, and the U.S. Army even sent observers to study his tactics. Now that he had split with Carranza, Villa had every reason to expect the United States government to continue backing him.

But Woodrow Wilson was hardly an unalloyed populist. He was, of course, an advocate of democracy, yet stability was of greater value to him in a nation that shared a border with the United States. Wilson's State Department formally announced U.S. recognition of the Carranza government, and Wilson promptly issued an executive order forbidding further arms shipments from the United States to Villa's army. As mentioned in Chapter 8, the president also extended Carranza the very practical courtesy of allowing him to use American railroads to move large numbers of troops against Villa. As the wealthy and powerful landlord's son had attacked his sister, so now the wealthy and powerful government of the United States betrayed him. The son had paid with his life, and so, too, the Americans would pay with their blood.

On January 8, 1916, Villa formally sealed an alliance with Emiliano Zapata. On this same day, eighteen American miners were bound by rail for Cusihuíriachic, where a U.S.-owned silver mine had closed down during the revolutionary unrest. General Alvaro Obregón, Carranza's minister of war and the navy, had urged the reopening of the mine, assuring American businessmen that it was safe to return to Mexico, where, he promised, "Villa is a thing of the past." After a two-day layover in Chihuahua City, the miners continued their journey on January 10. At about one in the afternoon, their train stopped at Santa Isabel, forty miles west of Chihuahua City, to take on more coal. This done, the train eased out of the station. Some five miles outside of Santa Isabel, air brakes hissed, coaches lurched, and the train slid to a halt. Several of the miners descended to the roadbed to see what was happening. Ahead of them, a railroad car was lying on its side across the tracks.

A derailment? But where was the rest of the train?

Gunfire punctured the miners' puzzlement. Twelve, perhaps fifteen Mexican soldiers—Villa's men—materialized behind the train, closing fast. Their fire split and splintered the wooden sides of the passenger coaches and shattered the windows. After a final paroxysm of gunfire, another thirty Villistas appeared in the doorway of the coach. Brandishing a German Mauser rifle, Colonel Pablo López walked through the car and began culling the American from the Mexican passengers.

"If you want to see some fun," he paused to announce to the Mexicans, "watch us kill these gringos." To the Americans he sputtered, "Tell Wilson to come and save you, and tell Carranza to give you protection. Now is the time to come here and protect you."

A Mexican passenger recalled what happened next—how López ordered his men to line up the Americans on the right side of the tracks a short distance from the train, then how he detached two men, who fired their Mausers, executing one man at a time. The pair trotted along the line, alternating their fire. Some of the victims broke away, but soldiers quickly herded them back into the line, where they were killed.

Throughout the procedure, the other Villistas stood and watched, chanting "Viva Villa" and apparently taking pleasure in the writhing of the wounded on the stones and cinders of the roadbed. A Mexican eyewitness later reported that the spectacle "seemed to drive the bandits to a frenzy. 'Viva Villa!' they cried and 'Death to the gringos!'"

At length, López authorized the tender mercy of a coup de grace for those who lingered in agony. Troops "placed the ends of their rifles at their victims' heads and fired." This operation completed, the Villistas retired to the express car, which they looted of silver and coffee beans. Then López ordered the train crew to carry himself and his men back to Chihuahua City.

Behind, beside the tracks, eighteen Americans, fifteen of them employees of American Smelting and Refining Company, lay dead. A nineteenth, Thomas Holmes, survived, through a fortunate accident having been overlooked by the Villistas. At the first burst of gunfire, he had leaped from the train, but then tripped, and, propelled by the momentum of his initial leap, rolled into the bushes near the tracks. There he played dead. Amid the executions, he lay motionless at first, then stealthily crawled deeper into the bushes until he came to a small stream. Sheltering himself under the cover of its bank, he crouched and shivered through the half hour it took for the Mexicans to finish their work. It was Holmes's report that was printed in the press—not only the lurid account of the executions, but the even more ghastly narrative of the postmortem mutilations, of eyes gouged out, of bodies transfixed by bayonets, of genitals crushed under the blows of rifle butts. America was outraged.

Two months after the Santa Isabel massacre, Villa led about five hundred men across the Mexican-American border, marched with them to the New Mexico town of Columbus, waited for the deadliest predawn hour, then sent his men through the underbrush and into town. Two groups, one under General Francisco Beltrán and the other commanded by Colonel Nicholás Fernández, swung north of the railroad tracks that divided Columbus proper from Camp Furlong, which domiciled a detachment of the 13th Cavalry. Two other contingents, one under Colonel Pablo López and the other, led by Candelario

Cervantes, struck south of the tracks, directly attacking Camp Furlong.

Colonel Herbert Slocum, commanding the 13th Cavalry, was awakened by the sharp crack of the Mexicans' Mausers, which were answered by the duller, to him more familiar pop of the cavalrymen's Springfields. As the colonel shook off sleep, he heard, below the gunfire and the dueling bugle calls of Villa's dismounted cavalry and his own troopers, snatches of the impertinent song long associated with Pancho Villa. "La Cucaracha," it was called. Somebody somewhere was scratching it out on a fiddle.

For days, there had been many warnings of the possibility of attack. Telegrams reporting Villa sightings had arrived regularly on Slocum's desk. Accordingly, he deployed his troopers to patrol a sixty-five-mile-long section of the international border, mostly west of Columbus. Slocum reasoned that, because this stretch of borderland was reasonably well supplied with water, it would be the likely route by which Villa would enter the country. He stationed two officers commanding sixty-five troopers at the Border Gate, three miles south of Columbus, and he stationed an additional 165 troopers under seven officers at a ranch outside of town. In addition, Slocum dispatched a number of roving patrols. Despite all of this, Villa's raid came as a complete surprise. Before it was over, ten civilian residents of Columbus had been killed and two wounded; eight 13th Cavalry troopers fell, and six were wounded. The raiders set fire to a number of the town's buildings, they stole horses and mules, made off with several machine guns as well as the ammunition for them, and they looted the general store and grocery.

Not that they got away scot-free. At least sixty-seven Villistas were killed outright, and many others were wounded, of whom perhaps thirteen later died. Five raiders were captured unwounded. But what made the Columbus raid even more of a Pyrrhic victory for Villa was the war it unleashed against him. It would be called the Punitive Expedition.

That Victoriano Huerta had been a brutal, bad man was sufficient reason for the United States to have backed Villa and Carranza against him. Wilson had found an additional motive, however, in Huerta's cozy relations with the Germans. The American president understood the game that the Kaiser was playing with Mexico. By destabilizing U.S.-Mexican relations, the chances that Wilson would ally his nation with France and Britain against Germany in the ongoing European War would be sharply reduced; Wilson, after all, could hardly send an army abroad if his own borders were threatened. The American president's subsequent decision to back Carranza against Villa was also partially motivated by his desire to foil German designs on an alliance with Mexico. The relatively moderate Carranza would be far more likely to recognize the benefits of civil, if not exactly cordial, relations with the United States than the mercurial Villa. Moreover, Germany would have a far harder time manipulating a stable Mexico under Carranza than a volatile one under Villa.

The raid on Columbus came as a gift to the Germans. Wilson hardly wanted to provoke war with Mexico, particularly not during these most perilous of times. But he couldn't let a cross-border attack on U.S. citizens and U.S. soldiers go unanswered—especially with his own prospects for reelection in November hardly bright. Worse, he had already alienated the electorate's more bellicose elements by refusing to go to war with Mexico over the Santa Isabel massacre.

Something had to be done. But what?

All-out war in the form of a full-on invasion would not only play right into Germany's hands, but would be costly in lives and treasure, as well as being a disproportionate response to a bandit raid. And what would be the object of an invasion? Occupation? Conquest? Mexico in Mexican hands was wracked by nonstop revolution. What would it be like in the grip of the hated gringos?

No. Invasion was out of the question, as was making no response. Instead of taking either of these courses, Wilson decided to wage the first deliberately "limited war" in United States history, a military adventure that anticipated such future Cold War conflicts as the Korean War and Vietnam War, wars fought to achieve narrowly defined objectives and prosecuted in a manner that fell far short of an all-out effort. He would send the army into Mexico for the purpose of hunting down, killing, or capturing Pancho Villa and his military followers. To the press and to Carranza, Wilson took pains to make clear that this was not a war against Mexico, but a "punitive expedition" against Villa for the sole purpose of "putting a stop to his forays into the United States. This can and will be done in entirely friendly aid of the constituted authorities in Mexico and with scrupulous respect for the sovereignty of the Republic."

The Columbus raid had put Wilson in a delicate position, but Venustiano Carranza now found himself in even more perilous straits. He would surely win popular support if he refused to let the American president send a gringo army into Mexico. But what would Wilson do? Back down? Almost certainly not—and thus Carranza would find that he had taken Mexico into a war it was bound to lose, and when it lost, Carranza would surely be overthrown. On the other hand, if he allowed the U.S. Army to range freely and deeply into Mexican territory he would quite possibly be ousted for this.

In the end, Carranza found a brilliant solution. Through his secretary of foreign affairs, Jesús Acuña, he cited the historical precedent of reciprocal cooperation in the pursuit of Geronimo in the 1880s. By formal agreement, U.S. troops had been permitted to operate in Mexico, and Mexican troops had been permitted to cross into the United States, all for the purpose of hunting down an Indian "renegade" who menaced the citizens of both countries. But now, instead of granting permission for American forces to enter Mexico, Acuña formally requested that "Mexican forces be permitted to cross into American territory in pursuit of the aforesaid bandits led by Villa, upon the understanding that, reciprocally, the forces of the United States may cross into Mexican territory if the raid effected at Columbus should unfortunately be repeated at any other point on the border." The stipulation with which the sentence ended was, of course, key to preserving the appearance as well as the fact of Mexican sovereignty. By way of response, however, Woodrow Wilson simply ignored the stipulation and, on March 13, 1916, his State Department replied directly to President Carranza by agreeing to the reciprocal arrangement his administration had proposed, adding that the U.S. government considered the agreement to be effective immediately. For his part, Carranza now chose to overlook the fact that Wilson had ignored the stipulation, critical though it was.

At first glance, the obvious choice for commander of the Punitive Expedition was Major General Frederick Funston, a Medal of Honor laureate who had become a national hero fighting Filipino nationalists after the Spanish-American War, and who singlehandedly took charge of disaster control in San Francisco after the 1906 earthquake. In 1914, Wilson had tapped him to lead the occupation of Veracruz—and therein lay ample reason for giving command of the expedition to someone else. Funston was highly unpopular with the Mexican people and government. Wilson's advisers suggested he look to a more junior officer, Brigadier General John J. Pershing.

Patton was thrilled as soon as he heard that Pershing was the choice to lead the pursuit of Pancho Villa. Whereas Patton was a stranger to Funston, he was serving under Pershing at Fort Bliss. He had instantly admired the handsome fifty-five-year-old brigadier, lean, mustache as crisply trimmed as a smart salute, impeccably military in utterance, carriage, and appearance, his Sam Browne belt as brightly polished as his riding boots. He had enjoyed the kind of career Patton coveted. A graduate of the West Point class of 1886, he fought in the Indian Wars, the Spanish-American War, and the Philippine-American War, so impressing President Theodore Roosevelt that, in 1905, he nominated the captain for promotion to brigadier general, effective the following year. As Patton saw it, even more important was his being the beneficiary of a terrible tragedy that had befallen Pershing just a year earlier. On August 27, 1915, Pershing's Fort Bliss orderly read him a telegram sent from the Presidio at San Francisco, where the general's wife, son, and three daughters were living. A fire had ravaged the house, the telegram announced, taking the lives of all but five-year-old Warren, his son.

The orderly later recalled that the news, horrific beyond imagining, failed to crack the general's martial composure.

"Is that all? Is that everything?" Pershing demanded after the telegram had been read.

"Yes sir," the orderly replied.

In truth, the tragedy had left John J. Pershing a shattered, profoundly lonely man, and so he remained when, early in 1916, Patton's sister Anne—"Nita"—arrived at Fort Bliss for a visit with her brother and sister-in-law. At twenty-nine, she was a tall blonde, handsome rather than beautiful—described by at least one admirer as an "Amazon"—and unmarried. Patton introduced her to Pershing, who brightened at the meeting beyond what mere courtesy might have dictated. As for Nita, she stayed at Fort Bliss much longer than planned. Patton had not set out to play matchmaker, but, like any good soldier, he was always prepared to exploit tactical opportunities when they presented themselves. He was eager to make the most out of what looked to be a budding romance.

On March 12, 1916, Patton wrote a long, sometimes nearly breathless letter to his father. Not only, he announced, did it seem certain that "we are about to go over the line [border]," but that the talk in Fort Bliss was of a "war and not simply a punitative trip." For Patton, the prospect was wonderful: "Personally"—the adverb was significant, setting him apart (as usual) from what he perceived as the prevailing sentiment favoring peace—"I hope that they [the Carranza government] break with us. . . ."

He looked forward to a hard and dangerous fight precisely because it promised to be hard and dangerous. "I think that we will have much more of a party than many think as Villa's men at Columbus fought well and the [Mexican] country [terrain] is very bad for regular troops. There are no roads and no maps and no water for the first 100 miles." Yet it was not all war fever for Patton. Immersed as he was in the thrill of anticipation, he never stopped thinking like a strategist, a tactician, and a leader. If Villa could be provoked to a stand-up fight, he wrote, "it will be all right but if he breaks up"—that is, if he deployed numerous guerrilla bands—"it will be bad, especially if we have Carrenza on our rear." It was a most thoughtful analysis; yet, in a manner that would prove typical of Patton, cold calculation, penetrating, unblinking, and objective as it was, failed to dampen his morale: "They can't beat us," but he predicted that "they will kill a lot of us," adding: "Not me though."

From the consideration of tactics, strategy, and fighting spirit, Patton turned to personal advancement. He predicted that if a long war developed, the government would create a lot of volunteer regiments, "so if I do well keep an eye out and get me a job," he urged his father, then quickly broadened his vision to a global scale: "It occurs to me that if Japan is after us now is her time as no one on earth can help us. So this may be the start of a very interesting period."

With this thought, Patton apparently left off writing to do something else. When he again took up his pen, it was to deliver the grim news that "Since writing the foregoing I have discovered that . . . [the 8th Cavalry] are not going but will sit here and watch the rest go past us." Never one to be thwarted without a fight, he explained to his father that it "is hell to be so near a fine fight and not get in it . . . so I went to General Pershing and asked him to make me as an aid[e]. He said he would if he could so I still have hopes."

Patton believed he knew very well why Pershing had decided to hold back the 8th Cavalry. Its commanding colonel was obese, obviously unequal to the rigors of overland travel in Mexico. "There should be a law killing fat colonels on sight," he grumbled to his father.

Patton launched a full-scale assault on General Pershing. After appealing to the adjutant of his own squadron to put in a personal recommendation, he immediately went over his head to Major John L. Hines, adjutant general of the expedition, asking him for a personal recommendation as well. Then, just for good measure, Patton went under Hines to Lieutenant Martin C. Shallenberger, one of Pershing's regular aides, and asked for his help as well. Having thus launched a massive preparatory barrage, Patton again called on Pershing in person, assuring him that he would accept any assignment, no matter how menial, as long as it meant joining the expedition. Because Pershing's disdain for reporters was already legendary, Patton suggested that he could handle the press for the general. Through the hindsight of the chronically disastrous state of Patton's public relations during World War II, this proposal seems laughable. Nevertheless, Patton insisted to Pershing that he was very good with correspondents—though he had yet to so much as speak to a reporter.

The well-known Pershing ice remained solid.

"Everyone wants to go," he replied to Patton. "Why should I favor you?"

The answer was immediate and absolutely truthful: "Because I want to go more than anyone else." But Patton recalled how Pershing fastened his "steely eyes" on him. Without even the "flicker of a smile," he dismissed him with a curt "That will do."

Early the next morning, the telephone in the Patton house rang. In "Personal Glimpses of General Pershing," an essay from 1924, unpublished during his lifetime, Patton recalled the terse exchange that followed.

"Lieutenant Patton, how long will it take you to get ready?" The voice on the other end of the line was unmistakable.

Patton responded that he was already packed.

"I'll be God Damned," Pershing allowed. "You are appointed Aide."

The Punitive Expedition was the biggest U.S. military operation since the Spanish-American War and the trouble that followed in the Philippines. Two cavalry brigades and one of infantry were assembled, a force of nearly fifteen thousand men. All those horses' hooves and human feet were augmented by two significant twentieth-century additions: automobiles and the half-dozen Curtiss JN-2 "Jennies" of the army's 1st Aero Squadron. The cars were Fords, homely but sturdy. The Jennies, kitelike and frail, were the best any American manufacturer could offer at the time, and they represented the state of the art in U.S. military aviation. Compared to the aircraft currently contending for control of skies over Europe's battlefields, however, they were already obsolete. Yet to Patton, the Jennies spoke of the future of combat. Whereas most army officers scorned the flying machines, Patton, this romantic cavalryman and diehard champion of the archaic saber, was fascinated by their potential. (In fact, the airplanes proved practically useless in the field. Desert sand clogged carburetors, and the propellers, which were fashioned of wood laminate, tended to fall apart in the dry air, their wooden layers curling up and peeling apart like the veneer on cheap furniture.)

In his diary, Patton recorded that he worked all day on March 14 "organizing the Expedition"; on the fifteenth, he participated in selecting "what part of the baggage was to go" then executed Pershing's order to take two Fords and seven Signal Corps soldiers to pick up and deliver the cumbersome Telefunken radio equipment that would accompany the expedition. On the next day, at 2:45 a.m., Patton started out for Mexico with an advance contingent, crossing the border at 3:16

in the morning. During a lunch stop, someone stole Patton's saddle blanket. Colonel George Dodd loaned him a replacement. Before the day was over, Patton noted in his diary, "I stole another one for him."

The full expedition began moving across the Rio Grande on March 18. Between this date and February 1917, Pershing and his men would trek about four hundred miles into Mexico, more than half of that distance through the unforgiving eastern foothills of the Sierra Madre as far as the town of Parral.

As with any aide, Patton's mission was to do whatever the CO ordered him to do. Some of his duties were personal, including making certain that Pershing was well fed and reasonably comfortable. This work extended to looking after the general's horses and automobiles, as well as the headquarters enlisted staff. Patton also accompanied Pershing on his tours of inspection and was repeatedly gratified to see just how demanding he was. Discipline was of the highest importance to Pershing, especially on a long march through harsh country. Patton recalled how he had been condemned at West Point for being "too damn military." Now, observing Pershing, he tasted vindication.

Of all his assignments, Patton's favorite was serving as a courier. Riding alone in rugged country, always the object of hostile eyes, was highly hazardous and, in Patton's mind, therefore highly desirable. A month into the expedition, in April, he eagerly volunteered to take a message to the 11th Cavalry, which had advanced miles to the south—though nobody knew quite how far. "Almost a needle in a haystack," Patton observed.

Before sending him on his way, Pershing took the lieutenant's hand and shook it. With unusual warmth, he admonished him to "Be careful, there are lots of Villistas." Patton recalled that Pershing was still holding his hand as he continued: "But remember, Patton, if you don't deliver that message don't come back."

Not only was the message delivered, Patton also had learned a valuable lesson in command. A great leader had the ability to convey his concern for his men even as he handed them a do-or-die ultimatum.

This was command presence. And Patton saw even more of it when he accompanied Pershing in a three-car convoy deep into the countryside. En route, the convoy was stopped by a detachment of Mexican soldiers.

"With halting Spanish and beating heart, I rushed forward to solve the problem," Patton recalled, "always most difficult, as to the friendliness or hostility of the Mexicans." Unsure of the soldiers' motives, the lieutenant did his best to conceal Pershing's identity with the lie that the small detachment was the advance guard of an automobile regiment. Just as he was putting the finishing touches on his fiction, "the General appeared at my side and . . . declar[ed] himself to be General Pershing, and demand[ed] Why in H— these people dared stop him." Patton anticipated an immediate storm of bullets, "but the commanding presence of the General and his utter disregard of danger over-awed the Mexicans and we went on, though personally it was more than a mile before I ceased feeling bullets entering my back."

By May, everyone, from Pershing down to Patton and all the way to dogface privates, was feeling the frustration of having marched very far without having found the slightest sign of Pancho Villa. Eager for results, Pershing decided to start fishing for smaller fry, beginning with General Julio Cárdenas, a top Villa officer who was believed to have been one of the masterminds of the Columbus raid. Scenting blood, Patton beseeched Pershing to include him in the manhunt. Accordingly, the general temporarily attached him to Troop C, 13th Cavalry.

Word had spread locally that Cárdenas was living on a ranch six miles north of the village of San Miguelito. On May 2, Patton rode to the ranch with a detachment from Troop C and there (as he sketchily recorded) "took a man the uncle of Cardenes. Surrounded San M found wife and baby of Cordenes. Allowed no one to leave. Camped near house [apparently lying in wait for Cárdenas] . . . Tried to get information out of uncle. Failed." In a letter to his father written shortly after the event, Patton was more specific: "The uncle was a very brave man and nearly died before he would tell me any thing."

Clearly, Patton had used torture on an old man in his quest for the Villa general, but to little or no avail. Nevertheless, he refused to give up on finding Cárdenas. On May 14, Pershing sent him with ten infantrymen, two civilian guides, and two civilian drivers in three automobiles to purchase corn from local farmers. "Went to . . . ranch[es] at Coyote, Rubio, Salsito, secured 250 hectaires of corn," he noted in his diary, then added off-handedly: "Decided to go to San Migel [San Miguelito] and see if I could find Julio Cardenes." He would later explain that his decision had been motivated by his sighting at the Rubio ranch some sixty suspicious-looking Mexicans, whom one of his guides identified as partisans of Villa and Cárdenas. Reasoning that this meant Cárdenas was likely nearby, Patton decided to return to San Miguelito and the ranch at which he had earlier found the general's uncle, wife, and baby. His diary entry narrating the results of this excursion is terse:

Did so [that is, found Cárdenas] and killed him and two of his men, a Captain named Isadore Lopez and an orderly Juan Garza. Saw 40 or 50 mounted men approaching at a gallop so left. Got five [ammo] belts three rifles one pistol two sabres two saddles. Fight started about 1230 pm lasted till 12:45.

Even in Patton's bare-bones entries, two elements stand out. The first is his initiative. Sent on a foraging mission, he did not hesitate to turn it into a combat mission when the opportunity presented itself. For Patton, there was no such thing as logistics troops versus combat troops. As he would explain repeatedly to subordinates, every soldier is a rifleman.

The second significant element here is that, even in a mere sketch of the encounter, Patton took the time and effort to give names to the men he killed. There is Cárdenas, the general, and also a captain, Isadore Lopez. But even the captain's lowly orderly—Juan Garza—is accorded the dignity of being named. Patton respected his enemies, including the "very brave man" he and his soldiers had tortured and the three men they had killed.

In writing about his maiden battle to Beatrice, to his father, and to his Aunt Nannie, Patton focused on what he himself took as the amazing fact of his absence of fear. "I have always expected to be scared but was not nor was I excited," he wrote to Beatrice on May 14, admitting that his only fear was that the enemy would get away. The next day, he wrote to his father: "I was much less scared than I had thought I would be, in fact all that worried me was the fear they would get away." And, on May 17, he expressed to his Aunt Nannie his amazement that the enemy's bullets "did not hit me," and confessed only to having been "worried for fear they would get away."

In later days and on several occasions, Patton described

in some detail the "Battle of San Miguelito." From his various accounts, it is possible to create a coherent narrative of an engagement that, minor though it was, claims the distinction of having been the first mechanized assault—three automobiles were involved—in the history of the U.S. Army. It was, therefore, a fitting baptism of fire for a commander whose name and career would be so intimately linked to mechanized warfare.

Patton's approach to the San Miguelito ranch revealed his exquisite awareness of the tactical implications of terrain. For about a mile and a half south of the hacienda, the ground was lower than the house, which was not visible until a traveler topped a rise. As soon as Patton had reached the high ground and saw the house—and therefore knew that he in turn was visible from it—he gave the car full throttle. (From his accounts, it seems apparent that he, not a driver, was at the wheel.) He purposely drove past the house at high speed, so that he could quickly reconnoiter. All he saw was four men skinning a cow in front of the house. One of them, however, ran into the house, then just as quickly returned to resume his work. This was entirely sufficient to raise Patton's suspicions.

Patton stopped his car northwest of the house and positioned the other two cars southwest of where he was. He jumped out of the car and ran around to a large arched door that led into the hacienda's patio. He rounded the corner, halfway to the door, and, when he was fifteen yards from it, he saw three men—armed—dash off on horseback. Patton now started around the southeast corner of the house. His army training had taught him to hold his fire until he was certain of his target. He therefore drew his revolver, and waited to see what would happen next.

When the three riders caught sight of Patton's men, they turned back. All three now opened up on Patton himself, one bullet hitting the ground close to him, spitting gravel up against his legs. Patton returned fire with his revolver, squeezing off five shots just as his men came around the corner of the house and started shooting.

Silence, unnaturally still, followed the fusillade. It did not last long. Three shots rang out, the bullets hitting the wall of the hacienda about a foot above Patton's head, showering him with adobe fragments.

Patton quickly deployed his men so as to cover all exits from the house, then reloaded his revolver. Glancing up from this work, he saw a man on horseback coming straight across his path. Reacting reflexively, he started to shoot, but almost immediately remembered what Marshal Dave Allison had taught him back in Sierra Blanca: Always shoot at the horse of an escaping man, not at the man himself. He took aim at the animal, his shot shattering its hip and sending the horse down on top of its rider no more than ten yards from where Patton stood. He and his men poured fire into the downed man. Patton later recalled that he just "crumpled up."

While this gun battle raged, another man managed to run out of the house, but was soon felled in a hail of rifle bullets. This made two men down, but Patton still had no idea of how many hostiles might yet be inside the house. Determined to find out, he clambered up onto the earthen roof of the building. As he stepped out toward the center of the roof, it dissolved beneath him. He fell through with both legs, coming to a sudden and painful halt when his armpits ended his fall. Acutely aware that two-thirds of his body dangled down from the ceiling of the hacienda, he strained every muscle to pull himself up and out. As he struggled, he heard the crack of a rifle. One of the civilian guides had just shot and killed a third man.

Having by now extricated himself from the hole in the roof, Patton reflected that, throughout the battle, the four men who had been skinning the cow had never stopped working. No one, he thought, is that brave—or that indifferent. He ordered his soldiers to round up the quartet, then, motioning for three of his soldiers to come to him, he told each to take one of the men. Patton grabbed the fourth, and, using them as human shields, he and the others walked into the house and searched it. All the while, he felt the eyes of Cárdenas's mother and wife (who held her baby daughter in her arms) drilling into his back and neck. He came at last to a wooden door, very old and very heavy. Gingerly, he pulled it open, pistol cocked and ready. Behind the door, crouched in prayer, rosaries in hand, was a clutch of leathery-faced old women.

So ended the Battle of San Miguelito. Patton pushed the cow skinners to the three bullet-pierced corpses, which were now laid out side by side.

Who are they? he demanded.

The cow skinners identified a Villista private, a Villista captain, and General Julio Cárdenas.

It had been a damn fine fight. Patton ordered his men to tie the three bodies across the hoods of each of the three automobiles. No sooner was this done than everyone froze at the distant thunder of hoof beats. Villistas were on the gallop toward them. Through the cloud of dust they raised, Patton estimated their number at fifty. As the riders closed in, he and his outnumbered "army" opened fire and took fire in return as they dashed to the cars and ran them for all they were worth. When their pursuers were no longer in sight, Patton ordered a halt and sent a man to shinny up the telegraph pole to cut the wires that ran alongside the road. This would keep word of the shootout from reaching the nearest town, Rubio, before they could get there.

But they did not stop at Rubio or anywhere else, not until they had reached Pershing's headquarters, where Patton was instantly swarmed by reporters. Little enough had happened during this Punitive Expedition, and they were desperate for copy. With Pershing's blessing, Patton gave it to them.

By the next afternoon, Patton was a national hero. It was, he well knew, the kind of heroism that is trumpeted briefly in headlines and lingers a few days before it is quite forgotten. No matter. He had won. He had suffered no casualties. And he had felt—to his surprise—no fear. He was confident that there would be many more occasions for heroism. Sooner or later, he would be remembered.

CHAPTER 10

THE DOGS OF WAR

"I saw the paint fly off the side of the tank and heard machine guns so I jumped off and got in a shell hole. . . . Here I was nervous."

—PATTON, ACCOUNT OF HIS RIDE ON THE OUTSIDE OF A TANK DURING THE ST. MIHIEL OFFENSIVE, FRANCE, SEPTEMBER 12, 1918

The Battle of San Miguelito consumed just fifteen minutes of a campaign that lasted nearly a year. For Patton, despite the exhilarating glory of the gunfight, this was a terrible problem. As the prospect of entering the European War became increasingly likely, President Woodrow Wilson grew commensurately more anxious to avert a major crisis with Mexico. Although the Punitive Expedition had failed to track down Villa, Patton and others had killed or captured many of Villa's top lieutenants, and the president decided that it was time to stop pushing the diplomatic envelope. He ordered Pershing to pull back the Punitive Expedition some 250 miles, to within just 150 miles of the border. Patton and some fifteen thousand fellow soldiers were still in Mexico, but they were now remote from Villa—and they knew it. Patton's diary entries became desultory and dull:

May 15: Staied around camp all day . . . Plaied horseshoes with Cabell, Kromer, and Collins.

May 16: I had a chil and went to bed early.

207

May 18: I did absolutely nothing but take a bath.

May 19: Terrible wind all day. No one did anything.

There was a flutter of excitement on May 22. Patton recorded that he and four enlisted men "Saw Mexican with gun on horse but he looked so powerful we did not chase him. We should have." Whether out of boredom or with a thought toward some future eye that might scan his diary, Patton revised the entry: "I saw a Mexican with a gun ride off from the mountain and at first I decided to kill him, but later I thought he might possibly be innocent and I let him go."

On the next day, Patton had the satisfaction of finally receiving his promotion to first lieutenant, but the rest of May and then June and July slithered by, dusty, dismal, and hot. Granted a few days' leave in August, he traveled in company with General Pershing back to Columbus, New Mexico, where he reunited with Beatrice. Sister Nita Patton was there as well to greet the general. Marriage between the middle-aged widower and the no longer girlish "Amazon" was expected. Patton looked forward to the prospect, lightheartedly remarking to Beatrice, "Nita may rank us yet." (She never would. Pershing proposed to Nita early in 1917, left to fight in the world war, but on his return in 1919 sent her a letter to the effect that his former ardor had cooled; Nita responded by formally breaking off the engagement.)

Then it was back to Mexico. "Nothing to report," Patton reported in a letter to Beatrice on September 24, 1916. "Even the wind did not blow today."

"Darling Beat," Patton began a letter to his wife on October 7:

You are indeed fortunate in not being able to kiss me right now. My face looks like an old after-birth of a Mexican cow on which had been smeared several very much decomposed eggs. I have a large and flatulent double chin and jawls [jowls] like the tipical Wall St. Magninate. Also both ears are red and inflamed and I have no hair nor eyebrows nor eye lashes. No I have nothing catching. I simply set my self on fire with the above distressing results.

Patton always considered himself a fortunate warrior, and more than once, he quoted Virgil, *Audaces fortuna iuvat* ("Fortune favors the brave"), though he at least once misattributed it to Caesar. During World War II, in Europe, he christened his advance field headquarters "Lucky Forward," and in his diary and letters, he often marveled that he consistently avoided becoming a casualty of combat. But in peacetime—or, at least, during what passed for peacetime—when the roar of musketry was not to be heard and the lead had stopped flying, Patton suffered one injury after another. Most of the accidents, which ranged from trivial to potentially fatal, arguably were designed, unconsciously of course, to punctuate—perhaps relieve—the tedium that came in the absence of war.

After nightfall on October 2, Patton attended the showing of some movies, then retired to his tent to write an article on "musketry" for the *Cavalry Journal*. He pumped up his lamp, which he fueled not with kerosene but gasoline, and lit it. When it failed to burn brightly enough, he pumped in more gas, even as a live flame flickered. Realizing that he had now pumped too much, he stopped, causing the gasoline, under pressure, to squirt directly into the flame. The fluid stream ignited as if it had issued from a flamethrower. "As it came," he wrote to Beatrice, "it hit me in the face and got in my hair. I ran out side and put my self out."

If self-inflicted injury was typical of Patton, so was keeping his head in spite of it. After putting himself out, he walked back into the tent to put out the lamp and to extinguish parts of the canvas that had started to burn, thereby preventing a major fire. "Then I reported to Gen. P. that I was burned and went to the hospital."

Although he emphasized in his letter to Beatrice that the doctors promised he would be unscarred and his eyesight had not been damaged, Patton described to her the extent and appearance of his injuries in gory yet clinical detail, clearly doing so with relish—though he assured Beatrice that he had written "this long letter to keep you from being worried," but adding, "I also had a couple of pictures taken which I will send you."

Although the burns were not deep, they were extensive, and Patton seems to have suffered some degree of infection. He was granted sick leave, once again met Beatrice in Columbus, then traveled with her by train to his childhood home, Lake Vineyard, and visited in nearby downtown Los Angeles his uncle by marriage, Dr. Billy Wills, who treated him. While Patton convalesced in California, Pershing wrote him a letter expressing probably as much warmth as he was capable of. "I hope you are rapidly recovering from your accident," the general began, then hit a rather awkward note with "and that your personal appearance has improved." But Pershing exhibited less concern for Patton's physical welfare than for the well-being of his career. Knowing that the senior Patton was running for the Senate (he would suffer a resounding defeat), Pershing cautioned Lieutenant Patton "not [to] be too insistent upon your own personal views" when he discussed "the Mexican situation" with his father. "You must remember that when we enter the army we do so with the full knowledge that our first duty is toward our government, entirely regardless of our own views under any given circumstances." As sage as it was prophetic, it was advice Patton would always find hard—often impossible—to follow.

The fame Patton enjoyed as a result of the Battle of San Miguelito quickly faded, as it should have, but the connection he had made with John J. Pershing proved more durable and of far greater consequence. The Punitive Expedition earned Pershing the second star of a major general and set his career on the highest possible trajectory. Patton continued as his aide until Pershing was named to succeed Frederick Funston as head of the army's Southern Department. After Pershing departed for his new San Antonio headquarters, Patton remained in El Paso, now as commander of a cavalry troop, and headed toward rapid promotion to captain. Add to this the likelihood of a Pershing-Patton marriage, and the still-young officer's prospects were about as bright as any could be in the peacetime American army.

On April 6, 1917, the peacetime American army suddenly ceased to exist. In response to President Wilson's request, Congress declared war against Germany and the other Central Powers. The United States was now a combatant in the "Great War," the war Wilson proclaimed America would fight to "end all wars."

Patton was unsurprised by the declaration. He had long believed U.S. entry into the European War was only a matter of time, and, of late, he had been following the news closely. Weeks before April 6, 1917, he had begun soliciting letters of recommendation from key officers under whom he had served. Captain in the regular army, the promotion toward which he was surely headed, was a company-grade rank. Patton aimed higher. His object was to obtain an immediate field-grade commission—a jump to major or even lieutenant colonel—which meant going outside of the regular army and into the volunteer forces that were being formed. (The National Defense Act of 1916 authorized creation of a Volunteer Army; the Selective Service Act, passed on May 18, 1917, would change this to the "National Army," consisting of draftees as well as volunteers. Under both guises, this force augmented the regular army for the duration of U.S. involvement in World War I and for many was a vehicle for rapid, if impermanent, promotion.)

As for Pershing, he left San Antonio and Southern Department headquarters to answer the War Department's summons to Washington. He had been ordered to organize a division, take command of it, then lead it to France as the vanguard of the American Expeditionary Force (AEF). Pershing's first step in his new assignment was to make a list of officers to appoint to his staff. Patton was near the very top. Even as the general set about cutting orders for Patton and the other appointees, the War Department sent Pershing new orders. His revised assignment was to lead the entire AEF. His command would consist of every soldier the United States committed to the Great War. At the same time that he received this vastly expanded brief, Pershing discovered that the War Department was about to send Patton to Front Royal, Virginia, to buy cavalry horses. With all that had been heaped onto Pershing's plate, he took the time and effort to get Patton's horse-buying order rescinded.

This done, on May 18, he directed the adjutant general to wire Patton—who had been promoted to captain just three days before—with an order to report directly to the commanding general, AEF, at the War Department.

Patton received the telegram at Pride's Crossing, the Massachusetts home of his mother- and father-in-law. He drove to Boston and boarded the first available train, which left for New York at half past midnight. Arriving at Penn Station at seven in the morning of May 19, he picked up a newspaper to pass the time while waiting for the Washington train. The headline said that Pershing was about to go to France in advance of the first wave of the AEF. As soon as he arrived in Washington, Patton called Beatrice to arrange for his uniforms and belongings to be shipped to Washington from El Paso. Next, he reported to Pershing at the War Department, where the general's aide told him that "we were leaving Wednesday" (it was now Saturday afternoon). Patton immediately took himself to a local tailor, who measured him for a uniform, promising that it would be ready in time.

Pershing gave Patton no reason to imagine that he was bound for martial glory. His assignment was as a staff officer, not a combat commander. As he noted in his diary on May 20, his job—at least his initial duty—was to supervise thirty "men who had been selected as Headquarters orderlies." In other words, he was the equivalent of a head butler looking after the lesser household staff. If this disappointed him, he did not let on, nor did he commit any expression of disappointment to the privacy of his diary, and all talk of getting a volunteer command was dropped. For Patton, the only thing that mattered was that he was going to France with General Pershing himself and would be one of the very first Yanks in Europe. For the time being, this was glory enough, and, in the fullness of time, he believed, there would be plenty of chances to get into the shooting.

In the rainy gloom at 6:00 a.m., Monday, May 28, George S. Patton Sr. accompanied his son to the Governor's Island ferry in New York Harbor. The two parted amid "much tears," after which, in what had now become a cold, driving rain, Patton directed "people where to go" and saw to the "placing of baggage." When General Pershing arrived at Governor's Island, all boarded a tender, the *Thomas Patten,* and steamed out to Gravesend Bay, Brooklyn, where, with harbor waters churned by a strong easterly wind, Patton, fifty-nine other officers, and a mixed bag of 120 enlisted men along with a few civilian clerks joined John J. Pershing in boarding the liner *Baltic*, bound for Liverpool in a heavy spring fog.

In 1620, the *Mayflower* carried 102 passengers to America. In 1917, the *Baltic* carried 188 military and military-contracted civilian passengers to England. In both instances, they were the first of many, many more. At the start of the Punitive Expedition, the U.S. Army numbered about 133,000 officers and men. By the armistice of November 11, 1918, it stood at four and a half million, of which number two million had been sent to France. Patton was in the first wave of the greatest mobilization in American history, headed for the greatest war the world had ever fought. Upon General Pershing fell the responsibility of building the army and deploying it along the Western Front, where Europe's mightiest military powers had been killing each other for some three years.

During the *Baltic*'s five-week passage, Patton drilled his orderlies, attended staff study sessions, and brushed up on his French. Lifeboat exercises were mandatory, especially with U-boats a constant peril. It was not until June 6, just two days from docking, that the *Baltic* was joined by a pair of destroyers. Patton had no illusions that these escorts could stop a torpedo attack, but they "could prevent the shelling of the [life]boats which is a comfort," he admitted to his diary. "It would be rather an experience to be torpedoed but one would not enjoy being shelled later."

At nine o'clock on the morning of June 8, the *Baltic* eased into a Liverpool dock, where it was greeted quayside by the city's lord mayor, a Royal Navy admiral, a British army lieutenant general, and the regimental band of the Royal Welsh Fusiliers, which struck up "The Star-Spangled Banner" followed by "God Save the King." After the requisite salutes and welcoming speeches, Pershing and his staff officers boarded a special train for London, where the U.S. ambassador to the Court of St. James's, Walter Hines Page; the British secretary for war, Lord Derby; the top commander of the British Home Forces, the portly, generously mustached General Sir John French; and U.S. admiral William Sims (who was already working with his Royal Navy counterparts) waited at Euston Station. After another round of greetings, Pershing was chauffeured off to the Savoy Hotel, a masterpiece of stately luxury that had been financed in the preceding century largely by proceeds from Gilbert and Sullivan performances at the Savoy Theatre. Patton, together with the sixty-seven men who now reported directly to him, was dispatched to quarters in the Tower of London, a venerable tourist attraction that, during the war, had reverted to its centuries-old status as an active military installation. The detachment was met with all the pomp and circumstance the Tower's Honorable Artillery Company could muster, including a brass band and cheering troops. "It was very thrilling," Patton cheerfully confessed, noting that the entrance of the men he led marked the first time in history that foreign troops had "ever marched through" the Tower's "venerable portal save in the guise of prisoners."

The London sojourn was brief. On June 13, Pershing and his staff, including Patton, left for Paris. It was here that the routine nature of his assignment finally sunk in with full dreariness. Patton's days were consumed in managing the orderlies and arranging for drivers to chauffeur the general and his staff. Nevertheless, he did make time to look at the latest French aircraft—"400 of them and wonderful," he noted in his diary, and to Beatrice wrote that he had "never before known what flying was. It is impossible to imagine the perfection which these people have attained." Clearly, French aeronautics was far in advance of the American air industry, which had succeeded in producing for military service nothing more than the awkward Jennies Patton had seen during the Punitive Expedition. Now Patton knew just how primitive they were. Awed by the French aircraft, the Master of the Sword was clearly not wedded to the technology of horse and saber.

Patton also found relief from routine in the occasions, few but significant, on which Pershing summoned him for confidential talks. Yet even these did not stem Patton's growing impatience. He was eager to see the front, and, as much as he admired Pershing, he believed the general should be even more eager; yet it was July before Pershing, with two colonels and Captain Patton (as aide-de-camp), visited Field Marshal Sir Douglas Haig at his forward headquarters.

Haig was already a controversial figure, having lost half a million men (killed and wounded) at the Somme in 1916. Patton was less interested in disputing whether such losses revealed determination or betrayed incompetence than he was in meeting, close up, one of the most aggressive commanders of the war. The instant and evident chemistry between Patton and Haig—tall and ramrod straight, he looked to be a blond and very British facsimile of Pershing—was almost unheard of in a meeting of field marshal with newly minted junior captain. Haig was as impressed with Patton as Patton was with him. He described the American captain as a "fire-eater," who visibly hungered to get into "the fray." The two spoke at length about polo and riding to the hunt. Haig was especially interested in what Patton had to say about the saber, and Patton came away from the conversation willing to admit that, where the sword was concerned, Haig was even "more of a charger than" he.

If San Miguelito was Patton's maiden battle, the summer of 1917 was his introduction to war. For many men, it is traumatic. To Patton, it was eye-opening. The sight of the latest French aircraft had opened his eyes to the pathetic inadequacy of American military aviation. The meeting with Marshal Haig had shown him a truly aggressive commander. On July 31, he rode in a staff car with Pershing, his chief of staff, Colonel James Harbord, and a French officer to St. Dizier to inspect newly arrived U.S. troops. Their route took them past the site of the First Battle of the Marne. Along the road were many graves, and where the field hospitals had been, there were now "large squair inclosures full of crosses." As sobering as this vision of the cost of war was, there was (as far as Patton was concerned) worse to come. On August 1, he accompanied Pershing in an inspection of American troops, recording in his diary that he was "disappointed. Men did not look smart, officers were lazy, troops lacked equipment and training, were listless." Patton well knew that there were many graves yet to be filled, and, as he looked at the sloppy, sorry troops of St. Dizier, perhaps he reflected on the drubbing he had taken at West Point for being "too damn military." Well, here were the consequences of failing to be military enough. Whether this vision of poor soldiering constituted for him a genuine epiphany, we cannot say, but Patton never wavered in his conviction that victory begins with training and the acquisition of discipline.

For his part, General Pershing stood firm against incessant French and British demands to begin throwing, piecemeal, his under-trained and under-equipped soldiers into the line. Like Patton, he was convinced that men of the low caliber of those at St. Dizier were prepared to be nothing more than cannon fodder. It was not until September 1917 that the general felt sufficiently confident in the quality of his troops to deploy a contingent to the front, albeit in a "quiet sector" in Lorraine. His idea was to ease this first contingent into combat, so that they would have a fighting chance against Germans hardened by nearly four years of war. On September 1, Pershing moved his headquarters from Paris to Chaumont, to be close to these troops.

The town quickly mushroomed into *the* major U.S. training center, which included general combat training facilities—Pershing quickly perceived that the basic training soldiers received stateside fell far short of what was necessary for actual combat—and military specialty schools. At Chaumont, Pershing expanded Patton's portfolio. He was to continue serving as one of his aides-de-camp, but he was also appointed post adjutant. This put him in command of a very large headquarters company—250 men, more than twice the size of the standard infantry company—as well as a motor pool of some ninety vehicles. Before he shipped out, Patton had answered a questionnaire on which he emphasized his experience with gasoline vehicles. This may have helped him gain command of the large motor pool, which, in turn, would later put him in a favorable position for a field command in the nascent U.S. Army tank corps.

Despite the impressive set of responsibilities assigned him, Patton did not relish running a headquarters outfit. Perhaps by way of venting his chronic frustration, he made no attempt to curb his "too damn military" inclination. Soon, Patton's company stood out from the run-of-the-mill American doughboys for its impeccable spit and polish as well as its combat readiness—even though these headquarters troops were unlikely ever to be sent into the trenches. It is not known what the members of HQ Company thought of their CO—surprisingly, "iron-ass" commanders often evoke as much approval as complaint from the men they ride—but General Pershing was wowed. As the AEF continued to grow, so too would the Chaumont facility, and Pershing decided that Patton was ideally positioned for promotion to major. That, of course, was the field-grade command he had craved, and had even been willing to go outside of the regular army to obtain; the only problem was that *this* command would not be in the field. Patton rapidly became depressed, getting a foretaste of the blues that would afflict him in the deadly peace between the two world wars. He confessed to Beatrice that he "would trade jobs with almost any one for any thing."

Anything?

In 1770, a Britisher named Richard Edgeworth cobbled together a system of metal links to create the world's first caterpillar track. No one quite knew what to do with it at the time, but at the outbreak of the Crimean War in the 1850s, smack in the middle of the "age of steam," military-minded inventors turned out a handful of steam-powered tractors that rode on the caterpillar instead of wheels. These vehicles could negotiate muddy terrain impassable for a horse and cart, but the war was over before the new inventions had even the slightest impact on tactics or strategy. It was 1890 before Benjamin Holt, in America, began tinkering with ideas for steam tractors to be used in farming. In 1904, he produced his first steam tractor based on a caterpillar track and, two years later, introduced a gasoline-fueled internal-combustion version. At the outbreak of World War I, the British government purchased several Holt tractors—not for combat, but for hauling heavy loads over difficult terrain.

Enter Sir Ernest Swinton. As a veteran of the Second Boer War, he had come to the attention of Lord Kitchener at the outbreak of the Great War. Britain's war minister was greatly concerned over what he deemed the demoralizing effect of news stories that had been coming in from the Western Front, and he appointed Swinton to serve as the army's "official" war correspondent, responsible for turning out combat coverage that would counteract the grim stories filed by civilian reporters. Swinton did his job, producing blandly comforting accounts intended to assure the British public that trench warfare wasn't "as bad as all that."

But, actually, Swinton was appalled by what he saw. In the late summer of 1914, after little more than a month of a brutal and breathtaking wheel of German troops through Belgium and northern France in execution of the infamous invasion strategy known as the Schlieffen Plan, the Western Front hardened into trench warfare as static as it was bloody.

At this moment in military history, the technology of weapons served defenders far better than it did attackers. Trenches, barbed wire, and the craters made by the impact of hundreds of thousands of artillery shells impeded any attack across no-man's land, whereas the machine gun, which had reached its first great height of development before the outbreak of the war, gave defenders an incredible advantage over anyone who dared raise his head above the lip of a trench, let alone climbed "over the top" to venture an attack. Two men operating a single machine gun from the cover of a trench or a "nest" could cut down an entire company of attackers within minutes. This is what appalled Swinton, and this is what set the wheels of his mind turning.

About Christmastime 1914, Swinton chanced to see one of the imported Holt tractors towing an artillery piece. It gave him a brainstorm. Why not develop the Holt tractor as a *combat* vehicle capable of rolling over trenches, barbed wire, and shell craters? As Swinton saw it, the tractor could be just the thing to reintroduce maneuver into the horrific stalemate of trench warfare. Predictably, Sir John French, at the time commander-in-chief on the front and a beefy Briton of remarkably little imagination, thought nothing of the proposal. But, acting on his own initiative, Swinton dashed off a note to Maurice Hankey, secretary of the government's War Council. Hankey was sufficiently intrigued to pass the memo to Winston Churchill, who was not at the time an army officer or official, but first lord of the Admiralty.

Churchill possessed—in great abundance—the vision French lacked. He was already quite familiar with the armored car, a rugged wheeled vehicle that the Royal Navy used to defend naval airstrips in Belgium. Churchill not only grasped Swinton's idea for a tracked vehicle that could traverse the most difficult of terrain, but he saw it as a highly feasible extension of the already existing military technology of the armored car. Churchill may have even been aware that, as early as 1899, Frederick Simms, a British inventor, had tried unsuccessfully to interest the War Office in what he called a "motor-war car," which was driven by a Daimler gasoline engine, was encased in "bulletproof" armor, and sported a pair of Maxim machine guns mounted in revolving turrets. What Swinton now proposed, Churchill understood, was seating such an armored car on caterpillar tracks. The result, this admiralty chief conceived, would be a battleship built for land war: a "landship." Churchill instantly established a Landships Committee to create specifications for a vehicle, which could be contracted out for rapid design and manufacture of a prototype.

The Landships Committee quickly discovered that the firm of Richard Hornsby & Sons had already produced the Killen-Strait Armoured Tractor, an open vehicle with two sets of caterpillar tracks, a short steerable set up front and a longer motor-driven set in the back, both track systems consisting of steel links joined together with steel pins. Churchill and David Lloyd George (at the time chancellor of the exchequer) witnessed a demonstration of the Killen-Strait machine in June 1915 at Wormwood Scrubs. It was a tractor, unarmed and with the driver seated in the open, but it was a sufficient proof of concept to prompt the Landships Committee to collaborate with another new bureau, the Inventions Committee, in commissioning Naval Air Service lieutenant W. G. Wilson and William Tritton of William Foster & Company to produce an armed and fully enclosed landship. Swinton code-named the prototype "the tank," because its unprepossessing rhomboid body resembled nothing more descript than some kind of—well—tank.

The "tank"—soldiers took to calling it Little Willie, though its official designation was Mark I—was rushed into production. It was turned out in two versions, a so-called "male" and "female." The twenty-eight-ton male sported two vaguely phallic 6-pounder guns and four 8-mm Hotchkiss machine guns. The female, at twenty-seven tons, was equipped only with machine guns, four .303 Vickers and two 8 mm Hotchkiss pieces. Top speed for both versions was about three miles per hour, and the crew of eight were crammed into the hull, which they shared with the engine. Internal temperatures climbed to more than 120 degrees, and carbon monoxide exhaust as well as other noxious vapors leaked into the confined space. When crews routinely vomited uncontrollably, passed out, or did both, they were issued gas masks, which they took to wearing most of the time. Additional protective gear included helmets, goggles, and even facemasks of woven chainmail. These were necessary because bullet and shell hits on the thin (eight-millimeter) armor often sent shrapnel and rivets ricocheting within the hull space. Impact by something more powerful than small arms fire or a tossed grenade—an artillery strike or a mortar hit—was likely to cause the gas tanks to explode, instantly incinerating the crew.

Maneuvering the Mark I was a Herculean labor that required the simultaneous effort of four of its crewmembers. The tank was steered by varying the speed of the two tracks relative to one another. One "driver," designated the tank commander, operated the brakes, the other tended the primary gearbox. Two additional "gearsmen" worked the secondary gears, one for each track. There was no accelerator. Speed, steering, and direction were all controlled by shifting gears. (The tank's other four crewmembers were gunners.) Maneuvering on the battlefield required exquisite coordination among the drivers and the gearsmen, even though no one could hope to make himself heard above the din of the engine and machinery, let alone the clatter of bullet impacts. All communication, therefore, was nonverbal, a combination of hand signals and raps on the helmet.

By the summer of 1917, when Patton had finally arrived at least close to the front, the British Mark I had evolved into the Mark IV and the Mark VI. The Mark IV was "up-armored" by the addition of plates varying from about a quarter-inch thickness to a half-inch; gasoline storage was improved sufficiently to reduce from inevitable to likely the probability of an explosion resulting from a direct hit; speed was upped from 3 miles per hour to 3.7; and the vehicle's operating range was extended from about twelve to thirty-five miles. The Mark VI was bigger and wider than either the Mark I or Mark IV—the two earlier tanks were "Little Willies," the Mark VI, "Big Willie"—but the most significant and visible advance was the installation of its gun in a top-mounted turret rather than in ungainly "sponsons" bulging from the tank's sides. The turret greatly enhanced the flexibility of the Mark VI's firepower, giving it the ability to shoot anywhere along a 360-degree radius without having to turn the tank. Crews also benefitted from a compartmentalized hull, which isolated the motor in a separate engine room on one side of the vehicle. Top speed, however, remained a walk.

Despite the fighting and safety improvements incorporated into the Mark VI, few soldiers, British or American, wanted to be tankers, but when the man Pershing appointed to create a U.S. Tank Department, Lieutenant Colonel LeRoy Eltinge, asked him if he'd like to become a tank officer, Patton, heartily sick of his desk, replied with an impulsive yes. He then recorded in his diary that another officer, Colonel Frank McCoy, advised him to write a letter directly to General

Pershing to make doubly certain that he would indeed grab himself a tank appointment.

Dated October 3, 1917, Patton's letter is especially revealing for what it says about the insight into armored mechanized warfare he possessed even before he had climbed inside of a tank. "I think my self qualified for this service for the following reasons," he began. "The duty of 'tanks' and more especially of 'Light Tanks' is analogous to the duty performed by cavalry in normal wars. I am a cavalryman."

Three points are significant in this remarkable statement. First, Patton distinguished between generic tanks and *light* tanks from the get-go. While the British were developing increasingly heavy tanks, moving from Little Willie to Big Willie, the French focused on lighter, smaller tanks. The Renault FT-17 weighed just seven tons, was sixteen feet long, and slightly less than five feet wide. Instead of an eight-man crew, it carried just two. Armor was light at twenty-two millimeters, but the primary gun, either a 37-millimeter cannon or a 7.92-millimeter machine gun, was turret mounted. A four-cylinder, thirty-nine-horsepower Renault engine made about four and a third miles per hour—still a walk, but a brisker one than any of the British Marks could manage. Most important of all, the light tank was much more maneuverable than the lumbering Big Willie.

That Patton preferred the light tanks to the heavies is the second important point in his appeal to Pershing. Patton was a cavalryman, and, to him, the light tank was analogous to a cavalry horse, whereas the British heavy was closer to something a horse might pull.

Finally, there was Patton's analogy between the tactical role of tanks in the current war and that of cavalry in what Patton interestingly called "normal wars." Although he admired modern technology, Patton apparently saw in the light tank a means of embracing the latest without having to abandon his beloved cavalry traditions (the traditions of "normal" wars). The cavalry of old were knights in armor. As Patton saw it, a tanker could be a latter-day knight, except that now it was the "horse," not the man, who bore the armor. More precisely, the modern knight did not wear his armor, he inhabited it. In a squalid war of trench against trench, the tank represented not only the possibility of tactical breakthrough, but the resurrection of chivalric glory in twentieth-century combat. For Patton, *this*, and not the static, anonymous slaughter that had marked the first four years on the Western Front, was "normal" warfare.

In his letter to Pershing, Patton went on to explain that he had commanded a machine-gun troop and knew "something of the mechanism of machine guns." Moreover, he had "always had a Troop which shot well so think that I am a good instructor in fire," and, as he reminded Pershing, "accurate fire is very necessary to good use of tanks." Patton also reiterated his experience with gas engines and automobiles, and he pointed out that his facility with the French language was "better than 95% of American Officers so could get information from the French Direct." Perhaps even more important was his having "been to school in France," which proved his ability to get "on well with Frenchmen."

These were all reasonable, rational qualifications, but Patton concluded his letter by enumerating some more personal qualifications for leadership in combat. They do say much about his style and philosophy of warfighting: "I believe I have quick judgment and that I am willing to take chances. Also I have always believed in getting close to the enemy and have taught this for two years at the Mounted Service School where

I had success in arousing the aggressive spirit in the students." Finally, he summoned up the Battle of San Miguelito: "I believe that I am the only American who has ever made an attack in a motor vehicle."

Patton was so proactive in writing to Pershing that, when the general received the letter, the tank service he called for had yet to be launched. He did not, therefore, even bring up the tank service when (as Patton wrote to Beatrice on October 9), General Pershing told him that "he was about to recommend some promotions in the national army." Pershing asked him if he would "like to be a major of cavalry or any other branch or staff department." Without waiting for an immediate answer, the general advised Patton to "think it over" then "tell him frankly what [he] wanted." Pershing promised that he would try to see that Patton "got it."

It was a remarkable vote of confidence from the senior American commander in Europe, and it set Patton to thinking. He explained to Beatrice that "the only chance for a man of my age is to command troops. For such staff jobs as I could get would not amount to much." He considered that commanding either a thousand-man infantry battalion or a twenty-machine tank battalion "would be something worth while and with luck I might go a long way." Significantly, he left cavalry out of the picture entirely, doubtless recognizing that his own branch, beloved though it was, had no significant role to play in this modern war. At this point, he seems to have been leaning toward an infantry command. "The Tanks are yet in an unsettled state but they may have a great future."

Within days after writing his letter to Beatrice, nature intervened in a way that put the whole matter of choice of command in abeyance. Feeling unwell, Patton looked at himself in the mirror. It was *not* his imagination: his skin had gone yellow.

He was duly hospitalized with what physicians diagnosed as "jaundice catarrhal," according to Dr. Adolf Strümpell's *Text-Book of Medicine for Students and Practitioners,* Third American Edition (1901), an inflammation and obstruction of the common bile duct, resulting in jaundice, vomiting, stomach pains, and languor. The only prescribed treatment at the time was several weeks of "rest and prudence." This misfortune had the happy consequence of introducing Patton to Colonel Fox Conner, an officer who would be revered as a mentor by George C. Marshall, Dwight D. Eisenhower, and Patton himself. At the time, Conner was laid up with "stoppage of the bowel," and Patton was assigned as his roommate. Conner did not hesitate to counsel him to turn his back on tanks and ask instead to be made an infantry major. Conner was so persuasive that when Lieutenant Colonel Eltinge visited Patton the next day, he was all ready to tell him that he had decided against the Tank Corps. But Eltinge spoke up first, announcing to Patton that a U.S. tank school was to be opened at Langres as soon as November 15. He wanted Patton to take command of it. To his diary on November 3, Patton confided: "Inspite of my resolution to the contrary I said yes." Yet no sooner did Eltinge leave his bedside than the usually decisive Patton found himself once again swamped by doubt. "I kept discussing it pro and con with Col. F. Conner," he wrote, "and again decided on Infantry."

That would seem to have been that. Yet when Patton was discharged from the hospital on November 3, he said nothing to Eltinge, and when he was ordered on November 10 to assume command of the tank school, he simply followed orders. The night before he was to report, he could not sleep. He had been handed the proverbial golden opportunity to write his own ticket in the biggest war the world had ever known, and he had chosen a teaching assignment in a branch that was not yet even a branch, working with men who were untrained and machines whose mechanical unreliability was already the stuff of legend. What *had* he done?

Sometime before dawn, Patton succeeded in persuading himself that it wasn't a matter of a right decision versus a wrong one. It was a question of destiny. With this realization, he was suddenly seized with the sense that he had acted in accord with his fate. Cavalry, infantry, tanks—all that really mattered was that he was no longer a staff officer, but a leader of troops. Patton went on to make a mental list of the virtues of tank service.

The infantry was crawling with majors, whereas he would be the only major in tanks. He had found a most exclusive service and therefore couldn't help but attract notice.

The life of a tank officer promised to be much like that of an air officer. The combat was hazardous, but, in between fights, there was no languishing in the cold, filthy misery of the infantryman's trench. Instead, there would be the convivial warmth of a pleasant headquarters.

The final point on Patton's inventory was the possibility that the tanks might prove effective, very effective, even war winning. He admitted to his father in a letter of November 6, that there was "about a fifty percent chance that [the tanks] wont work at all but if they do they will work like hell."

And if they did work like hell, Patton could see before him what he called "the golden dream":

1st. I will run the [tank] school. 2. Then they will organize a battalion. I will command it. 3. Then if I make good and the T[anks] do and the war lasts I will get the first [tank] regiment. 4. With the same "IF" as before they will make a brigade and I will get the star [of a brigadier general].

It was heady stuff. On a roll now, he reasoned to his father that if he had taken the conventional route by accepting an infantry command, there was a real chance that his outfit might be held in reserve and that, therefore, he would miss out on battles. Tanks were so new and so few that there was no danger of any being held in back. Moreover, because they had the appeal of a cutting-edge technology, they would be "a great drawing card in the papers and illustrated magazines." It was easier to be hailed as a hero commanding tanks than serving as just another infantry officer. Patton did concede that tank service looked very dangerous. One-fourth of the machines did become casualties of war, but, he added, tank crews had a casualty rate of 7.5 percent, "much lower than the Dough boys. Also in the tanks you are not apt to be wounded. You either get blown to bitts by a direct hit or you are not touched." He closed his musings by returning to the issue of destiny: "I have a hunch that my Mexican Auto Battle was the fore runner of this. Who can say?"

In preparation for opening the U.S. tank school, Patton was sent to the French tank school near Compiègne, where he spent two weeks of total immersion in the state of the art of armored warfare. He learned how tanks worked, he learned what they could do, and, just as important, what they could not do. His "golden dream" letter to his father had been thoroughly self-serving, as most of his correspondence and conversation had been ever since his West Point days. But in the fortnight he spent continually engaged with the French light tanks, his focus shifted from advancing his own career to advancing the strategy, tactics, and doctrine of armored warfare. The issues quickly fell into place for him. The British tanks were little more than artillery pieces rendered mobile by virtue of being mounted on a heavy, slow-moving body. The light French tanks, however, seemed to Patton a truly revolutionary weapons system, highly maneuverable (at least by comparison to a Mark I, IV, or IV) and almost speedy.

It was, however, the British heavies that first proved their mettle. Nearly five hundred of them had spearheaded a seven-mile-deep infantry penetration at the Battle of Cambrai in northern France (November 20–December 5, 1917), fought while Patton was still at the French tank school. In a trench war in which advances were typically measured in yards, seven miles was a near infinity of gain. Even though German counterattacks subsequently forced the British to give back all that they had won, no one could question the success of the tanks. The problem at Cambrai had been the failure of infantry commanders to follow up on and exploit what the tankers had won. To Patton, it was clear that the function of tanks was to punch holes into the defensive line, but then it was the job of infantry to pour through the breaches to flank and enfilade the enemy. The tank was a tool, wondrous in its potential, but a tool only.

Cambrai left everyone suddenly excited. Everyone, it seemed, now wanted to get into the Tank Corps. All doubts about the course he had chosen melted away. The Tank Corps was hot, and Patton was at the very heart of the flame.

He should have been thrilled. But Patton the romantic warrior was always counterbalanced by Patton the realist. To Beatrice he wrote that everything had to be created from scratch at Langres: "there is nothing to start with nothing but me that is." Over him was a senior officer, Colonel Samuel D. Rockenbach, commander of the entire Tank Service (which was interchangeably also called the Tank Corps). In addition to administering the service, Rockenbach also took charge of indoctrinating U.S. tankers in the hard business of operating the heavy British tanks. Patton was turned loose with orders to create a cadre of American *light* tankers.

On the verge of allowing himself to feel overwhelmed by the task at hand, Patton saved himself by realizing that the first step was to ensure that his students were good soldiers. Make them good soldiers, and they could learn tanks, and making good soldiers was something Patton already knew how to do. Even so, his work was cut out for him. He had made the case to Pershing that light tanks were analogous to cavalry, but the army sent him as his first students not cavalrymen or even infantrymen, but twenty-four Coast Artillery Corps officers. This was not an auspicious crop of candidates. Coast artillery soldiers were essentially garrison troops, trained to man the permanent artillery fortifications that defended the U.S. coasts from an enemy sea attack that never did come. Assigned to tend fixed guns from permanent installations, the officers and men of this branch were the bottom of the army's barrel. Patton did not complain, not even in his diary. Instead, he began teaching his tank course by keeping his students away from the tanks and instilling in them the almighty importance of looking like a soldier, moving like a soldier, and following orders like a soldier. Before you could become a good tanker, you had to be a good soldier. Whereas an infantryman has to be trained to prevail against an enemy, a tanker needed that kind of training in addition to lessons on how to master the machine and prevent it from mastering him. Locked in an iron coffin, bombarded by gunfire, deafened by the roar of the machinery, the tanker could finally rely on one thing and one thing alone: discipline. Every tanker had to be more reliable than the notoriously unreliable machine that carried him. That meant creating a level of discipline enabling "instant, cheerful, unhesitating obedience" to orders. Patton was unremitting in his demands. At the same time, however, he cozied up to the quartermaster to ensure that his soldiers had the most comfortable quarters and best food to be gotten anywhere. If you are going to demand the best from your soldiers, Patton reasoned, you had better treat them like the best.

Having hammered out a unit of disciplined soldiers, Patton set about imparting all that he had (just recently) learned about tanks. In the back of his mind, however, yet another issue lurked. It was one thing to teach the basic operation of tanks, but quite another to present on anything like a thoughtful level strategy, tactics, and doctrine. In 1917, these were very much in flux. Tanks were such new weapons—and, as of yet, only marginally reliable—that there was no consensus on just how they should be handled in combat. As usual, the loudest voices were the most conservative. Infantry commanders strongly believed that the role of the tank was as an infantry support weapon, period. Its use on the battlefield, they insisted, had to be wholly subordinated to the needs of the infantry commander. Issues of doctrine aside, there was a sound technological argument to be made for this approach. Since even the light tanks were relatively slow, they were not especially well suited to operating far in advance of infantry, let alone acting independently from the foot soldiers. Both the machines and the men moved at a walk.

Even at this early stage of his own experience with armor, Patton was persuaded that the future of this arm lay in its eventual independence from the infantry. To be sure, ground operations would have to be coordinated, but it made no sense, as Patton saw it, to force a machine to operate within human constraints in a battle environment. Yet, uncharacteristically, he held his tongue. He understood that most of his colleagues and seniors had little knowledge of and even less interest in tanks. If they thought about them at all, it was to express concern that they would somehow interfere with tried-and-true infantry tactics. In speaking to those outside of the Langres school circle, Patton took care to meekly define the role of the tank as strictly subordinate to infantry. His object was to win support for the tanks from even the most hidebound infantry commander. After enough of the traditionalists had bought into the new weapons system, there would be time to allow the tanks to fully come into their own.

The only question was, would they come into their own before the war was over and done with?

Even as he became increasingly committed to armor, Patton found himself assailed by his own second guessing. He might never get to lead tanks into battle, after all. Suddenly, that seemed like a real possibility. Had he made the conventional choice, had he taken an infantry command after all, he would probably be in combat right now. Yet even as he longed for combat, Patton accepted an appointment to attend the Army General Staff College, a branch of which had been set up with the other schools in Langres. As anxious as he was to get into combat, he was not willing to sacrifice the education that was a prerequisite for command at the strategic level. Even as he fretted that the war was being fought without him, Patton knew he had made the right choice as a professional soldier. His experience at the General Staff College also brought him into contact with George C. Marshall, Adna R. Chaffee, and others who, in the years leading up to World War

II, would come to hold some of the most influential positions in the nation's military.

Even before he graduated from the war-accelerated course of study, Patton became a lieutenant colonel in the National Army. He juggled his teaching duties with his student duties, and continually wondered when, if ever, he would get into combat. Yanks were pouring into France by now, but, back home, American firms were struggling to begin production of battle-worthy tanks. Aware that the Langres school was on the verge of graduating the first class of U.S. tank officers, General Pershing decided that he could no longer afford to wait for American industry to turn out, let alone ship, its first vehicles. Appealing to the French, Pershing secured twenty-five light tanks, which, in August 1918, he turned over to Patton, who now had fifty officers and nine hundred enlisted tankers to man and maintain them. On the twentieth of the month, while he was listening to a General Staff College lecture, a runner approached Patton with a note. Colonel Rockenbach needed to see him—immediately. Patton left the lecture hall and presented himself to his CO. The AEF was slated to make its first major independent offensive of the war at St. Mihiel. Since 1914, the very start of the war, German troops had occupied in the vicinity of this Lorraine town a massive salient that bulged into Allied lines as if it were a malignant growth. This intrusive enemy strongpoint perpetually threatened an attack that could split the Allied lines in two. Repeatedly, the British and French had attempted to reduce the salient, failing each time, and each time incurring substantial losses. Now it would be up to the Yanks to do the job. What is more, Rockenbach added, American-commanded, American-driven tanks would be part of the offensive.

Even Patton had not expected to make the leap from teacher to combat commander so suddenly. On August 24, he formally organized and activated the 304th Tank Brigade, which was alternately (and more accurately) dubbed the 1st Tank Brigade. In preparation for the St. Mihiel operation, the French shipped 225 light tanks to Pershing, of which 144 were earmarked for Patton's brand-new brigade. He fully appreciated that taking delivery of so many machines at one time was no simple task in itself. Accordingly, Patton plotted out every phase of delivery and reception, from unloading at the rail head to deployment at the front. With regard to the latter, he believed that the most critical piece of intelligence he could acquire was the condition of the no-man's land ground that separated the Allied from the German lines. Reports were trickling in that the ground was marshy and probably would not support the weight of the tanks.

Reports? Patton was not about to base his first major operation on secondhand reports. Taking another officer with him, he attached himself to a French night patrol, which sortied some 1,500 yards into no-man's land. "I was out on a patrol in No mans land last week," he wrote Beatrice on September 1. "It was most interesting," he reported, "and not at all exciting." He and the others did what Patton characterized as a "burglar's crawl" for a full mile and a half, creeping right up to the German barbed wire. They were not unobserved. Patton wrote, "the Bosch whistled at us and we whistled back and having seen what we wanted went home. No one shot at us . . . . I picked some dasies for you in the bosch wire and will send them back." More important, Patton had seen for himself that, while the ground was soft, it would surely support light tanks.

Shortly after Patton returned from this hazardous patrol, he learned that higher headquarters had changed the location of the tank operation, thereby obliging him to draw up a whole new plan of attack. If he resented having risked his neck for nothing, he never said as much. The truth is that he was probably grateful for the opportunity to risk death without having actually suffered it. For it was precisely this kind of experience that Patton periodically needed to prove to himself that he had not lost his nerve. With the revised requirements in hand, he set out to reconnoiter the new ground and put together a new plan. Then he turned to the necessary logistics, including the delivery of ten thousand gallons of gasoline for his thirsty machines.

With the attack and logistical plans locked down, Lieutenant Colonel Patton turned to his troops. He ordered their assembly on D-Day minus one, September 11, the day before the operation was to commence. He explained that, tactically speaking, the operation was "easy," but that upon its success depended "the future of the Tank Corps in which all have shown by their long and cheerful work that they are fully interested." He reviewed the mission's key objective, which was to mow down the German wire to make a path for the infantry while also taking out German machine-gun nests. He admonished his crews to get no more than 150 yards ahead of the infantry assault, but also never to allow the infantry to outrun the tanks. As in every battle he would ever lead, his chief admonition was to keep moving and to attack unceasingly. As he pictured it for his men, these most modern of machines were really the old dogs of war, the vicious beasts unleashed by the most ancient of warriors. The men were to drive their dogs without remission:

No tank is to be surrendered or abandoned to the enemy. If you are left alone in the midst of the enemy keep shooting. If your gun is disabled use your pistols and squash the enemy with your tracks. By quick changes of direction cut them with the tail of the tank. If your motor is stalled and your gun broken . . . You hang on, help will come . . . You are the first American tanks [in combat]. You must establish the fact that AMERICAN TANKS DO NOT SURRENDER . . . As long as one tank is able to move it must go forward. Its presence will save the lives of hundreds of infantry and kill many Germans. Finally This is our BIG CHANCE; WHAT WE HAVE WORKED FOR . . . MAKE IT WORTH WHILE.

What seemed to Patton a monumental operation on which the future of American armor depended was, in fact, a small part of a gargantuan offensive that hurled against the Germans more than half a million American soldiers augmented by 110,000 French troops. Pershing's plan was to use the French to harass the Germans from the west while the Americans attacked the southern and western faces of the salient. All of the tanks were used to support the U.S. infantry attack on the southern face of the salient. A French-led armor battalion supported the right of the infantry attack, while Patton's tanks (which included a French battalion under his command) supported the left.

Patton divided his forces into three large elements. He placed under the command of Captain (later Colonel) Sereno Brett an element that would lead the 1st Infantry Division. Patton's French battalion was tasked with following the 1st Division while Captain Ranulf Compton would lead another contingent to trail the 42nd Infantry, then, once positioned opposite the German defenses, would roll through the infantry ranks and assume the lead for the rest of the advance. Brett had the bolder role, but it was also the simpler maneuver. Judging him to be his most aggressive subordinate, Patton was confident in his decision to put him in the vanguard. He was less certain of Compton, who was expected to lead a more complex movement through infantry troops. Patton therefore decided to stay as close as possible to him throughout the assault.

In classic Great War fashion, the offensive was preceded by an intense artillery barrage beginning at one in the morning. At five, the guns fell silent, and the advance began. After starting his units off, Patton withdrew to a hilltop observation post he had prepared. He was in position by 6:10, but lasted there less than twenty minutes. Through his field glasses he saw a number of tanks sink down into the watery trenches. Determined to get them moving again, Patton descended the hill and walked two miles through live fire to personally supervise the extrication of his dogs of war. Along the way, he passed many dead and wounded but, seeing one man apparently comfortably seated in a shell hole holding his rifle, he "thought he was hiding and went to cuss him out." In fact, the soldier "had a bullet over his right eye and was dead."

After getting the stuck tanks moving again, Patton decided against returning to his hilltop observation post. Instead, in company with some of his staff officers, he walked among his dogs, directing them personally and individually in their advance. The tankers had at least a quarter-inch of armor to protect themselves. All Patton had was the crook cane favored as a swagger stick by English officers—that, and a holstered Colt revolver.

When he reached the end of the telephone wire that had been laid, he used motorcycle messengers and runners to maintain a flow of reports from the nose of the attack. At about 9:15, a runner from the 327th Tank Battalion—Compton's tanks—reported to him that they were bogged down in unfavorable terrain. Fearful that Compton lacked the wherewithal to get them moving again, Patton corralled another officer and three runners, then, hunching forward like men in a hailstorm, they walked toward the distressed tanks. Shells burst all around them. "I admit," he recalled later, "that I wanted to duck and probably did at first but soon saw the futility of dodging fate." Besides, it suddenly dawned on him that he was the only officer in the beleaguered vanguard who had not stripped off his shoulder straps, the badges of rank that made so attractive a target for snipers. Patton believed his role was to lead his men. He wanted them to see his shoulder straps, partly so they would know who to follow, but also so that they would see the example of an officer who cheerfully offered himself as a target. Strangely enough, the farther he advanced thus exposed, the better he felt. "It was much easier than you would think," he wrote, "and the feeling, foolish probably, of being admired by the men lying down is a great stimulus."

Near the village of Essey, Patton walked upright among the front-line infantry who were lying down. "As there was only shell fire" as opposed to rifle fire, he walked on, vigorously puffing away at his pipe. Making his way along the firing line of one brigade, he encountered Brigadier General Douglas MacArthur, who was standing unperturbed on a little hill. "I joined him and the creeping barrage came along toward us, but it was very thin and not dangerous." In fact, Patton later mused, "I think each one wanted to leave but each hated to say so, so we let [the barrage] come over us." As nonchalantly as possible, the two men conversed, though Patton guessed that neither of them "was much interested in what the other said as we could not get our minds off the shells."

After the creeping barrage had passed over the little hill, Patton took his leave of MacArthur and advanced to another

rise at which he lingered to observe German troops withdrawing behind Essey. With the town now emptied out, Patton went
in for the kill, ordering five of Compton's tanks to roll into the
village. A French officer rushed up to turn the advancing tanks
back, shouting that the bombardment falling on Essey was
simply too heavy. Patton quickly intervened. Dismissing the
Frenchman, he ordered the tanks to press on and, determined
to lead them, he strolled out in front of the slow-moving vehicles—a shepherd leading his flock, a master driving his dogs.

Patton hesitated ever so slightly at the bridge that led into
the village high street. Might the retreating Germans have lingered long enough to rig it for demolition? That would have
been the logical thing to do. Patton gambled on their not having had the time, and he strode across, the tanks rumbling
behind him.

Behind the tanks came the infantry, and Essey was soon the
property of the U.S. Army. Following his own directive to
keep moving, Patton rounded up the machines that had rolled
into the village and ordered them to drive two more miles to
Pannes. It was a good idea, but Patton had pressed his luck—
or, at least, had exceeded the available supply of gasoline.
Every tank but one ran dry, sputtered, and stopped. Absent
the comforting cover of the Renaults, the infantry stopped just
short of Pannes.

Figuring that the doughboys didn't necessarily need five
tanks but would be content to follow one, Patton trotted up to
the lone vehicle that hadn't run dry and ordered the sergeant
to lead the infantry in. When, unwilling to face the fire alone,
the sergeant hesitated, Patton wasted no more words. Instead,

with rifle fire pouring out from Pannes, he hoisted himself onto the top deck of the tank and pointed his cane in the direction of the village. Flabbergasted by Patton's defiance of shot and shell, the sergeant put the machine into gear, Patton rode it clear through Pannes, and the infantry followed. He clung to the tank until the enemy fire became so thick that bullets began chipping the green paint from off the armor. Amid the rattle and ping of multiple ricochets, Patton finally jumped off and rolled into a convenient shell hole for cover.

He did not stay hunkered down for long. Noting that the reluctant infantry had fallen back some three hundred yards, Patton climbed out of the shell hole and zigzagged through rifle fire back to the infantry. He located the unit commander and demanded that he catch up with the tank, which was still rolling forward. When the ashen-faced officer refused, arguing that there was now too much exposed territory between his men and the lone escort tank, Patton once again put action in place of words. Turning on his heel, he zigzagged back to the lumbering tank and brought his heavy cane down against the back door several times. When the long-suffering, sweating sergeant opened the hatch, Patton ordered him to turn around, head back to the infantry, and cover it. His mission was to support the infantry, and if that meant turning back, that is what he meant to do.

By this time, the four other tanks, having been refueled, appeared. Satisfied that he had followed his orders to support the infantry—even if it was with just one tank—Patton directed the refueled four to continue their advance, without infantry in train. Thus they rolled through Pannes in pure armored assault, which continued into the neighboring village of Beney, Patton trotting along so as to be there when the town fell to the Americans.

Heartened by the performance of Compton's battalion, Patton now felt sufficiently confident in that commander to leave him and hike out to Brett's tanks. He found all of them idled in the town of Nonsard, their fuel spent. *A tanker never leaves his tank* was a maxim Patton had drilled into his students. Unwilling now to take a crewmember out of his tank, Lieutenant Colonel Patton assumed the role of lowly runner and dashed several miles to the rear, where he put in an order for gasoline to be carried up to Nonsard immediately. Since he was close to corps headquarters, he dropped in to file a report stating that all armored units had attained their assigned objectives. In fact, they had slightly outrun the infantry, and Patton ordered them to pull back to the infantry line under cover of darkness.

Day one of the battle had cost two tanks lost to artillery fire. Another three succumbed to engine failure, and two were sidelined with broken tracks. Forty of the small Renaults got hung up in trenches, but were extricated. Thirty ran out of gas, but were duly refueled. When combat resumed the following day, Patton was able to muster 105 operational tanks, and by the end of that day, the Germans were in full retreat. The St. Mihiel salient, an unwelcome Western Front landmark since virtually the start of the war, had been vaporized.

In the end, of the 174 tanks under Patton's command, a total of three fell victim to enemy fire, another twenty-two wrecked (in tankers' parlance, "ditched"), and fourteen suffered catastrophic mechanical failure. Nine tankers were killed in action, fifteen wounded. In the vast St. Mihiel Offensive, Patton's role had been small. Nevertheless, he had demonstrated the effectiveness of the light tank in combat, he had proven himself as a commander, and he gave the newspapers plenty to write about—especially his ride atop the machine, cane at the ready.

He had also given Colonel Rockenbach heartburn. The resolutely conventional commander did not approve of a field-grade officer personally leading an attack. But he couldn't be too hard on Patton, not after General Pershing sent a personal letter of congratulations—a letter Rockenbach knew he owed to Patton.

In any case, Pershing issued his next action directive hard on the heels of St. Mihiel, leaving little time for scolding lectures. The Tank Corps was now tasked to support the next major offensive in which U.S. troops played a big role, Meuse-Argonne. Patton and his tanks were deployed just west of Verdun to support I Corps infantry.

As quickly as Pershing moved, Patton moved even faster. Days before U.S. forces were scheduled to relieve the French in the sector assigned to his tankers, Patton decided to reconnoiter the ground his dogs were to traverse. As at St. Mihiel, he wanted to be certain that he wasn't sending his men into a bog. To avoid standing out in a sea of French soldiers, Patton borrowed a French uniform and, on September 19, "Went to Front line and found trenches not very wide. And ground rather better than I expected." This being the case, he laid out a particularly aggressive attack in which the tanks would do more than merely support the infantry. He aimed to make a narrow, violent thrust directly through the heavily fortified German lines, which extended to a depth of a dozen miles. After this breakthrough had been completed, the tanks would re-form as the pointy end of the spear, leading a massive infantry pursuit of the retreating Germans. Patton had fewer tanks to work with than at St. Mihiel—140—which he divided into two battalions, plus a group of French-crewed tanks. In a letter written on the eve of the battle, Patton told Beatrice that he was about "to play a little part in what promises to be the biggest battle of the war or the world so far."

As at St. Mihiel, the usual "artillery preparation" preceded the attack beginning at 2:30 in the morning of September 26. After a massive three-hour barrage, the troops and the tanks began their advance. A dense autumn mist hugged the battlefield, serving to screen the tanks from the enemy, but also making it impossible for Patton to direct the operation from his observation post. Rockenbach had warned him about leaving his OP to lead in the field, but he simply could not see; therefore, laying hands on two officers and a detachment of about twelve runners, he marched through the mist. As a helmsman follows the sound of the foghorn in a pea-souper at sea, so Patton followed the rattle of machine guns and the crack of rifle fire.

He was thrilled to find that his tanks had already advanced about five miles in a remarkably short time, but when he reached the village of Cheppy at about nine in the morning, he was overrun by retreating doughboys wide-eyed with panic. Under heavy fire, they were making for the rear—until Patton stopped them, re-formed them, and rallied them with a promise that he would personally take them to the advancing tanks, which would cover them through the rest of the advance.

The men responded, but then, looking ahead, Patton saw a large number of his tanks hung up across trenches. The newfound courage of the men he had rallied, Patton knew, would have a short shelf life. It was critically important to get those tanks moving again, and so he sent some men forward with orders to do just that.

As the mist burned off in the morning sun, Patton peered through his field glasses. The tanks remained motionless. Taking the binoculars from his eyes, he announced that he was going to find out what the problem was. He walked briskly toward Cheppy and instantly sized up the situation.

The men he had sent pitched in with the tankers to dig the vehicles out, but every time they began working in earnest the scream of an incoming shell or the spasmodic burst of machine-gun fire would send everyone scrambling for cover. At this rate, Patton realized, the tanks would never be dug out. His first step was to organize the men into efficient work parties, then, after personally unstrapping the shovels from the tanks, he distributed them, making a great show of standing up to the rifle and machine-gun fire that ricocheted wildly off the tank hulls.

Following Patton's example, the men dug furiously, now seemingly oblivious to the artillery fire, but for a lone doughboy who remained frozen in fear. Patton awakened the man to his duty by means of a sharp shovel blow to his helmeted head. In no time, the tanks were moving, and once they got going, Patton lofted his cane, swinging it over his head in circles of widening circumference as he called out to the infantry: "Let's go get them." Pausing a beat, he continued, "Who is with me?"

Clustered around five tanks, Patton and his men advanced. Ahead was a gentle hill, but, gentle or not, every hill hid what was behind it. Sure enough, as he and the men nearest him crested the rise, machine-gun fire opened up on them from what seemed every direction.

George S. Patton Jr. was terrified. That fact shocked him, and, as he trembled, there was no escaping that fact. He was afraid, and he wanted to run. The urge coursed through him in a great rush of desire. Run, run, *run!*

That is when, looming "in a cloud over the German lines," he saw his "progenitors," the fallen Pattons of the Confederacy, the names he had heard ever since infancy, the faces he had seen time and again in old daguerreotypes and tintypes. With this vision, the trembling stopped. The desire to run, so powerful just an instant earlier, melted away. Aloud, he said: "It is time for another Patton to die." Much louder, he called out: "Let's go."

Of the six or so soldiers within hearing of his call, all rose to advance, and all were cut down. Joe Angelo, Patton's orderly, was still unhurt.

"We are alone," he remarked, stunned into matter-of-factness.

Quietly, Patton replied: "Come on anyway."

And that is when the machine-gun round ripped into his left thigh. It tunneled through flesh, fat, and muscle, finding its way out near the rectum. It brought Patton down, hard.

Angelo laid a heavy hand on Patton's uniform, grabbing it up in a large bunch and using it as a handle to pull him into a shell hole. There, the orderly hurriedly cut away his trousers, pulled a field dressing from his pack, and bandaged the wound as tightly as he could. The blood flowed rather than pulsed. That meant the bullet had torn a vein or two, but not an artery, and thanks to the tight bandage, the flow soon eased to an ooze.

Satisfied that he wouldn't bleed to death anytime soon, Patton ordered Angelo to run toward the tanks approaching and direct their fire against the machine-gun nests.

The orderly did as he was told, the tanks opened up on the German positions, and the enemy machine guns fell silent. A tanker sergeant ran back with Angelo to the wounded lieutenant colonel. Patton told him to go find Brett, to tell him he had been hit, and to pass the word to Brett that he was now in command. Before dismissing the sergeant, Patton cautioned him to hold off sending stretcher bearers to pick him up—at least until more of the enemy fire had been suppressed. To Angelo, he reeled off a series of targets for the still-advancing tanks. He told his orderly to start those tanks firing against them.

At least an hour passed before a medic finally came to Patton. The wounded man asked him to change his bandage, but then insisted that he tend to the more seriously hurt first. Another hour went by before it was feasible for stretcher bearers to fetch him. Three men trundled Patton two bone-shattering miles to an ambulance. Even then, Patton ordered the driver to take a detour to division headquarters. He wanted to make his report before continuing on to the evacuation hospital.

It was as if Patton did not want his ordeal to end. The wound was as grand a thing as the battle had been, and he wanted, it seemed, to savor it. Perhaps he also wanted others to see that he had been hit. In either case, it was the closing act of this particular drama, and as any actor knows, you don't rush your lines just before the curtain comes down.

His exploits had put him in the newspapers again: VALIANT YOUNG COLONEL BLEEDS IN A SHELL HOLE. The papers were full of such stories. For a time.

While he convalesced, promotion to full colonel came through. "Peace looks possible," he wrote Beatrice from his hospital bed, "but I rather hope not for I would like to have a few more fights." It was the end of October before he was released. At the Meuse-Argonne, the battle continued without him. Before long, his thirty-third birthday rolled around: November 11, 1918. On the eleventh hour of that day, the guns, as all the histories record, fell silent. It was not a welcome birthday present.

Patton had become a warrior in Mexico and a combat commander in France—a combat commander compounded of chivalry, an atavistic thirst for bloody glory, a mastery of fear, a genuine feel for the technology of combat, and the emergence of the first stirrings of tactical brilliance. He was made for war. He was ready for war. The twenty-three years he would have to wait for another war would very nearly kill him.

PATTON IN HELL

Behold yon statue picturing

A hero slane in strife!

And then in pity gaze upon

That comrade still in life.

The one a glorious super-man,

Replete with life and fire,

The other a poor doddering wrathe,

A witch light in the mire.

—George S. Patton Jr., from
"Anti-Climax," May 30, 1922

Twice—maybe—it could all be blamed on a horse. At least that was how the family wanted to see it. The first time was in Hawaii, during the 1936 Inter-Island Polo Games. Lieutenant Colonel George S. Patton Jr. was G-2, chief of intelligence, for the army's Hawaiian Division, headquartered in Honolulu. Ever since his cadet days at West Point, Patton had been not so much an avid polo player as a thoroughly savage one.

As with everything having to do with men on horseback, this cavalry officer played the game with a lethal seriousness that was driven by at least two linked motives. The first was ostensibly military. Back in the fall of 1922, Patton had published a paper titled "Polo in the Army," in which he argued that, "from the standpoint of the Army officer, polo is not simply a game, it is a vital professional asset . . . it is the nearest approach to mounted combat which can be secured in peace. . . ." That the "physical hazards" presented by polo were both "constant and real," Patton counted as invaluable experience for the army officer-player, for "talk as we will of the necessity for cold judgment in combat it is none the less a fact that no man can stay cool in battle unless he is habituated to the exhilarating sense of physical peril." In a second paper, "Army Polo. (No. 2)," written at the same time, Patton elaborated on the "element of personal risk," judging it "not a drawback but a decided advantage. No matter how brave a man may be he is none the less a creature of habit. If his most lethal experience prior to battle has consisted of dodging automobiles on city streets the insinuating whisper of bullets about his sacred person will have more disquieting influence on him than would be the case had his same person received a few cuts and broken bones on the polo fields." And if this "last statement seems a trifle harsh . . . such is the nature of truth." Patton argued that "The War Department . . . in encouraging polo is doing a very economical thing," because the faculty of "quick decision while engaged in rapid movement under the disconcerting influence of profuse perspiration resulting from vigorous exercise" was precisely what war demanded, and "Such practice is not acquired behind the steering wheel, at golf or while riding at a walk."

Then there was the second, more personal, motive. "Do not take counsel of your fears" was always a favorite maxim of Patton. It is a most revealing expression. It does not brashly proclaim fearlessness; quite the opposite—it admits to fear. Nor does it suggest ignoring the existence of fear. Rather, it is a bid to defeat fear by refusing to heed its commands. Of all the enemies Patton faced, fear was both the most familiar to him and the most formidable. Paul Robinett, who served under him when Patton commanded the 3rd Cavalry at Fort Myer, Virginia, in 1938–1940, recalled that, one day, after playing polo, Patton brought his horse into the fort's indoor riding hall to practice for a scheduled steeplechase-style exhibition ride. Robinett watched as his CO rode the horse toward a post-and-rail jump. When the mount faltered, hesitated, and showed signs of refusing the jump, Patton dug in with his spurs and brought down his riding crop, hard. This was sufficient to prompt the horse to jump, but too late. The horse hit the upper bar with his knee and fell, catapulting Patton out of the saddle and onto his head. Fortunately, the rider was still wearing his polo helmet and, after shaking off the impact, swore mightily at the animal, remounted him, then forced him over the jump—successfully—time and time again. Dismounting at last, he walked over to Robinett.

"Do you know why I made my horse take those jumps?"

A wide-eyed Robinett replied that he imagined it was to instill discipline in the animal.

"Not at all. I did it just to prove to myself that I am not a coward."

It was in precisely this spirit that George S. Patton Jr. played a polo match or fought a war—when, that is, fortune smiled on him by furnishing a war to fight. But there was no war in 1936, and polo, especially the Inter-Island Games, was the next best thing—second best, to be sure, a very distant second.

Patton had seen war. He had led men in what he liked to call "desperate battle," and he had been victorious. Maybe most important of all, he had been wounded in war. His first experience in combat came during the Punitive Expedition against Pancho Villa in 1916–1917, and his next, hard on the heels of the first, was in the Great War, in 1918. He was in his early thirties back then, six feet tall, handsome in a becoming military manner, with an athlete's body, his strong-jawed visage already set in the slightly frowning mask he himself dubbed his "war face," a look he practiced religiously in front of a mirror, like an actor preparing for a part he hoped would never end. If Patton had a gripe back then, it was only that his baptism of fire had not come even earlier. Still, he could count himself lucky. He'd had his moment of glory.

By 1936, it must have seemed to him to have been no more than the distant blink of an eye. It had been a mere span of months a long time ago, a whetting of an appetite for combat rather than its satisfaction. Chasing Pancho Villa in Mexico and fighting the Germans in France were, Patton felt, no more than a fitting overture to what he hoped would be a lifetime of war. But the dream of such a lifetime ended, on November 11, 1918, and what followed could only be described as a long, empty anticlimax. In 1936, Lieutenant Colonel George S. Patton Jr. was fifty-one, his body no longer quite as hard—though his "war face" harder than ever—a middle-aged soldier without a war, an officer in a shrunken army belonging to an isolationist, pacifist nation bent on absolute neutrality.

So the fifty-one-year-old resolved to ride, to play polo—to *fight* a match—and to do it like a man half his age. In a scrimmage preparatory to the Inter-Island Games, he rode with an abandon far in excess of what this practice called for. It was too much even for his pony, which suddenly came up short, hurling Patton to the ground—once again hard on his head.

To those looking on, it was apparent that he was badly dazed, but, lying in the grass, he angrily waved off all offers of assistance, struggled to his feet, remounted, and finished the practice scrimmage. Only afterward did he consult a doctor, who, learning that Patton had immediately resumed play, made a cursory examination, and diagnosed nothing more serious than a mild concussion. That evening, Patton did what he and his wife, Beatrice, often did during the languid evenings among Honolulu's wealthy and prominent. With her, he attended a cocktail party, and, the next morning, boarded their forty-foot schooner, *Arcturus,* for a weekend of sailing. It was a pleasant weekend on the water, all the more so because it took place during a tense and dreary period marked by very little that was pleasant between Patton and his wife of twenty-five years. But the weekend came to a close late on Sunday, with Patton helming *Arcturus* toward the yacht harbor. He turned to Beatrice and asked, quite matter of factly, "Where the hell am I?" Then he went on to explain, "The last thing I remember is seeing the ground come up and hit my face!"

Those who saw Patton in World War I and even on the front lines in World War II were convinced that the man conducted himself in battle in a way that simultaneously invited and defied injury or death. The fact was that he engaged in practically everything he did the same way. Polo? He played it like a man who wanted to get hurt, and that spill in 1936 was just one in a thick catalogue of injuries Patton sustained during the years. Preserved in Patton's papers is a record of a physical exam conducted by army surgeons in 1925. At that time, the physicians noted fractures of the radius and ulna, just below the right elbow joint, and a fractured nose, all sustained in 1905; a dislocation of the left ankle (1906); a fracture of the left radius, a fractured nose, and one fractured rib (1907); a fracture of the third right metacarpal (1910); the onset of prepatellar bursitis—a bum knee (1911); a five-inch laceration at the top of the skull, requiring sixteen stitches (1912); a concussion with partial paralysis of the right arm (1914); a lacerating head wound, requiring five stitches (1915); a lacerating wound over the left eyebrow, requiring three stitches, plus second-degree burns of the head and neck and third-degree burns of the ears (1916); a lacerating wound on the right side of the neck and over the right eye (1917); a penetrating gunshot wound in the left thigh (this was Patton's major war wound, sustained in 1918); a fracture of the left pubic arch (1921); a lacerating head wound requiring two stitches, along with a penetrating laceration of the upper lip (1922); two rib fractures, a sprained knee, and a lacerating head wound requiring three stitches (1924).

To label Patton as accident prone would be an understatement, even for one who drove himself to the limits of physical endurance. Yet, to those who knew Patton most intimately, there seemed to be something very different about the head injury he suffered in 1936. Popular mythology paints General Patton as a hard drinker. In fact, most of his life, he was a moderate drinker, the kind people used to call a "social drinker," a man who never seemed to be drunk. His daughter Ruth Ellen wrote that the blow to his head in 1936 dramatically "cut down his capacity to carry alcohol and whereas he had never shown his liquor his whole life, just a couple of drinks would make him quite tight." After the 1936 accident, Beatrice Patton was frequently worried and embarrassed by the displays of her husband's obvious drunkenness, and although she made it a practice (according to Ruth Ellen) never to criticize him, even in private, she did express her displeasure over his drinking at this time. "That," Ruth Ellen recalled, "upset him and he got very disagreeable." By way of response, "he would take an extra drink while she was looking at him; just to 'show her.'"

And when he was drunk—at least following the 1936 accident—he was no fun. "He did not appear well," Ruth Ellen observed. "He got tearful and sentimental; recited poetry out of place and context and picked on Ma." What was most painful to his daughter was seeing "feet of clay where the winged heels once were."

The drinking and drunkenness would remain a problem for some time to come—at least until he finally went off to war again. There was, however, a more immediate and startling episode of bad behavior. Having apparently shaken off the head injury incurred during practice scrimmage, Patton, as captain of the army team, entered the Inter-Island Games, which were a weeklong polo extravaganza that attracted the upper crust of Hawaiian high society. The army team faced off against the Oahu team, which was captained by Walter Dillingham, a close friend of the Pattons. In attendance was an audience of Hawaii's civilian and military elite, including General Hugh Drum, commanding officer of the army's Hawaiian Department.

Patton's play was, as usual, utterly savage. In itself, that was not unacceptable; indeed, it probably thrilled spectators and teammates alike. It was, however, when the savagery crossed over into the ungentlemanly that Patton got into trouble. The ponies slammed into one another in a species of combat that would have been familiar to Genghis Khan, and the pounding violence was accompanied by a string of shouted curses readily identifiable as Patton's own. Whether they liked him or not, all who served with Patton remarked on his extraordinary "command presence," the military phrase used to describe officers who, by their very physical being and demeanor exude the aura of authority and inspiration. Obviously, his "war face" and strapping six-foot frame contributed to his command presence, but what was more remarkable was that his voice did not totally undermine it. Incongruously high-pitched, strained, even whiny, it fit neither the body nor the man from which it emanated. But it was distinctive, and it unmistakably marked as exclusively Patton's the stream of expletives that sprayed over the match that day. The crude language must have been distasteful enough to the ladies and gentlemen watching the match, but it finally and irretrievably crossed the line when Patton fiercely charged after Dillingham, seeking to ride him off.

"Why you old son of a bitch," he screeched, "I'll ride you right down Front Street."

At this, General Drum rose from his box seat and shouted an order to suspend the match. He motioned for Patton to approach.

Patton rode up to Drum, dismounted, and, before everyone assembled, faced his commanding officer. As he stood there, what were his thoughts in the moment before the notoriously proper and humorless Drum opened his mouth to speak? For as long as he could remember, George S. Patton Jr. had burned with a thirst for martial glory. "I am different from other men my age," Cadet Patton wrote to his parents in 1909. "All they want to do is live happily and die old. I would be willing to live in torture, die tomorrow if for one day I could be really great." Even at this young age, the conviction was not novel for him. As he wrote to his father at the beginning of his West Point career, "I belong to a different class," a class as far removed from the ordinary American soldier "as heaven is from hell."

Convinced from an early age that he was a man apart, Patton nevertheless understood that the fulfillment of his "destiny," the slaking of his thirst for glory—a real, urgent, utterly physical thirst—required the tribute of cheers from the crowd, especially the kind of crowd assembled on the polo field that day. Instead, now standing beside his mount before those very people, he listened as Drum's voice finally boomed, stiff, angry, and loud enough for everyone around to hear each word. Drum shamed Patton for his profanity and, far worse, for what he called conduct unbecoming an officer and gentleman. Drum told Patton that he was, then and there, relieving him as captain of the army team "for using offensive language in front of the ladies and insulting your competitors." Then he drove the dagger home: "You will leave the field at once."

From the spectators, there were neither cheers nor jeers. Just a stunned, dead silence, made all the deader by contrast with the pounding, shrieking cacophony that had preceded it.

Patton braced to attention.

"Yes, sir."

With that, he saluted his commanding officer and slowly led his pony from the field.

What happened next was almost even worse for Patton. Dillingham, together with Frank Baldwin, captain of the Maui team, approached Drum, and asked if he had indeed relieved Patton. When the general answered in the affirmative, Dillingham turned to Drum and declared, loudly enough for the spectators to hear, that this would mean the end of polo for the rest of the year. Fixing his eyes on Drum, he declared that he would immediately lead his own team off the field and end the tournament right there and then.

Hugh Drum was the most powerful military figure in Hawaii. Dillingham and Baldwin were among the most prominent civilians in the territory. The last thing Patton wanted was to trigger a showdown between army authority and civilian influence. Yet that is precisely what he had done. For his part, Drum had no desire to be seen as responsible for ruining the most important social event of the season. Both personally and professionally, it was crucial that he maintain good relations between the army and the islanders. He therefore called Patton back, issued a stern warning that he mind his language henceforth, then restored to him the captaincy of the team. Having done this, he summoned the members of his family, packed them into his automobile, and drove off the field.

Even in wartime, of course, Patton would be notorious for his profanity and impulsive behavior, both of which would repeatedly put his command in jeopardy. But in wartime, his outrageous words and actions might be seen and excused as the excesses of a consummate warrior, whereas, in peace— the peace Patton openly loathed—these things were simply offensive, irrational, unacceptable, and, to Patton, deeply humiliating. His family ascribed much of his behavior to his injuries, especially the repeated blows to the head, and as serious as his 1936 riding accident was, there was indeed worse to come.

In 1937, Patton left Hawaii for a new assignment as executive officer of the 9th Cavalry and the Academic Division of the Cavalry School at Fort Riley, Kansas, an assignment that heralded promotion from lieutenant colonel to colonel in the regular army, the highest rank he had held in the wartime National Army. Before taking up his new duties, he was given an extended leave, part of which he spent at the palatial Massachusetts home of his wife's family. On July 25, he was riding with Beatrice and their son-in-law, Johnnie Waters. Patton later said that he had entered what he himself called the "danger zone"—drawing the head of his horse even with the stirrups of Beatrice's mount. The veteran cavalryman was well aware of this "danger zone," and he made it a point to warn both his subordinates and the civilian friends he rode with that, of all the risky things one might do on horseback, straying into it was the most dangerous and the most foolhardy, especially during the horsefly season, when an animal was likely to kick unpredictably at a marauding insect.

And that is precisely what occurred. The hind leg of Memorial, Beatrice's horse, suddenly flared out, its shod hoof crashing into Patton's lower leg. Later he said that he distinctly heard the sound of "a dry stick snapping." It was a fracture so severe that thrombophlebitis instantly set in, sending clots into Patton's bloodstream. He was rushed to the hospital, where his physician reported that an embolism had come within seconds of ending his life. The stricken man did slip into unconsciousness, a state, however, that was for him no black void. Instead, as he later recounted, he became aware of having fallen on a battlefield and was lying on a Viking shield, borne up by a pair of Norsemen arrayed in cloaks and armor and bound for Valhalla, the heavenly reward that awaits all true warriors. But then one of the bearers shook his head no, the shield was lowered to the ground, and Patton awoke to the reality of his hospital bed.

He was not dead, not yet, but he would soon often find himself wishing he were. In 1937, there were no effective anticoagulant drugs to combat phlebitis, and antibiotics were all but unknown. There was, in fact, no medical treatment for Patton's injury other than to set the fracture and immobilize the patient in bed for a long, long time. Complications, possibly resulting in amputation or even death, were an ever-present possibility, and even if nothing so dire occurred, it seemed highly likely that the long-term effects of the injury would end Patton's military career. This was all the worse because, with the deteriorating situation in a Europe menaced by Hitler, Mussolini, and Stalin, a new war was at long last looking to be practically inevitable. Would he miss it?

The army certainly was not sympathetic. Although the accident had occurred while Patton was off duty and, indeed, on leave between assignments, an ad hoc board was convened to investigate whether he had been drunk or otherwise intoxicated at the time of the incident. The board duly exonerated him, but the fact that it had been convened in the first place suggests the pervasiveness of Patton's reputation as a hard drinker and, worse, a habitual drunk.

Presumably, the board members did not visit Patton in his hospital room, at least not when the liquor was flowing—as it did—in abundance. The invalid staged a show of raucously stoic festivity before a stream of well wishers. Fortified by drink, he regaled those visitors as well as fellow patients and even nurses with crude, often downright obscene jokes.

Beatrice Patton saw through the façade, recognizing that her husband was actually sinking into a deepening depression. Perhaps acknowledging that her mere presence and concern were no longer sufficient in themselves to rally her man, she searched for something else to cheer him up.

Back in the spring of 1935, when he received his orders to report for duty in Hawaii, Patton announced to Beatrice that he would rather die than consign himself to life as a nonentity, and, applying his own rather bizarre logic, he converted this into a decision to purchase the schooner *Arcturus*, which he intended to sail the nearly 2,500 miles from San Diego to Hawaii. His original impulse had been to go it alone, but Beatrice insisted that she would not let her husband "drown without her." The pair was joined by four additional amateur crewmembers and one seasoned sailor. Patton had taken cram courses in celestial navigation, but it could hardly have inspired Beatrice with confidence when he turned to her, as they left port, with a rhetorical question: "We can learn, can't we?"

Beatrice never complained about that voyage, in which Patton took her life, his, and those of the others in his hands for the sake of the thrill of making a spectacular crossing to his new

261

assignment. She was violently seasick throughout the fifteen-day passage, which, however, was a cakewalk compared with their return voyage from Hawaii to San Diego in June 1937. On that trip, *Arcturus* was caught in a bad storm and limped into San Diego with major damage. "Captain" Patton and his crew, Beatrice included, were very lucky to be alive. But whatever fears and doubts she may have had, she now reminded her husband, languishing in the hospital, of how they had talked airily back then of building a new, bigger schooner, a kind of dreamboat. Even as they voyaged out to Hawaii in 1935, she and Patton had kept a journal of the passage, headed "When and If We Ever Build a Boat." The title had been suggested by Patton's remark that the boat would be built *"When* the next war is over, *and if* I live through it." Beatrice now decided that her suffering husband—and her suffering self—could afford to wait no longer. She called in John G. Alden, the world's most celebrated marine architect specializing in yachts, and asked him to work with Patton on designing a new yacht to be christened the *When and If.*

The collaboration did cheer him, at least for a time, and the result, launched in 1939, was a sixty-five-foot craft displacing forty-three tons and sporting 1,700 square feet of sail. It could comfortably accommodate seven—and even more on short hops. As it was being built, Patton dreamed of sailing the *When and If* around the world, but he had more immediate business to take care of first. After his release from the hospital and having recovered sufficiently to hobble about on crutches, he resolved to punish the horse that had injured him. What unfolded was beyond ugly. He stumped out to the stable, confronted Memorial, cursed him wildly, then began beating the animal with one of his crutches, vowing that he would not stop until he had beaten him to death. A stable hand intervened, and Beatrice exploded, telling him that only a child would blame an animal for an accident that he himself had admitted was entirely his fault. Patton was unrepentant. Growling at Beatrice, he complained that one of the very few pleasures he could still contemplate in his miserable life was to kill her horse.

He may have had more motive for his equinicidal thoughts than mere vengeance. Lately, Beatrice had been spending more time with Memorial than she did with him, riding the horse at every opportunity. Patton felt—probably quite correctly—that she was trying to get away from him. To be sure, she had nursed her husband faithfully during his hospital convalescence and well beyond, but he showed little to no gratitude and was often brutally confrontational. It got so that she would deputize her daughters to visit their father daily, who lay for hours brooding in a porch hammock. It was a mission the girls dreaded, and they took to drawing straws to decide which one would be sacrificed this time.

The family blamed the increasing darkness of his mood on the lingering effects of his latest injury. Yet it seems clear that his irrationality went beyond what might be expected even of an active man forced to endure a long, confining convalescence. To his thirst for alcohol was added a voracious appetite for sugary snacks. If Patton was, at least periodically, an alcoholic, so he was, during these same periods, addicted to sugar, a substance closely resembling alcohol biochemically, save for a single molecule. Patton would gorge on fruitcake, whole, or consume several boxes of candy at a sitting. Such was his compulsion that he more than once made himself so acutely sick that the only remedy was a trip to the hospital for a stomach pumping. Increasingly ashamed of his sugar habit, he took to stealth and would carefully unwrap filled chocolates, suck the filling from them, then delicately rewrap the hollowed-out chocolate shells and return them neatly to their boxes, presumably to be consumed by some unsuspecting family member.

Binging, drinking, and boozy sentimentality became a way of life. The approach of a birthday created an agony of emotion and a torrent of tears. Some of his outbursts were downright comical, as when, disturbed by the sound of a military band, he hollered out his window, "Quit playing that goddamn music!" The "goddamn music" was "The Star Spangled Banner."

More often, the behavior was sad, humiliating, and even grotesque. When one of the family's favorite horses came up lame, Patton proclaimed that the animal deserved better than to be injected with poison by some anonymous vet, and he announced that he would shoot the horse himself: a hero's death. His son, George, watched as his father took aim, fired—and succeeded only in wounding an animal that was already writhing in agony. Weeping uncontrollably, Patton tried to hold the struggling horse with one hand while endeavoring to get into position to administer the coup de grace. At last, he gave up and ran from the stable, leaving a groom to finish the grisly work he had begun. Patton holed up behind the closed door of his bedroom for the rest of the day and night.

On February 2, 1938, he was at last pronounced sufficiently recovered to assume his new assignment at Fort Riley. This did for him what neither Beatrice nor any other member of his family could. He suddenly felt much better. His promotion to full colonel on July 1 helped as well, and, days after the promotion, he was transferred from Fort Riley, Kansas, to Fort Clark, Texas, as commanding officer of the 5th Cavalry Regiment. Located near the border town of Eagle Pass, Fort Clark put Patton in mind of his early glory riding with

General Pershing in pursuit of Villa. Never mind that it was a dirty, dusty backwater outpost, Patton reveled in the assignment and did not hesitate to shake up the cavalrymen under him. He started training them for war—a brutally rapid war, he said, in which machines, not horses, would play a leading role. He, for one, looked forward to it, and they had better get into shape to fight it.

Training men for war, making them hard and smart—that was halfway to war itself and proved a strong tonic for Patton. But his deliciously violent Texas idyll was shattered all too soon. In December 1938, he received word that he was being transferred yet again, this time to Fort Myer as commanding officer of the 3rd Cavalry. Most officers would have greeted the news with a cheer or even a prayer of gratitude. If Fort Clark was an assignment to nowhere, Fort Myer, Virginia, as Patton knew from firsthand experience, was a beautiful setting for an urbane military life, full of high-level social gatherings that outdid even Hawaii. Indeed, that was the very reason for Patton's reassignment. The officer he was replacing, Jonathan Wainwright, had to support himself and his family on nothing more than his colonel's pay, and he simply could not afford to meet the many social obligations imposed by life at Fort Myer. The War Department took pity on Wainwright and, knowing that Patton was independently wealthy and knew Fort Myer well, called him in. In truth, his wealth was not entirely independent. The bulk of his fortune came from his wife, and, devastated now by his cruel translation from the rough-and-ready soldiering of Texas to the mostly ceremonial world of Myer, he leveled bitter curses on Beatrice, accusing her and her "goddamn money" of having ruined his career.

This accusation was very nearly the proverbial last straw for the Patton marriage. Not that it hadn't already survived worse. Beginning in the 1920s and continuing year after year, Patton fell into the habit of repeatedly embarrassing Beatrice with displays of foul language, calculated insults aimed at her sister Kay Merrill and her husband, and even by his adolescent insistence that certain women view the wound he had sustained leading the tank assault at Cheppy in the Great War, a gunshot to the upper left thigh, which "came out just at the crack of my bottom about two inches to left of my rectum." But his marital outrages came to a head in the mid 1930s, in Hawaii. To everything else he had dragged into his marriage, he now added infidelity. Biographer Martin Blumenson wrote of his engaging "in casual affairs," presumably more than a few, but at least one was far more than casual.

In 1936—the year of Patton's polo injury and his humiliation at the Inter-Island Games—Jean Gordon arrived in Honolulu. Twenty-one years old, the daughter of Beatrice's half-sister, Louise Raynor Ayer, she was the best friend of the Pattons' daughter, Ruth Ellen. Jean Gordon was also a vivacious beauty of singular charm and intellect, and when she visited Ruth Ellen on her way to a tour of Asia, she made no attempt to hide her spontaneous attraction to George Patton, despite his being, after all, her half-uncle as well as the father of her closest friend. For his part, Patton melted to her. To a man who felt himself oozing helplessly into middle age, the attentions of this fresh beauty proved irresistible.

At first, Beatrice paid no notice to what was going on, whether through obtuseness or through a conscious act of will. According to other members of the family and to friends, the pair made no serious attempt to conceal their feelings for one another, yet when Patton invited Jean to accompany him, alone, on a horse-buying excursion to one of the other Hawaiian islands, Beatrice raised no objection. Perhaps she had simply decided to bide her time, knowing that Jean would soon be leaving for Japan. But when the longed-for day of departure finally arrived, the spectacle of Patton adoringly adorning his niece and lover with lei upon lei—the traditional significance of which, when presented on departure, was a wish for a speedy return—was nearly too much for her.

"It's lucky for us that I don't have a mother," she confided to Ruth Ellen, "because, if I did, I'd pack up and go home to her now."

But Beatrice Patton decided that, despite everything, her husband needed her—and really did love her—and so she stayed with him. She stoically endured the rest of Patton's Hawaiian duty and his assignments to Forts Riley and Clark, but, shortly after arriving at Fort Myer in December 1938, she was felled by what army physicians diagnosed as renal colic, a pain associated with kidney stones, which came on in spasmodic waves, sometimes as a series of unrelenting dull aches, other times in sharp agonies far more excruciating. Patton responded not with a show of strength, a pledge to a reform, or a demonstration of sympathy, but by collapsing himself. He suffered a kind of nervous breakdown, which, whatever else it did, served to draw the ministrations of the army doctors away from Beatrice and to himself. Even in illness, he could not bear to let anyone else occupy center stage.

Flailing in the gloom, Patton meted out his misery to those closest to him. His family might blame their collective troubles on his injuries, and, to be sure, his wounds contributed to his depression, but, almost certainly, his many accidents were symptoms of his mental and spiritual malaise more than they were contributing causes. Peace was George Patton's long winter of discontent.

As we saw in Chapter 8, much of the Pershing Punitive Expedition was so much tedious marching and fruitless pursuit, but, in May 1916, Patton fought his maiden battle, a spectacular shootout with Villistas at the Rubio Ranch (Chapter 9), and drank deep of what was for him the delicious springtime that was war and thoughts of war.

The newspapers brimmed with this exploit of the dashing young lieutenant, and, better yet, a much bigger war was just around the corner.

In 1916, President Woodrow Wilson gained election to a second term largely on the slogan "He Kept Us Out of War." The conflagration, which Americans called the "European War" and the rest of the world the "Great War," had broken out in the summer of 1914, and Wilson had studiously steered a neutral course. The Punitive Expedition ended just weeks before April 4, 1917, when the peace president asked Congress for a declaration of war so as to make the world "safe for democracy."

When his CO, John J. Pershing, was named to command the American Expeditionary Force and headed off to France, Patton, promoted to captain and appointed commanding officer of the AEF's Headquarters Troop, sailed with him on May 28, 1917. Thrilled to be among the very first U.S. soldiers in Europe, Patton also knew that he would never see combat as the captain in charge of a headquarters outfit, and in October he sought and received a transfer to the U.S. Army's embryonic Tank Service. Thus the anachronistic warrior, cavalryman, and swordsman, became the American military's premier practitioner of mechanized warfare, twentieth-century warfare, warfare at the cutting edge.

As told in Chapter 10, Patton led his tanks personally, walking ahead of them, deliberately exposing himself to fire, and receiving a severe wound, a wound, he believed, that betokened an even greater destiny to come. But, as Patton lay in the hospital recovering, September became October and October November, the eleventh month, which advanced to the eleventh day and the eleventh hour of that day, the hour at which the shooting stopped. The Great War ended, and George Smith Patton Jr. saw his destiny deferred.

Fulfillment turned to anticlimax. How long before the next war? How long this winter of discontent that passed for peace? Far worse to contemplate, would there even be another war?

Patton was indeed like a character out of Shakespeare—not the tragic civilian hero Hamlet, but one of the tragic military heroes, a Caesar, Titus Andronicus, Othello, one of the captains on whom a people call when they are menaced by force of arms but whom the people shun, fear, and loathe after they have been saved and want only to live in peace. Like the military heroes of Shakespeare, Patton could find no place and therefore no peace in a nation without war.

Thus, year after year, from 1919 on, the middle-aging warrior fell deeper into depression and self-destruction, embarking as well on a course of outrageous—literally antisocial—behavior. Drink, women, polo, all might soften the dullness of despair momentarily, but as for a cure, one and only one remedy was sovereign.

On September 1, 1939, the second world war of the twentieth century began as Adolf Hitler's land and air forces blasted across the Polish border. As a new "European war" raged, the army promoted Patton to brigadier general in September 1940. With spelling as idiosyncratic as everything else about him, he wrote on September 30 to his friend Terry de la Mesa Allen, who had also been promoted: "Haveing made us, all that is now needed is a nice juicy war." And on December 20, 1941, that war having come to the United States at Pearl Harbor less than two weeks earlier, Patton assembled the members of his command at the time, the 2nd Armored Division.

"At all times we have been preparing for war," he told them, but he might as well have been talking to himself, of himself.

On that December day, he addressed his remarks in particular to those who "have not been fortunate enough to have engaged in combat," admonishing them to ignore the "foolish writings of sob-sisters and tear-jerkers" who write of "men— imaginary men—who on the eve of battle sit around the camp fire and discuss their mothers, and their sisters, and their sweethearts, and talk regretfully of their past life and fear foolishly for their future." No, Patton told his men, "the night before battle you do not sit around a fire. . . . You go to sleep and have to be kicked in the butt in the morning so as to start the war. You have not dreamed of dying or worried about your boyhood. You have slept the sleep of fighting males eager for the kill."

Perhaps he knew, perhaps not, that the sleep of which he spoke was the long, troubled sleep in which he himself had languished since the armistice of 1918. "Battle," he told the men of the 2nd Armored Division, "is not a terrifying ordeal to be endured. It is a magnificent experience wherein all the elements that have made man superior to the beasts are present: courage, self-sacrifice, loyalty, help to others, devotion to duty."

For Patton, belonging to a "different class," the customary order of things was inverted, and war, with all its obscene horror, was for him the occasion for those basic virtues of human decency he was unable to summon up in time of peace. So if, he told his soldiers, you find yourself "perhaps . . . a little short of breath, and your knees . . . tremble . . . this breathlessness, this tremor, are not fear. It is simply the excitement every athlete feels just before the whistle blows—no, you will not fear for you will be borne up and exalted by the proud instinct of our conquering race. You will be inspired by magnificent hate."

He might as well have been talking to himself, of himself.

After more than two decades as a "fighting male" asleep, Patton was about to fight the war for which his experience between 1916 and 1918 had been first blood. Primed, prepared, bloodied during that brief two-year span, he had then been forced to sleep. Now, inspired by magnificent hate, he was eager for the kill and would lead others in it as no other modern general, Axis or Allied, possibly could. "This is a helluva way to die," Patton said as he lay bleeding and paralyzed on the floor of his Cadillac staff car shortly before Christmas 1945. It had been, in fact, a helluva way to live.

A NOTE ON SOURCES

The Bibliography that follows this note is by no means exhaustive of the works devoted to Patton, let alone relevant to him. It is intended only as a list of the principal sources for *Patton's Drive*.

Unless otherwise noted in the text, material from Patton's letters, dispatches, diaries, speeches, and reports is quoted from transcriptions compiled by Martin Blumenson in *The Patton Papers 1885–1940* and *The Patton Papers 1940–1945*. Patton's account of his September 12, 1918, tank ride during the St. Mihiel Offensive is summarized from material cited in Blumenson's *1885–1940* volume.

Unless otherwise noted in the text, quotations from Dwight D. Eisenhower's official correspondence are from *The Papers of Dwight David Eisenhower: The War Years*, edited by Alfred D. Chandler Jr.

In addition, Dr. Perrin H. Long's report (August 16, 1943) concerning the Patton "slapping incident" in Chapter 1; Hobart R. Gay's account of Patton's ultimately fatal automobile accident in Chapter 7; and details concerning Patton's affair with his niece presented in the Epilogue are all drawn from material cited in Carlo D'Este's *Patton: A Genius for War*. Quotations from Patton's poetry are drawn from Charles M. Province's *The Unknown Patton*, except for "Anti-Climax," in the Epilogue, which is quoted from D'Este's *Patton*.

The Blumenson, Chandler, D'Este, and Province works are all cited in the Bibliography.

BIBLIOGRAPHY

Allen, Robert S. *Drive to Victory.* New York: Berkley, 1947.

———. *Lucky Forward.* New York: Vanguard Press, 1964.

Anders, Curt. *Fighting Generals.* New York: Putnam, 1965.

Army Times Editors. *Warrior: The Story of General George S. Patton.* New York: Putnam, 1967.

Axelrod, Alan. *Bradley: A Biography.* New York: Palgrave Macmillan, 2008.

———. *Patton: A Biography.* New York: Palgrave Macmillan, 2006.

———. *Patton on Leadership: Strategic Lessons for Corporate Warfare.* Paramus, N.J.: Prentice Hall Press, 1999.

Blumenson, Martin. *Kasserine Pass.* Boston: Houghton Mifflin, 1967.

———. *Patton: The Man Behind the Legend, 1885–1945.* New York: Morrow, 1985.

———, ed. *The Patton Papers 1885–1940.* Reprint ed. Bridgewater, N.J.: Replica Books, 1999.

———, ed. *The Patton Papers 1940–1945.* Reprint ed. New York: Da Capo, 1996.

Bradley, Omar N. *A Soldier's Story.* New York: Henry Holt, 1951.

———, with Clay Blair. *A General's Life.* New York: Simon and Schuster, 1983.

Bryant, Arthur. *Triumph in the West: A History of the War Years Based on the Diaries of Field-Marshal Lord Alanbrooke, Chief of the Imperial General Staff.* Reprint ed. Westport, Conn.: Greenwood Press, 1974.

Butcher, Harry C. *My Three Years with Eisenhower—1942–1945.* New York: Simon and Schuster, 1946.

Carpenter, Allan. *George Smith Patton, Jr.* Vero Beach, Fla.: Rourke Publications, 1987.

Chandler, Alfred D. Jr., ed. *The Papers of Dwight David Eisenhower: The War Years,* 5 vols. Baltimore and London: The Johns Hopkins University Press, 1970.

Codman, Charles R. *Drive.* Boston: Little Brown, 1957.

Collins, J. Lawton. *Lightning Joe: An Autobiography.* Reprint ed. Novato, Calif.: Presidio Press, 1994.

Coram, Robert. *Boyd: The Fighter Pilot Who Changed the Art of War.* Boston: Little, Brown, 2002.

Cray, Ed. *General of the Army: George C. Marshall, Soldier and Statesman.* New York: Cooper Square Press, 2000.

D'Este, Carlo. *Eisenhower: A Soldier's Life.* New York: Henry Holt, 2002.

————. *Patton: A Genius for War.* New York: HarperCollins, 1995.

Dyer, George. *XII Corps: Spearhead of Patton's Third Army.* Baton Rouge, La.: Army Navy Publishing Co., 1947.

Eisenhower, Dwight David. *Crusade in Europe.* Reprint ed. Baltimore and London: The Johns Hopkins University Press, 1997.

Essame, H. *Patton: The Commander.* London: B. T. Batsford, 1974.

Farago, Ladislas. *The Last Days of Patton.* New York: McGraw-Hill, 1981.

Forty, George. *The Armies of George S. Patton.* London: Arms and Armour Press, 1996.

————. *Patton's Third Army at War.* New York: Scribner's, 1978.

Gavin, James M. *On to Berlin: Battles of an Airborne Commander 1943–1946.* Reprint ed. New York: Bantam, 1984.

Gilbert, Martin. *Churchill: A Life.* New York: Owl Books, 1991.

Harkins, Paul D. *When the Third Cracked Europe.* Harrisburg, Pa.: Stackpole, 1969.

Hatch, Alden. *George Patton: General in Spurs.* New York: Julian Messner, 1950.

Hirshson, Stanley P. *General Patton: A Soldier's Life.* New York: Harper Perennial, 2003.

Ingersoll, Ralph. *Top Secret.* New York: Harcourt, Brace, 1946.

Irving, David. *The War Between the Generals: Inside the Allied High Command.* New York: Congdon and Lattès, 1981.

Kershaw, Alex. *The Longest Winter: The Battle of the Bulge and the Epic Story of WWII's Most Decorated Platoon.* New York: Da Capo Press. 2004.

Larabee, Eric. *Commander in Chief.* New York: Harper & Row, 1987.

Lengel, Edward G. *To Conquer Hell: The Meuse-Argonne, 1918, The Epic Battle That Ended the First World War.* New York: Henry Holt and Co., 2008.

MacDonald, Charles B. *A Time for Trumpets: The Untold Story of the Battle of the Bulge.* New York: William Morrow, 1985.

Mellor, William Bancroft. *General Patton: The Last Cavalier.* New York: Putnam, 1971.

———. *Patton, Fighting Man.* New York: Putnam, 1946.

Merriam, Robert E. *Dark December.* New York: Ziff-Davis Publishing Company, 1947.

Montgomery, Bernard Law. *Memoirs of Field Marshal Montgomery.* Reprint ed. London: Pen and Sword, 2006.

Odom, Charles B. *General George S. Patton and Eisenhower.* New Orleans: Word Picture Productions, 1985.

Patton, George S. Jr. *War as I Knew It.* Reprint ed. Boston and New York: Houghton Mifflin, 1995.

Pearl, Jack. *Blood and Guts Patton.* New York: Monarch, 1961.

Province, Charles M. *The Unknown Patton.* New York: Random House Value Publishing, 1988.

Semmes, Harry H. *Portrait of Patton.* New York: Appleton-Century-Crofts, 1955.

Strümpell, Dr. Adolf. *A Text-Book of Medicine for Students and Practitioners,* Third American Edition. New York: D. Appleton, 1901.

Third U.S. Army, *Third Army After Action Reports, July 1944–May 1945.* CD-Rom version. Beverly Hills, Calif.: Paperless Archives, n.d.

Toland, John. *Battle: The Story of the Bulge.* New York: Random House, 1959.

Truscott, Lucian K. *Command Missions.* New York: E. P. Dutton, 1954.

Vandiver, Frank E. *Black Jack: The Life and Times of John J. Pershing.* College Station: Texas A&M University Press, 1997.

Wedemeyer, Albert C. *Wedemeyer Reports!* New York: Henry Holt, 1958.

Welsome, Eileen. *The General and the Jaguar: Pershing's Hunt for Pancho Villa.* New York: Little, Brown, 2006.

Whiting, Charles. *Bradley.* New York: Ballantine Books, 1971.

———. *Patton.* New York: Ballantine, 1970.

INDEX

ABOUT THE AUTHOR

Alan Axelrod, who holds a Ph.D. from the University of Iowa, is the author or coauthor of more than twenty books, including *Patton: A Biography,* a Military Book Club Editor's Choice; *Patton on Leadership; Miracle at Belleau Wood* (Lyons), a Main Selection of the Military Book Club; and *Blooding at Great Meadows: Young George Washington and the Battle that Shaped the Man.* He has appeared on Discovery Channel documentaries. He lives in Atlanta, Georgia.